# HERMAN CHARLES BOSMAN
## - Between the Lines

# HERMAN CHARLES BOSMAN
## *- Between the Lines*

VALERIE ROSENBERG

For
HELENA,
who 'opened up the long-rusted locks on
the cupboard of her spirit',
as well as Bosman's 'future ages'.

## Acknowledgments

Initially, writing *The Life of Herman Charles Bosman* was a team effort. Even though most of these people are no longer with us, on *Herman Charles Bosman - Between the Lines*, I forever thank: Helena Lake, Bosman's widow whom I shall always miss; likewise Gordon Vorster, poet, painter, film-maker, Bosman's disciple and drinking mate; Lionel Abrahams, Bosman's pupil, literary executor, editor and author of *Mr Bosman: A Protégé's Memoir*; Aegidius Jean Blignaut, Bosman's colleague from 1930 to 1932; likewise George Howard, Bosman's friend for over 20 years, who gave me access to his own unpublished manuscript; John Webb, his colleague of the 1930s; Bernard Sachs, school friend, editor of the *South African Opinion* and biographer; my old friend Leon Feldberg, Bosman's employer, editor of the *Jewish Times* and proprietor of *The South African Opinion*; Bosmanophile Craig MacKenzie for giving me access to his doctoral thesis, 'The Oral-style South African Short Story in English'; and all of Bosman's relatives, friends and acquaintances who have helped piece together the segments of this mosaic.

Further research was made possible by: the Human Sciences Research Council, under whose auspices I was able to research the Bosman papers at the Harry Ransom Humanities Research Center in Austin, Texas, USA; municipal and state libraries throughout South Africa; and the British Newspaper Library, Colindale Avenue, London; Potchefstroom College; Jeppe Central and Jeppe High schools; the University of the Witwatersrand; and the Teachers' Training College, Johannesburg.

I am also grateful to the media for their fruitful appeals for missing information, namely *The Sunday Times*, the *Rand Daily Mail*, *The Star*, the *Transvaler*, the *Cape Times*, *Die Burger*, the *Pretoria News*, the *Northern Review* (formerly the *Zoutpansberg Review and Mining Journal*), and the SABC.

# Contents

# To begin with

When I first wrote Herman Charles Bosman's life story, *Sunflower to the Sun*, I put in just about all my research findings.

In this publication, approximately 26 years later, I needed to prioritise and streamline the material, and also to deal with information I hadn't really *wanted* to find (and wished that I could *un*-find). Above all, I wanted to share the story of the Bosman explosion over the past 20 odd years ... as well as some favourite passages.

As Gordon Vorster, Bosman's friend, disciple and drinking mate, once wrote to me:

*Let's open a bottle of wine. There now – it's a common Chateau Libertas, and I've taken down one of the pale Van Dyk brown-stemmed glasses that came from the old Langham Hotel where Herman and I often drank. I wish I had a rough claret from a bottle with a red triangular label. He liked that.*

*If I were to write a biography of Herman, the first sentences would go something like this: Herman Charles Malan Bosman was probably born, spawned of what were possibly parents. His mother was X and his father may possibly have been Y. I think his father was Edgar Allan Percy Bysshe John François Oscar Fingal O'Flaherty Wills de Sade Rossetti Dante Shakespeare Oliver Onions. And he had a sister, night, and a brother, desert. And he was educated, in his own soul, by fine fires.*

*He hated, he loved, he praised and condemned, was voluptuary and priest. He wrote waves and clouds, winds and the sun's rays, a Kalahari thorn and a Marico dust. But he also wrote an adultery, a seduction and a murder.*

*Bosman was a man, a woman, an angel, a devil, a tenderness, a cruelty, a brave man and a coward, an emasculated satyr, a womaniser, a racist and a liberal. He searched for purity in filth, and, like Wilde, found stars in the gutter.*

*You are probably shocked or dismayed by what you have found, but I expected it to happen that way. It is impossible to think that a three-year probing of Bosman's life would produce only the known facts or factors, and what has been found is only the natural result of properly investigating a life more multi-faceted than the most intricately cut diamond. And he is many-faceted, most intricate as a subject, so you must try to present all the facets you can without fear. I am sure that Herman himself would have been delighted by all these colours you have found to paint his portrait. So, now there is a lens to bring him into focus, remove forever the shadowy image, show him sharp and clear, and then you will have found out how wraith-like he really is.*

GORDON VORSTER

# 1

## The roots from which he sprang

In the wet season Porterville in the Western Cape is laced with a network of sparkling streams, from which a particularly lovely area derives the name 'Vier-en-Twintig Riviere'. It was there that Piet Malan and Bettie du Plessis grew up, met and married.

Piet, with his goatee beard, was a true patriarchal figure. He smoked a long, curved pipe and when he spoke he used it to give weight to his words with emphatic gestures. And he shyly wrote poetry.

The quick, darting rhythms of Bettie's spirit also invested her movements, which were slightly offset by a modicum of Victorian mannerisms. From her Huguenot forebears she had inherited a sparkling Gallic wit and an adventurous, innovative intelligence that contrasted with her husband's gentler, more reflective disposition. Together they created an environment that shaped their three sons and three daughters into extraordinarily gifted human beings.

According to the family Bible, Piet and Bettie's offspring were all born in the Cape. They were:

*Elizabeth Helena Malan, born 24 May 1875*
*Charles Steven Malan, born 13 August 1877*
*Nellie Petronella Malan, born 19 September 1881*
*Hester (illegible) Malan, born 15 October 1883*
*Victor Emanuel Malan, born 6 July 1885*
*Alfred Christiaan Malan, born 25 December 1889*

The first-born was Elisa, from whose womb would spring the quicksilver spirit of Herman Charles Bosman. His life course would run like a flashing stream, leaping its banks and leaving in its wake the bounty of his own particular vision. Sometimes havoc engulfed him and those close to him.

Charles Steven was born two years after Elisa, then followed Nellie, Hester, Victor and Fred, all of whom grew up in Porterville.

Charles read for a degree in law at the old Victoria College (later to become the University of Stellenbosch), and there he became a close friend of the Afrikaans poet C J Langenhoven, one of his fellow students. A brilliant student,

*Elisa Malan (Herman's mother as a child) with her own mother, Bettie Malan*

Charles scored 85 per cent on aggregate in his finals, creating a record in the annals of Cape law studies. He then entered the Civil Service and set another record when he was appointed magistrate of Vryburg at the age of 23 – the youngest person to have held this office in South Africa up to that time.

At the outbreak of the South African War in 1899, the Cape Boers were divided into two camps. Charles, inspired more by a spirit of adventure than a serious commitment to a cause, could just as cheerfully have thrown in his lot with either side. He accepted a commission with the Kimberley Light Horse Brigade and, in his tailored uniform with its shiny buttons, fought as readily for the British as he might have done for the Boers, had they been able to offer him the same inducements.

Initially, his was a war of euphemisms, of officers and gentlemen, in which his bilingualism and administrative abilities were utilised during pleasant sojourns at the Cape. But after Pretoria fell, the Boers regrouped and fought on as guerillas. When British General Kitchener realised every farm was a source of Boer food, shelter and intelligence, he cut off their supply lines, burned their farms, and put Boer families in concentration camps where many died of dysentery. The cleft between Boer and Briton would fester and refuse to heal.

In the peace that followed, the fertile banks of the Mooi River in the Transvaal beckoned with their promise of rich grazing and lush lucerne fields. The village that the Voortrekker leader Andries Potgieter had founded in 1838 had grown from a cluster of farms to the prosperous town of Potchefstroom. Lured north from the Boland, Piet and Bettie Malan and their six children relocated there. They came well equipped to contribute to the academic, cultural and administrative development of their new home.

They brought with them their legendary Cape hospitality, unbigoted attitudes and a gift for the written word; for in the newspapers of those times, now lost and untraceable, there appeared poems signed 'Pietie', the *nom de plume* of the reticent Piet Malan.

The Malans bought a tract of land in the country and a house in the village. There they and their children, now grown to maturity, began their new life. With its high water table, Potchefstroom was studded with tall oaks, cypresses and great willows bending to sweep their fronds over the river. The dirt streets were flanked by water furrows, and gardens and orchards stretched beyond the houses to hedges heavy with rose climbers that justly earned the town its reputation as 'the garden of Transvaal'.

During Nagmaal times the market place would seethe by Friday. Farmers came long distances; they outspanned their oxen, securing them with a yoke hewn especially for this purpose and a peg driven into the ground. Thereafter

*The market place, Potchefstroom, in the period after the South African/Anglo-Boer War*

they left them with drinking water and a couple of bales of forage within reach. On Saturdays farmers traded in the market place, and on Sundays the Hervormde Kerk, opposite the old Town Hall, became the focus of activity. Rural people had to be buried on the farms, but during Nagmaal time babies were christened and couples were married in church.

From one end to the other, the square would be packed with wagons, some of which would stay as long as a fortnight. After the last Sunday service, the farmers would inspan and disappear in different directions, leaving behind only their wagon tracks.

The South African War was followed by a period of reconstruction under the Milner regime. Four hotels – King's, Queen's, Royal and Crown – testify to the imperial leavening in the country loaf.

*The Potchefstroom Budget* (later to become *The Potchefstroom Herald*) carried advertisements for the brewers and distillers, as well as for patent medicines. Very likely, the latter were used to cure the effects of the former, and if Ohlson's and Castle breweries, Ingram's and Blommestein's bottle stores and Apostle and Picardie brandies were well known to all and sundry, so were Dr Cassell's tablets for indigestion and a weak heart. Even the most gifted men in the Malan family subscribed to the distillers' blandishments. This was passed on to the next generation, skipping Herman and some of his cousins at the cost of laying a double burden on the shoulders of Herman's younger brother Pierre.

*King Edward Street, Potchefstroom, as it appeared c 1900*

But Herman Bosman inherited something else. Encoded in the Malan DNA was the gene that made him prone to fits of ungovernable rage. It beset Charles, and would later exact a toll from Herman and – to a lesser degree – from Lex, Charles's son.

Potchefstroom had become a lively educational centre and Elisa Malan, a sharp-nosed, myopic woman with a remarkably incisive brain, was recruited as a teacher at the old South School. While attending Potchefstroom College, Herman first encountered library books and often lingered late – captive to a whole new world.

Meanwhile, Charles Malan had gone into legal practice with a prominent lawyer, George Louw. He also bought himself some farming land at Elandsheuwel but continued to live at his parents' home in Potchefstroom.

Whatever the reason for such an unexpected turn of events, at the age of 28 Elisa suddenly left Potchefstroom and on 26 April 1904 married a mine labourer, Jacobus Abraham Bosman, at Kuilsriver, near Cape Town.

On 3 February 1905, according to the Malan family Bible, Elisa gave birth to a son, whom she named Herman Charles. The birth date entered in the family Bible is the only record there is, and no birth certificate for Herman can be traced anywhere in the Republic.

The only early memory baby Herman retained of the Kuilsriver period is a revealing one, as indicated in 'Hometown' in the 'Talk of the Town' column in *Trek*, June 1947:

*I had only one conscious memory of Kuils River. That was when I was about two. I was seated on the grass wrapped around in a blanket, and there was a soft wind blowing, because it was getting on towards sunset, and two young girl cousins a few years older than me were dancing about me in the grass. And I suddenly burst into tears, just like that, without any reason. And the sadness of that memory has, at intervals, haunted me throughout the rest of my life ...*

Surrounded by girl cousins playing happily, why did he feel so threatened? Melancholy? Depression? This is the earliest record of Bosman's fragile biochemistry, possibly induced by neurotransmitters of a brain depleted of vital chemicals such as seratonin and norepinephrine.

Elisa's family, at a loss to explain her sudden marriage to a miner, and so far away from them, speculated as to whether it might have been a rebound liaison or the result of a disappointment in love, and mourned amongst themselves that she had married beneath her station.

Elisa must have thought so too. She was certainly frustrated, condemned to an unsatisfactory marriage with a man whose lack of education was always an

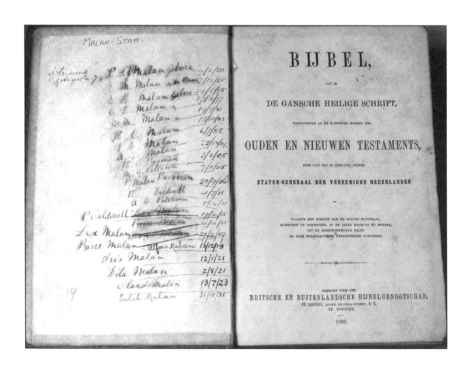

*The Malan family Bible, the only record of Bosman's birth (ninth from the top)*

16

*Above: The Malan grandchildren (Herman on the chair on the extreme right). Inset left: Uncle Charles Malan*

embarrassment and source of irritation to her. She would later confide to a friend that Herman had been a 'love child', and her marriage to Jacobus Bosman merely a necessary evil to provide a name for her baby and a measure of respectability for herself.

Here the Bosmans' trail runs dead for a while. It is uncertain how Jacobus supported Elisa, Herman and their younger son Pierre, born 18 months later at Kuilsriver. Since he was a mine worker throughout his life, it is likely that he found employment with the Kuils River Tin Mines, a crushing syndicate that operated in the districts of Kuilsriver and Stellenbosch, from 14 July 1906 until 10 July 1912.

According to school records, the Bosmans were in Krugersdorp by 1916, where Jacobus found employment on one of the West Rand mines. Midway through 1917, Elisa and the boys were once again in Potchefstroom, where Herman and Pierre were enrolled at Potchefstroom College, while Jacobus left to seek work in Johannesburg.

In some respects, Potchefstroom had changed from the town Elisa had left in 1904. Although it was still a farming community, regular stock fairs brought the farmers to town more frequently than had the old Nagmaal gatherings, and the livery stables were fighting a losing battle with motor car dealers selling Fords.

Even though the British troops had been withdrawn to fight another war in other lands, their influence, which had conditioned an entire generation, persisted in an empire-orientated lifestyle. Hotel names perpetuated a reverence for the monarchy, and English-style tearooms, with waitresses uniformed in black aprons and caps trimmed with white broderie anglaise, plied their patrons at Christmas with puddings, cakes, crackers and bon-bons, to muted background music provided by an 'eminent pianist'.

Bettie had coined a family maxim: 'Small minds discuss people, mediocre minds discuss things and great minds discuss ideas.' Among the Malan family the 12-year-old Herman came into his birthright and entered the realm of ideas. The Malans were prolific readers with retentive memories. Information enriched by their own thought processes gave birth to original comment and a philosophy of life. Conversation flowed from mythology to poetry, from metaphysics to ethics. It was a well from which the thirsty intellects of Bettie Malan, her son Charles and her grandson Herman drank deeply.

Charles Malan was, in appearance and intellect, the matrix in which Herman might most easily have been cast. Apart from the striking physical and non-physical resemblance between Herman and the uncle whose name he bore, they were bound by ties far closer than the one between him and his legitimate father, from whom he appears to have derived no more than a surname.

According to Charles's son, Lex, if the influence of a father figure existed in Herman's formative years, it was exercised by his gifted and accomplished uncle Charles, and they were the closest together of all the family.

In 1914 C V Bate, editor of *The Potchefstroom Herald*, had asked Charles to found an Afrikaans newspaper that would support the South African Party. The paper was called *Die Westelike Stem*. Its circulation grew rapidly, until eventually it gained the reputation of being the best Afrikaans country newspaper in South Africa. For this it duly received an official award.

Charles Malan's friendship with fellow Boer War veteran, General Smuts, was further cemented when he became secretary of the South African Party for the Transvaal. Because Herman was sometimes privileged to be present during political and historic discussions, he developed a precocious appreciation of both. Another member of the group was Charles's brother Fred, then an advocate, and later considered to be an outstanding judge of the Appeal Court. His legal mind dealt with facts and he was less at home in literature and poetry than were Bettie, Charles and Herman. The intellectual stimulation Herman received showed in his school results: for the humanities he scored close on an A aggregate, a mark he was never again to reach within the accepted academic disciplines.

This year at Potchefstroom College in his grandparents' home would be the happiest of Herman's childhood.

*Herman Bosman at Jeppe Central School, 1918, in the third row from the bottom, third from the left*

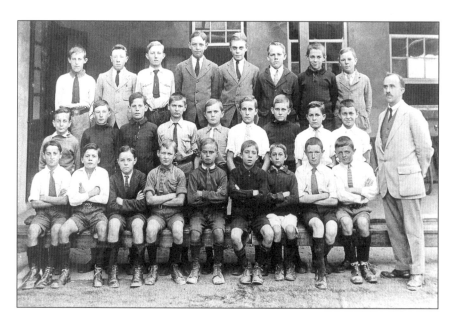

*Herman Bosman at Jeppe Central School, 1919, middle row, third from the right*

# 2

## Jeppe

By the middle of 1918, Jacobus Bosman had found employment as a waste-packer on the Johannesburg mines. He brought his family from Potchefstroom and installed them in a modest little cottage at 14 Grace Street, in Jeppestown, near the tickey stage of the Malvern tram.

A typical miner's cottage of the period, under a corrugated-iron roof, it was fronted by a red granolithic stoep with a wooden, lozenge-shaped balustrade and was set in a neglected garden bordered by a *Carissa macrocarpa* hedge. The single patch of shade cast by the large pepper tree was a poor exchange for the bounty the oaks and willows had yielded in Herman's much-loved Potchefstroom.

At the back of the kitchen was a detached ablution block on piles. The waste water from there and from the kitchen ran into a storage tank, where it stagnated to form a breeding ground for mosquitoes, until the municipal slopcart made the next of its tri-weekly visits and the water was baled out in buckets. The drop bucket-and-bench toilet housed in a corrugated-iron structure at the bottom of the garden was emptied by the municipal sewage carts in the dead of night – an image that Herman affectionately hoarded in the recesses of his memory for later use in his writing.

The local dairyman employed two delivery men who roamed the neighbourhood like the vendors in Dickensian London with their cries of 'Milk!' The neighbourhood children charged with these transactions exchanged pennies for pitchers of cool, creamy milk. The dairyman lived opposite the Bosmans in Grace Street, and was always ready to serve customers from his home.

Often, on a hot, bee-buzzing afternoon, an ice cream cart would appear with its tantalising call: 'Hokey-Pokey ice creams! Suckers and Eskimo Pies!' The Bosman brothers and other Jeppestown youngsters would emerge as if at the first call of the Pied Piper's tune, that set their sun-burnt legs pumping after the cart before it disappeared with its promise of bliss.

Herman started school mid-year at Jeppe Central with a hiccough. Like fellow plattelander Harry Rajak, he spoke 'Dutch' and was complexed about being of Afrikaner stock among a sea of predominantly English-speakers.

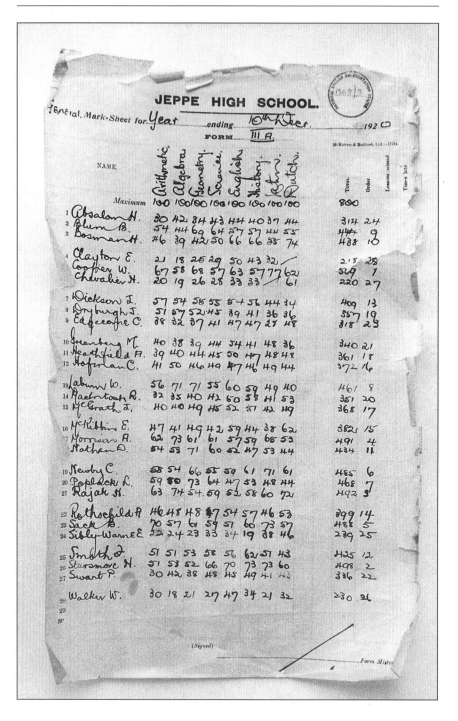

*Herman Bosman's class mark sheet from Jeppe High School, 1920*

The following year he entered high school where he first encountered mathematics, the complexities of which he was never to master and which would eventually cost him his matric.

On the positive side, Herman was fortunate enough to fall under the spell of his English master, William Cogie. By October he was top of his English class and, so motivated, he challenged those born to the language and excelled at it for the rest of his life.

His home life was unhappy. If Pierre was delighted to be reunited with Jacobus, Herman was not. With his ready wit, he was difficult for Jacobus to handle and Jacobus was never one to 'spare the rod and spoil the child'. Elisa felt little more than contempt for Jacobus. Having long deserted the conjugal bed, she neglected him to the point where he was expected to scratch together his own meals in an untidy house.

If Elisa loved Pierre, she worshipped Herman. Her sole concession to domesticity was to hang his framed sketches on the walls. Interested only in their academic achievements, she indoctrinated them with the credo: 'You must be successful!' She wanted them to reach for the stars; and in a way she may have been right, for stars were the stuff with which Herman later studded his poetry.

Higher up Grace Street in Jeppestown lived the McKibbin family: David and Bertha and their two sons, Robbie and Edwin. The neighbourliness of the two families was to ripen into close friendships for the boys and to cast Bertha McKibbin as Elisa's only companion and confidante.

Robbie McKibbin thinks it must have been after one of Jacobus's corporal punishment sessions that Elisa unburdened her soul. She told Bertha that she hated Jakoos, that she hoped the day would come when he would be killed in a mining accident; then she would take the proceeds from the insurance and catch a rich man. She bided her time and, almost as if in uncanny obedience to her will, that was close to what eventually transpired.

Elisa particularly entrusted to Bertha McKibbin the confidence that Herman was not Jacobus's son. As to his true origins, Elisa gave Bertha three clues: firstly, that Herman was the 'dead spit' of his genetic father; secondly, that his father was a brilliant man she was unable to marry; and thirdly, that Herman's middle name, Charles, had been given after his real father. To quote Robbie McKibbin, 'His middle name Charles wasn't for nothing.' Later in my research, Robbie McKibbin would send me on a hunt for his identity.

However, young Herman's attention was distracted from the problems of the family hearth by the discovery of the school library, and by his close friendship with Robbie McKibbin's younger brother, Edwin, with whom he'd attended Jeppe Central.

At the beginning of 1919, Herman and Edwin followed Robbie McKibbin to Jeppe High. It was a school steeped in a tradition of dedication to the war effort: 300 old boys and nine masters had seen active service, 23 had been decorated and 31 had not returned. The headmaster, a Mr Manduell, who assumed office in 1919, had been awarded the Military Cross and the Croix de Guerre. He took pride in the school's academic and sporting achievements. On the athletics track the runner L B Betts and later the young cricketer Horace Cameron reached heights that covered their school and themselves in glory.

Jeppe's cadet corps was attached to the Senior Imperial Light Horse, which had so distinguished itself during World War I. Cadet Herman Bosman, however, was a total embarrassment. One Thursday, late for parade, and with his shirt incorrectly buttoned, he caused the section corporal to demand, 'Cadet Bosman, where is your tie?'

'Around my neck, Corporal,' Herman replied mildly, thereby earning himself pack drill for that afternoon.

But Herman had his own agenda.

During science someone said, 'Look, Sir, Bosman's bleeding.'

And he was – from a self-inflicted wound on his throat. On his way to the first-aid station, he winked at Harry Rajak: 'No pack drill for me today.'

Both Harry Rajak and Bernard Sachs would later recall this instance of inappropriate behaviour in a petition to show that Herman Bosman was prone to moments of diminished responsibility.

Jeppe High held other attractions for Herman, though. In its library he discovered Edgar Allan Poe, who made a deep and lasting impression on him, and whom he once described as 'a leak in the cosmic secret'. O Henry also fascinated and inspired both him and Edwin McKibbin. They entered a partnership and collaborated in writing short stories for *The Sunday Times*. They made frequent contributions to the 'Sunday Sallies' column, one of Herman's first pen names being Ben Eath.

Their collaboration extended into the entrepreneurial field as well. First they rented a box at the Rissik Street post office in the name of Floydd B Warrington, after which tantalising advertisements began to appear in the daily press to the effect that anyone who wanted to know how to save money should send a shilling to the quoted box number, and they would be advised in due course.

Postal orders to the value of a shilling each flooded Floydd B Warrington's box. The two investment advisers responded by sending each subscriber a list of insurance companies. Drunk with success, they sent a letter to General Jan Smuts designed to net them ten shillings.

With the depression breathing down Johannesburg's neck, Edwin McKibbin left school to start work, and the task of emptying the post office box fell to Herman. One day, just as he was about to make his call, he saw a man loitering in the vicinity, whom he instinctively suspected to be a detective. Herman didn't clear the box, but the detective tailed him just the same. Herman led him on a wild-goose chase that started with their taking a tram to Fordsburg and ended at nine o'clock that night, when Herman – after extensive peripatetics and much backtracking – finally threw off his pursuer.

The following morning a visitor called on Edwin McKibbin and asked whether he knew anything about Floydd B Warrington. Major Trigger was then head of the CID, and the two boys were summoned to appear – Herman for the first time, but not the last – at the old Magistrate's Court. They admitted with disarming honesty that they saw this as an avenue of revenue. Major Trigger glared, so the magistrate smothered his grin and warned them that while this was not exactly illegal, it was perilously close to it.

The Jeppe High school magazine of July 1921 contained a contribution titled 'The Mystery of the ex-MP'. It could have been the work of almost any schoolboy of unremarkable talent, except for three characteristics: it showed flashes of a distinctive, if unorthodox, sense of humour; it took a dig at the establishment; and it had that double-pronged ending that would become familiar to all future Bosman readers. Besides, the initials at the bottom read H C B. The contribution, in part, read:

> *One morning, having hurriedly drunk my breakfast, I emerged from the 'Edward the Professor' to find my friend, Lockjaw Bones, the criminologist, waiting for me outside ...*
>
> *'Hist!' he breathed between his teeth, pointing a finger at a passing citizen. 'Time was when that man could have written M.P. after his name.'*
>
> *I was absolutely dumbfounded at this intelligence. 'Bones!' I gasped, 'is he actually as unscrupulous – as unprincipled – as to be a Member of Parliament?'*
>
> *'Not quite as bad as that,' was Bones's reply: 'M.P. merely stands for Mounted Police. In other words, he had the Mounted Police after him ...'*
>
> *At length we had run the Ex-M.P. to earth. This, I conjectured, would be the penultimate scene; the end would probably be the gallows. The web which Bones had spun round our prey was perceptibly tightening. Ah! now we had him! Coming to a standstill before a barrow, he thrust his hand into his pocket, and – oh, horror! – drew something shiny from his pocket! Already Bones's fist was*

*raised high above his head, till at the alcoholical moment, when he*
*was about to send the instrument clattering to earth.*

*'Give me a thrupp'ny packet, please,' the prospective victim said, as he*
*flung the still glittering coin at the pop-corn merchant.*

*Bones came out of hospital the following Sunday.*

After Edwin McKibbin left school, Herman widened his circle of friends to
include Bernard Sachs, who had an absorbing interest in the classics and
English literature. Sachs's friendship with Bosman was to endure on one level
or another right through university, normal college and their later
involvement in the *South African Opinion*, and finally cast him in the role of
pallbearer at Herman's funeral.

Benny Sachs, as his friends called him, was quick to realise that Herman's
rebelliousness and recklessness placed him squarely against the
establishment. He was always on the side of the underdog, and only changed
his stance when times and circumstances threatened to catch up with him.
Later Sachs was to make this penetrating observation about his friend:

*There are two kinds of misfits: those who are deficient in the elementary*
*qualities of adaptability, and those who are over-endowed. Bosman*
*belonged in the second category. The voltage he carried was too high.*

# 3

## A miss-spent youth

Herman left Jeppe High in 1921 to attend yet another educational institution, which he later described in the following manner:

*Houghton College is an unpretentious-looking building in one of Johannesburg's northern suburbs. It is run primarily for the purpose of cramming students for the Cape Matriculation. As its matriculation students consist largely of boys and girls who have failed the ordinary Transvaal Form Four or Five examinations, this educational institution does not really comprise the pick of South Africa's youthful intellect. The examination results obtained at Houghton College prove this fact conclusively. For it would be unfair to attribute the long list of failures exclusively to the lack of initiative displayed by the teaching staff.*

He spent part of his time at Houghton cramming for his matriculation, and a great deal more of it plaguing the masters with practical jokes.

Retribution was dealt Herman when he finally wrote his matriculation examination, and he still couldn't do maths. Confronted with the algebra paper, he wrote the examiners a letter confessing his regrettable deficiencies in this subject, and suggesting that they overlook these since he made up for them with his talents in English.

In 1922, Herman's matriculation year, the rumblings of the worst industrial confrontation in the history of the Rand grew louder. From the City Hall steps self-styled orators inflamed the passions of the miners to fever pitch. On street corners there was the insistent rattling of money-boxes collecting for the soup kitchens that fed the distressed miners and their families, who were obstinately facing starvation rather than concede.

Jacobus Bosman, more intent on keeping a roof over his family's head than on throwing in his lot with the miners, elected to work on. He was labelled a 'scab', severely beaten up, and his furniture was thrown into the street and set alight. Pierre had empathy with his father and suffered, but Herman kept his own counsel.

Laughter at any price had become the central doctrine by which Bosman had chosen to live. So when in the following year, 1923, Jacobus Bosman died

*Herman Charles Bosman, age 20, prior to his departure to teach in the Marico*

of multiple injuries in a mining accident, it was not really out of character for Herman to remark to a friend: 'I was almost moved to tears.'

Herman's brother Pierre, who resembled Jacobus physically and was close to him, told Robbie McKibbin that the shock of his father's death had driven him to his first bottle of brandy, his first step on the road to alcoholism.

For Herman, nothing was sacred if it provided him with scope for his peculiar sense of humour. It was a strange trait of freakish proportions, operating on every possible level – from rapier wit to corn-ball slapstick, from the sly ambiguity to the vulgar belly laugh, even plumbing the depths of the unorthodox and macabre, where few had ever previously found cause for laughter.

In 1923, under the pretext of studying for his T2 teaching diploma, Herman became a student simultaneously of the University of the Witwatersrand and the Normal College, and proceeded to raise havoc at both.

He joined the Young Communist League with his friends Benny and Solly Sachs, Eddie Roux and befriended Raymond Lake – a 'worker' from the City Hall steps. Characteristically, Herman saw his association with the Young Communist League more as a chance to take the mickey out of things than as a serious commitment to a cause. He preferred to be near the action rather than at the core of it, and hanging posters and heckling on the City Hall steps suited him very well.

For Herman the City Hall steps were invested with a certain glamour. Of the four perpetrators of a certain poster-pasting escapade, Raymond Lake was the only 'worker' in the literal sense of the word, and he was understandably nervous of being out of his depth one evening when Herman took him to a lecture at the university. 'Don't worry about it,' Herman reassured him. 'The others have got their education at the university; but we got ours at the City Hall steps.'

The Wits Philosophical Club was revived in 1924 with a tightly knit team of office bearers: Professor Hoernlé (president), Professor MacCrone (chairman), and Herman Bosman (secretary), who reported it in *The Umpa*, the Wits student magazine for which he'd begun to write. This was an early foray into *real* journalism where he not only reported the news, but made it.

In his final year, he submitted an entry to the University of the Witwatersrand literary competition of 1925. A committee consisting of professors Hoernlé, Maingard and Haarhof awarded third place to a poem entitled 'Time', which appeared under the *nom de plume* 'Ridens'. This, translated from Latin, means 'laughing', which Bosman was when he revealed that the poem had been lifted in toto from Shelley. Wind of the affair reached the press, much to the embarrassment of the literary adjudicators. But Bosman coolly presented himself to A V Hatfield, news editor of *The Umpa*, in which this little fraud had appeared, and claimed his ten-bob prize for coming third in the competition.

This same Hatfield once had the temerity to strike out the word 'accordingly' with which Bosman had begun an essay submitted to *The Umpa*, because, he said, it was incorrect style to begin an essay in this way. In later years, one of Bosman's favourite ways of beginning an essay was to be with the word 'accordingly'.

And many years later, in 1944, Bosman would describe in the *South African Opinion* what he thought should be the essential qualities of a seat of learning – qualities which, in his view, were sadly lacking at the University of the Witwatersrand.

> *I have seen many a stately pile, heavily encrusted with history, thick with dust and tradition, sanctified through the intimacy of its association with a nation's fortunes, through the centuries a silent witness of dooms and splendours – I have seen such a building, cathedral, abbey, palace, mausoleum, and I have not been impressed.*
>
> *But because the walls of Oxford did not tower, but seemed sunk into the earth, almost, and because with what was venerable about the masonry that had lasted from the Middle Ages there went also a warmth and richness of life that time could not chill, I realised that if I had gone there as a student, I would never have been able to do any work in the place. I would have gone to Oxford and spent too many years in the more idle kind of dreaming.*
>
> *When I was a student at Wits I had a contempt both for the buildings and the professors. I could not reconcile myself to the idea that any really first-class man from Europe would bring himself to apply for so obscure and – as I then thought – Philistine an appointment as a professorship in a South African mining-town university where the reinforced concrete slabs were still wet inside.*
>
> *Needless to say, my views in this regard have since that time undergone a very profound change. I have seen some of the things that first-class men get reduced to doing in this life. Myself included. And I feel only a sense of humble gratitude towards those men from overseas who came to the Witwatersrand University when it was first started, bringing with them that vital breath of culture that includes the Near East and Alexandria and the Renaissance, that rich old world of thought in whose inspiration alone the soul of man can find a place for its abiding.*

By this time, too, Bosman had begun to reveal unusual ability in the art class. His sketches reflected an extraordinary ambivalence: he could set down the essentials with absolute economy of line, and at the same time enrich the sketch with his own original approach, achieving what the art master called 'the harmony of discord'.

At the end of 1925, Bosman received his T2 diploma from the Transvaal Education Department, securing a pass in the following subjects: English, Afrikaans, Theory of Education, History of Education, School Organisation and Discipline, Child Psychology, Physiology and Hygiene, Ethics, Penmanship and Blackboard Work, Cardboard Modelling, Woodwork and Drawing.

Through his university career Bosman had lived by the credo: 'If you can't be famous, be notorious.' And by the time he left Wits, he was.

But something else happened in Bosman's last year at university. In 1925, after two years of widowhood, Elisa's wish that she would marry a rich widower came true, when on 29 June 1925 she married William Russell. But she didn't take into her calculations that ancient curse: 'Beware of what you wish for, for you may get it.'

*Vera Sawyer, 1926, on the occasion of her marriage to Herman Bosman*

# 4

## Vera and the teacher in the bushveld

In the October issue of 1925 there appeared in the Wits student magazine, *The Umpa*, a poem that had about it a strange tenderness:

*Vera*
*All else is now forgotten wholly,*
*All but the broken roses there,*
*Whose ghostly breath stirred sadly, slowly,*
*The rain was in her hair.*
*Though new age-old things have shaken*
*The placid course of passing years,*
*Yet vague are still the thoughts they waken*
*And dim as dream-shed tears.*
*But softly memory's page discloses*
*What sleepless lives forever there,*
*That haunting scent of broken roses,*
*The raindrops in her hair.*

Professor Max Drennan, Head of the Department of English at Wits, said 'Vera' was to be highly commended, and though second in merit overall, it was first in originality; the writer had the makings of a good poet and should be encouraged to write. The poem was unsigned, and quite out of keeping with any of the writer's previous contributions.

William Waldman, then editor of *The Umpa* and a young man of insight, recalled having seen Herman one rainy day sheltering a pretty girl who lived near the university in Ameshoff Street, with a waterproof raincape. He looked at the poem and thoughtfully repeated to himself: 'The raindrops in her hair.'

The Vera of the poem was clearly derivative of Edgar Allan Poe's lost loves, but the real Vera was very much alive. She was a slight, gentle, brown-eyed young bank clerk whom Herman Bosman had met the previous Christmas eve.

Many years later he recalled the circumstances and tried to recapture the atmosphere in the first chapter of a novel he was never to finish, and which lies, faintly yellow in its plastic envelope, among his unfinished manuscripts in the archives of the Harry Ransom Humanities Research Center, Austin, Texas.

This fragment is titled 'Johannesburg Christmas Eve':

*There was laughter and shouting and the swish-swish of plumes. Hurried words and an excited squeal and a melee that resolved itself when the confusion was at its thickest. There was an inextricable pattern of plumes and faces, of jackets and trousers and shoes and dresses. It was all in one moment. By the next moment the crowd had sorted itself out into its component elements. All that was left were a dozen young men and women, each separate and each lonely under the electric lights of the city and under the stars. But in the next moment they would mingle again, body and jacket, and wide-swung skirt and dark hair and shoe ...*

On such a night, when a smile was an invitation and a kiss a promise, Herman Bosman had found himself hurled like confetti into delicious proximity with – and kissing – two girl cousins, Vera and Mavis. Another six months were to pass before, passing a house in Ameshoff Street on his way to university, he met Vera Sawyer again.

They began to spend time together, and Herman invited Vera to a party at his home. Elisa, although herself virtually a bride of seven months, was critical of her and refused to be introduced. Instead of deterring Herman, this lack of approval enhanced Vera's appeal. Besides, tensions were looming in the Russell household and he warmed to the intimacy of the Sawyer family circle.

When Bosman finished his teaching diploma at the end of 1925, he was appointed to a rural school in the heart of the Bushveld. In his growing insecurity he needed an anchor. A little over a year after the Christmas eve Herman had first met Vera, on Friday 21 January 1926, he borrowed £5 from her and married her by special licence.

His mother had married without his blessing, and now he was reciprocally marrying without hers. The marriage was more like a minor's prank and a continuation of the fiction he'd made up about himself that Christmas eve they met. Vera's middle-class sense of propriety pervaded all facets of her life. She took enormous pride in her job as a clerk for a life insurance company. It would be the single preoccupation of her life while the years leaked away – interminable book entries, all fastidiously neat, years and years with wedges of three weeks' paid leave annually. And, at the end of it all, the carrot of a retirement pension.

She had told him she would never vote anything other than United Party, she would never marry anyone younger than herself and she would *never* marry an Afrikaner. Accordingly, when she'd asked his name and age, he replied: 'Herbert Charles Boswell, 26.'

34

*Above: The Marico
bushveld at the time
Bosman lived there
Left: The school at
Heimweeberg where
Herman taught in 1926*

Throughout his life Bosman played games with names and the identities they represented or conferred. Giving a spurious name on his marriage certificate permitted him to enter into a Freudian marriage that wasn't a real marriage to him.

*Oom Christiaan Geel, an Anglo-Boer War veteran and the inspiration of many of Bosman's stories*

The marriage did not change anything. Herman was 20 and in no position to enter into a marriage – legally or financially – and expected Vera to remain in her job and continue to live with her mother. It was a romantic gesture without commitment and responsibilities. Two days later he took the train bound for his first teaching post in the Bushveld. Vera, accompanied by her mother (still unaware of the marriage), rode with him as far as Krugersdorp, and returned to the little cottage near the university.

Herman Bosman sped on into an unfamiliar world. He did not know it then, but the flora and fauna had names that would sing to him and images that would 'ensnare the imagination'.

The Marico district to which Bosman went so reluctantly derives its name from the Groot Marico River along its northern border. According to the government surveyor's map, the Marico magisterial district of Bosman's time was bounded in the north and north-west by the Bechuanaland Protectorate (now Botswana). The eastern boundary followed a line southward from the Dwarsberge through – the names are pure poetry – Silkaatskop, Pachsdraai and Haakdoornbult towards the Lichtenburg district on to its southern boundary. In the west it was divided from the Cape Province by a barbed-wire fence known simply as the Convention Line.

There *is* a dot on the map labelled Groot Marico, but I'll come to it much later. Although it's now famous for its annual Herman Bosman Festival, this is *not* where Herman Bosman was sent. He was sent to an even smaller dot on the map in the Groot Marico district, an hour's car drive away. Near the Botswanan border, Zwingli boasted the nearest post office. It was to Zwingli that Vera posted all her letters to Herbert Boswell.

I know this because I've been there twice: once when Willie and Joey Flattery (the surviving children of the family with whom Bosman boarded) took me on my first research hunt, and again some years later when I went on a location hunt for an SABC TV series of Bosman's stories, which was unfortunately later shelved.

About 20 years later I went for the third time in my life. But I'm going to save that for now because it's part of the last chapter, and you're all in it.

The Groot Marico district where Bosman went was a vast dust bowl studded with the whole panoply of thorn trees – again with evocative names – from the *haak-en-steek* to the *apiesdoring*, the *kameeldoring* and the ubiquitous *soetdoring*. There were also groves of *tambotie* trees whose hard wood could be put to domestic use, and the *witgat* with its rambling trunk structure and mushroom top, whose roots yielded an ersatz type of coffee. In addition there were marulas with potent fruit and *moepels* (red milkwoods) with their 'yellow blossoms', and the *sekelbos* with its pinky-mauve or yellow flowers, not forgetting the *blouhaak*, which appears in Thomas Baines's paintings, and the *withaak*, which was to appear later in Herman Bosman's stories.

The majority of farmers were granted government loans to sink boreholes and erect windmills. However, there was seldom wind and the boreholes had to be pumped manually with a rudimentary hand-pump called a 'bitterhoutjie'. Veteran farmers remember their grandfathers' stories of long hours of toil on windless days under a stubbornly cloudless sky.

Before geologists mapped underground water courses, they located them with a 'stokkie' – a stick that twisted downwards towards water points. Earth dams were then built in these natural catchment areas, but these took several seasons to fill.

Times were hard and market prices low, adding to the woes of minimal veterinary services and rampant animal diseases. Calves perished from 'lewersiekte' and all cattle were prone to heart-water disease. In 1926, the year Bosman came to the Marico, the Dwarsberg farmers' union appointed the first veterinary surgeon. Then followed roads, government transport, postal services, the telegraph and telephone – slowly dragging into the twentieth century the farmers whose children Herman Bosman had come to teach.

In the June issue of *The Umpa* that year, Bosman gave his first impressions in his piece, 'A Teacher in the Bushveld':

> *A teacher's post having been assigned to me, I packed up and left – for the Crocodile River. After I had passed matric and had completed the three-year course at the Johannesburg Training College, they sent me to the Marico Bushveld. I'm glad I didn't take the four-year course, though, because with a full T2 and a B.A. I might have been thrown clean across the border: into Mozambique, perhaps, or else the Nubian Desert.*

This was a land settled by people within one generation of two Boer Wars and three Republics, and within living memory of a party of Boers attacked and killed by Chief Makapan. Transport riders stayed to become farmers. Hunters stayed to become conservationists. It was a land where 50 000 people – farmers, teachers and preachers – rushed to the diamond diggings at Grasfontein, while one or two wiser opportunists contented themselves with selling the water they transported there and sold at a premium.

And so this world that Bosman found was filled with images and folk whose grandparents told him stories of war veterans and *predikants*, constables and veld maidens – the faithful and the faithless who walked his Mafeking Road.

The stories they told teemed with images of violence and compassion, of fidelities and betrayals. And there were those other images and dreams that haunted Herman Bosman – the rain-washed gravestones with half-obliterated names, the love he felt doomed to pursue in the certain knowledge that he would never find her.

Above all, the theme of death held him in thrall through a lifetime twisted by its presence:

> *Sometimes, at night, when the world is very still, a soft wind comes sweeping across the veld. Then if you are outside, and listen very carefully, you can hear the story it has to tell. It is thoughtful, this little*

*One of the archetypal characters who might have appeared in any of Bosman's Schalk Lourens stories (courtesy of the Africana Museum, Johannesburg)*

*wind, and the tale it tells, as old as the world and as time-worn, has about it something that is yet new and sweet and strangely stirring. And this story is one that we all love to hear, for, steeped as it is in the fragrance of some romance of long ago, it awakens memories of far-off things – of trees that are dark in the moonlight, of crumbling garden-walls, of star-dust and of roses.*

*The Flattery household photographed outside the sleeping porch where Bosman boarded for the first six months of 1926*

*Then the little wind grows rather wistful, because the last pages of its story are sad. The ending has to be mournful, of course. Either Tristan, returning after seven lonely years and finding his Iseult false and in the arms of another, rides away broken-hearted into the west – to die. Or else Iseult gazes wearily and with tear-dimmed eyes across the plains for him who cometh not; gradually the crimson fades from her cheeks, the cyclamen from her lips, and in the early autumn, just when the first brown leaves are beginning to flutter to earth, she too breathes her last. Oh yes, the ending must be sad. All these old tales are that way, and the little wind, knowing it, perhaps, and heaving a tired sigh, sinks quietly to rest.*

*The Umpa*, 1 June 1926

This was the soil where Bosman's quirky humour would germinate and his wistful dream thrive.

In summer the Bushveld stirs early. Long before the first light washes across the eastern horizon where Abjaterskop rears up in all its sorcery and might, the insects, animals and birds begin preparing for the day in accordance with an ancient rhythm. On cue at half past four, Oom Jim Flattery, half a lifetime away from his native Ireland, would rise for his solo part in this Bushveld concerto. With his paraffin lamp in one hand, his mug of coffee in the other and his 12-year-old daughter Joey at his side, he strode out to reaffirm his sovereignty over the 2 800 morgen that represented Middelrand. Jim Flattery had bought the farm in 1906 at four shillings and sixpence a morgen in terms of a Land Bank scheme designed to assist Bushveld farmers. For those of their children who could be spared from labour on the lands or in the home for long enough, the government provided education up to Standard 8 in rural schools, and loaned the animals to transport the children to school by donkey-cart.

Tall and spare, Jim Flattery had been a transport-rider on the road between Johannesburg and Rhodesia when he met Kitty Pyper, a young woman of Boer stock. She was a trained midwife, had a rudimentary training as a pharmacist, and had grafted onto this her legendary Boer remedies.

Jim and Kitty were married in Gaborone and came to the Groot Marico district to carve out a livelihood in cattle farming, to build their home and to rear their family. The homestead of Middelrand was built on a slope between four mountains, in the shadow of Abjaterskop. It faced due south in order to shelter the front stoep from the fierce heat of the Bushveld summers. Most of the bedrooms faced east and the kitchen west. There was no bathroom as such, and water had to be pumped from the borehole and carried into the bedrooms. Almost as an afterthought, a portion of the verandah was partitioned off as a sleeping porch for Bertie Boswell, as he was then known.

The floor of the house was paved with slate slabs quarried from the farm. The window frames and doors, as well as much of the simple furniture, were fashioned from tambotie cut from the natural groves on the land. Apart from the furnishings, the corrugated-iron roof and glass windows were Jim Flattery's only concessions to sources other than those provided by the Lord.

The outbuildings consisted of a dairy and coachhouse, the loft of which was used to store preserved and dried fruits garnered in season from the orchard Jim had planted – peaches, plums, apricots, pomegranates, pears, figs – and vegetables from the carefully cultivated garden. When necessary, oxen, pigs and goats were slaughtered and the meat preserved in ten-gallon drums. Chickens, ducks and turkeys from their own pens were supplemented by the wild duck and guinea fowl that roamed the farther reaches of Middelrand. Jim Flattery also did his own iron-mongery, and taught young Bertie Boswell – a skill he would have reason to use 20 years later in the 1940s.

Survival made high demands on the Flatterys, and nothing ever went to waste. Like all other women of the district, Kitty Flattery made her own soap from prickly pear leaves, boiled bones and beef fat, and when times were hard she would take a load by donkey-cart into the kraal at Thebestat, where she bartered it for mealies, sorghum and sometimes a goat or sheep. Coffee could always be made from the root of the *witgat* tree. But no matter how hard things were, no-one ever crossed Middelrand without her giving him a large helping of mealie-pap, so she was known as 'Madapalachi' (mother of porridge).

Kitty, the acknowledged midwife for all races, even went as far as Ramoutsa in Bechuanaland (Botswana) to deliver babies and she ran an informal clinic to treat patients with her Boer remedies.

Through Bosman's stories, the names of the families whose children Bosman taught now have a familiar ring to them. On the Abjaterskop side of Middelrand lived John Callaghan, the first to teach in the Heimweeberg school, where Herman Bosman was appointed. There were the Geels, the Wellmans, the Swanepoels, the Bekkers, the Grobbelaars, the Swardts, the Odendaals, the Lemmers, the Nienabers and Dominee Ziervogel – all part of a hierarchy in which the Fouries were the poorest and Gielie Haasbroek the wealthiest.

Every morning Jim Flattery would welcome his family and their guest, young Bertie Boswell, to the breakfast table with his Irish-Afrikaans greeting, 'Die beste van die môre', or 'Top of the morning', after which they tucked into the porridge, fruit and slabs of homemade bread spread with a thick layer of homemade jam, all washed down with large mugs of coffee. Then Bert would climb into the donkey-cart next to 18-year-old Flo, the driver, and together with Jimmy, Maxie, Joey, Lucy and young Willie they jogged along the seven kilometres of country trails that separated Middelrand from Heimweeberg.

Heimweeberg school stood on the Haasbroek farm, a mile or so away from the Zwingli post office on the main road. It was a single-storey thatch-roofed shelter for children living too far from Nietverdiend (the only other school in the district). Every morning the sounds of high-spirited greetings and the braying of donkeys mingled as drivers jockeyed for shady spots to park.

Jan Loedewyk Terblanche, a graduate of Potchefstroom University College and the principal, shared the syllabus with Bosman, as stipulated by the 'Groen Boek'. When Bosman told Terblanche that he contributed to the *Sunday Times* under the name of Ferdinand Fandango, he was put in charge of English, while Terblanche used the wealth of local flora and insect life to teach nature study.

School politics and expedience were another matter. Boreholes were deep and water had to be carted a considerable distance. One school committee member spotted a gap in the market, and awarded himself the contract for delivering water to the school twice a week in barrels, and would then inspect the school at the same time.

After school, teacher and pupils would all pile back onto the donkey-cart and return famished to steaming mugs of rooibos tea, pancakes, hot scones or bread fresh from the brick oven that stood outside, a little way from the kitchen. In between, young Willie Flattery was sent on furtive excursions to the coachhouse loft for dried fruit and biltong.

The evening meal was hearty, with conversation and teasing sandwiched between the rites of saying grace and the rosary. Oom Jim Flattery warmed to the stimulus Bertie Boswell's quick brain brought to his dinner table, but he worried it was too heavy a burden for a young person to bear and was uneasy about the price it might one day exact. Even at this stage it was clear that Herman Bosman was a disturbed personality. Night after night, when Oom Jim was awake, he would hear the creak of the stable door of the sleeping porch, which meant that Bertie was abroad. He would softly call to Joey to fetch the hurricane lamp and wraps, and they would take off down the trail through the fruit trees towards the thorn trees. There they found Bertie unnerved and dazed – so much so that he had to be soothed and led gently back to bed.

Bosman kept a 'six-by-eight' portrait of Vera on his chest of drawers, and they wrote to each other via the Zwingli post office. However, he referred to her only as his sweetheart in Johannesburg – as truthfully she must have seemed to him – and considered himself entirely free to flirt with Flo and take her for long walks full of serious discussion, and to caper with the nubile young Maxie, who teased him constantly. In fact, she did this once too often.

One day, when the Flattery family had just returned from the orchard laden with pomegranates, Herman tried to persuade Maxie to sit next to him on the *riempie* bench. He had shifted up to make room for her while they pared their fruit. Maxie made a gesture as though to accept, but then teasingly pinched his shoulder and darted away instead. In a flash he had flung his red-handled penknife at her. Only when she passed the mirrored sideboard on her way to the kitchen did Maxie notice from her reflection that the red handle of Bosman's knife was protruding from her back, slightly above her kidneys.

In the kitchen, Kitty Flattery carefully withdrew the knife and stanched the blood. At this point Maxie was more dazed than hurt, but Bertie (Herman) stood cowering, white-faced in the corner by the door, repeating over and over in a half-whisper: 'Please, Mrs Flattery, please, Mrs Flattery.' In his state of shock he had more need of Kitty Flattery's ministering skills than Maxie.

It wasn't until a few days later, when Maxie's wound, exacerbated by the pomegranate juice on the knife blade, began to turn septic, that Kitty Flattery really had to nurse her daughter with poultices. Meanwhile young Joey, terrified by the thought of what might have been, had crept outside and buried the red-handled penknife in an ant heap.

Jan Terblanche, having already spent two years in the Marico, intended to make his home there. Herman Bosman was distinctly a transient, and remained a loner. Yet Bosman did penetrate the mystique of the veld with his highly attuned powers of perception. He absorbed whatever it would yield and, while he may not have become part of it, it became a deeply ingrained part of him.

There was one other respect in which Herman Bosman was quite keen to conform to the Bushveld code, and that was to possess a gun. Here, where people had carved out their destiny through several wars against the black population, two Anglo-Boer/South African wars and a score of commando raids, owning a rifle was the equivalent of a Mtosa blooding his assegai (that is, using it for the first time). The constant need for protection against wild animals and snakes, and the necessity to hunt for food gave the gun the same status in peace or war. When Herman Bosman bought an ex-military 303 rifle adapted for sporting purposes from At Geel for ten shillings, it was the proudest moment of his Bushveld life.

Moreover, when he left to spend the July holidays in Johannesburg, Oom Jim could not dissuade him from taking his gun with him. From the day he bought it he had fantasised about his triumphal return to the city, his hat bristling with guinea-fowl feathers, a buckskin or two in one hand and his gun, the symbol of his manhood, in the other. No, there was no way Oom Jim could persuade him to leave behind these symbols of the veld that could have no proper place in the city.

And it was to haunt him. For if he had left the gun behind, Herman Bosman's life might have been very different.

# 5

## The Bellevue tragedy

On 29 June 1925, in Herman's last academic year, six months before he left for the Marico, the second part of Elisa's wish had come true. She had married a man who was 'comfortably off', but she was not to know then at what cost.

Her second husband, William Russell, a Scots mechanical engineer, had been a widower for 17 years. He had a married son and daughter from his previous marriage, but three adult children, Peggy, Jean and David, lived with him and Elisa.

With Herman and his brother Pierre so aware of their Afrikaner roots, and the Russells equally so of their British colonial ones, they were politically ranged to refight the Anglo-Boer War. Earlier, Pierre had been living with his grandparents, then in Melville, but during July 1926 the two families, comprising Elisa, William and five young adults were awkwardly cramped into 19 Isipingo Street, Bellevue.

The front of the house led onto a garden where occasional fruit trees yielded their annual harvest, but inside conditions were conducive to disharmony and half-smothered tensions grew like fungi. The emotional climate between Elisa and William Russell was scarcely an improvement on that of her first marriage, and the younger generation found themselves flung together in uncomfortable proximity, rife with resentments. The Russells probably believed themselves a cut above the 'uncouth colonials', whereas the Bosman brothers considered the Russells almost illiterate.

The 23-year-old David Russell was well known in motoring circles and an enthusiastic member of the Harley-Davidson Motor Cycle Club. Pierre, officially a customs clerk, was then primarily interested in medical pathology and was constantly conducting a series of experiments on guinea pigs or snakes, which didn't endear him to the Russells.

It was to this mismatched company that Herman returned during the Easter holidays and by the July holidays of 1926, the discord between the two families had ripened into a boil in need of lancing.

A week before his mid-year holidays ended, Bosman overheard his mother and stepfather arguing. This event must have disturbed him deeply because shortly thereafter he left the house and took a room in President Street. It

*The body of David Russell after Herman Bosman shot him on the night of 17 July 1926*

is also possible that the argument and Bosman's reaction had an Oedipal dimension: it was Bosman's first experience of having to compete for his mother's attention. It may even have been an act of straight rebellion against the hostile environment at Isipingo Street.

The apex of this triangle could have been his own conflicted relationship with Vera (who still believed he was Bertie Boswell) and he may have simply wanted to spend the night with Vera but wasn't sure how else to arrange it. This three-way conflict, where he was married, yet not married, and juggling identities, had him both confused and troubled.

Herman left most of his belongings at the house in Bellevue East, continuing to see his mother every day, but probably spent most evenings with Vera. According to Pierre, as the weekend prior to his departure approached, Herman brooded over his reluctance to return to the Bushveld. On the Friday he brought home the belongings he had removed to the room in President Street and, too restless to sleep, prowled the streets until dawn.

The following day, 17 July, was the anniversary of Delville Wood and the eve of his return to the Marico. While thousands of people gathered near the cenotaph in silent remembrance of their fallen, Pierre dispiritedly helped Herman to pack his things. Among his kit was the service rifle Oom Jim Flattery had wanted him to leave behind in the Marico. It had been cleaned, oiled and loaded, ready for use.

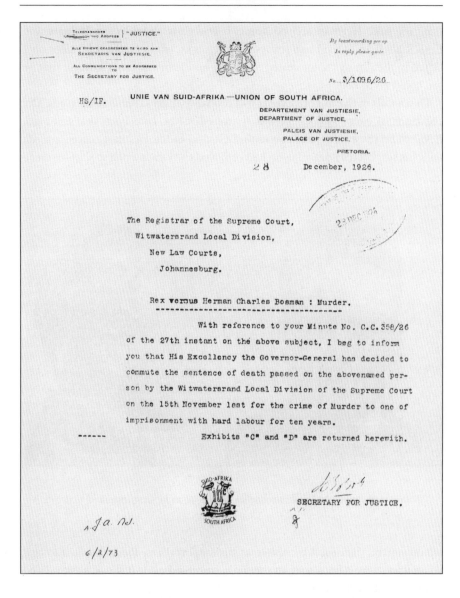

*The commutation of Bosman's death sentence to one of imprisonment for ten years*

After dinner that night, when Herman said goodbye to Vera at the cottage in Ameshoff Street, he thrust a little package into her hand and hurried away to catch the last tram. She carefully peeled away the tissue wrapping and in the palm of her hand nestled a little necklace, a fragile token of a relationship that could only be expressed in terms of 'raindrops in her hair'.

By the time Herman arrived home, it was close to midnight. William and Elisa Russell and David had retired for the night, while Pierre, who slept on a settee in the dining room, waited for Peggy and Jean's guest to leave so that he too could go to bed.

The details of that night's events will probably always remain uncertain. The sequence of cause and effect was shattered in the cataclysm that followed, never to be reconstructed in an entirely logical order. Herman shared a room with his stepbrother, David, who had removed the light switch so that his sleep

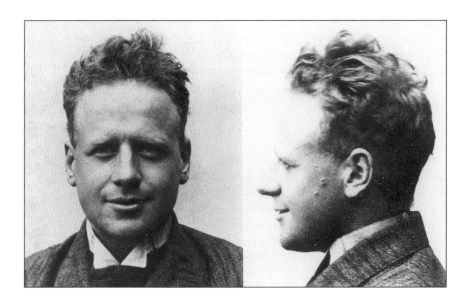

*Bosman photographed full face and in profile when he was sentenced to death*

would not be disturbed by either of his stepbrothers. Pierre went into this room to retrieve a book and, in the dark, stumbled against the washstand and did indeed disturb David.

One minute David and Pierre were exchanging blows in the darkened room, and the next there was the shattering report of a gun being fired. As David slumped towards the bed, Pierre cried out: 'You have shot David!' In the doorway of the unlit passage he could barely discern Herman with the rifle butt wedged under his armpit.

Despite the speculation of news-hungry reporters and the deliberations of a judge and his assessors, no-one could pinpoint precisely where the truth lay – Herman Bosman probably least of all.

Herman fled to the kitchen, followed by Pierre. William Russell burst into the room just as David rolled off the bed onto the floor, his head striking his father's foot. By the time William stooped to examine his son, his eyes were already glazed in death.

To Herman it must have seemed as though the dark echoes of Edgar Allan Poe had suddenly assumed a terrible reality. It has been suggested that he subconsciously wanted to remove William Russell from the scene. One way or another, he was obsessed with death and wanted to be involved in it.

Hysterically he pleaded with William Russell and Pierre to shoot him. Next he tried to slit his throat with a kitchen knife. He had actually inflicted a wound before Pierre managed to wrench it from his grasp. The realisation of what he had done was more than he could cope with, for the next moment Herman was sucked into the oblivion of a fainting fit. When he recovered, he was taken into custody.

For much of his life, Herman must have harboured this explosiveness, a volcano that could erupt with frightening unpredictability. Apart from his attack on Maxie Flattery, and the fatal one on David Russell, there were others, even much later during the last five years of his life. These ended less catastrophically, perhaps only through the intervention of a third party, and in every case the attack was followed by a trance-like state in which he appeared to be bewildered, confused and emotionally disturbed.

The fainting fit after the shooting of David Russell suggests a postepileptic state of dissociation. Psychiatrists and neurologists are unable to conclude whether this was a 'brain event' like epilepsy, or caused by a 'mind event'. But they agree that Herman Bosman acted in a state of diminished responsibility. The thread that outlines his emotional makeup is a nervous system too fragile to adapt to the world.

The next day was Sunday. Vera sat on the granolithic verandah of the cottage in Ameshoff Street when a policeman came up the steps and handed her an empty cigarette box. Scrawled on the back in Herman's pointed handwriting was the message: 'Am being held for murder at Marshall Square. Try to come and see me.' Vera did try, but he was being held incommunicado.

He recalled that wintry afternoon in 1926. There were about a dozen in a cell three-quarters underground. The barred window at skylight level afforded them their only tenuous link with the outside world: a view of the trouser turn-ups and the high-heeled, silk-stockinged feet of passers-by.

Those first hours in the cell were the most miserable in Herman Bosman's life. In *Cold Stone Jug*, that 'unimpassioned record of a somewhat lengthy sojourn in prison', he later recalled how the prisoners were idly cataloguing for one another the offences for which they had been arrested:

*A dapper little fellow who had been doing the questioning worked his way through the whole lot until he came to my turn. 'Say, what are you pinched for?' he asked eyeing me narrowly. 'Murder,' I said. And in my tone there was no discourtesy. And I did not glower much. I only added, 'And I'm not feeling too good.'*

*'Struth!' my interrogator remarked. And his jaw dropped. And that bunch of prisoners in the cell, the whole dozen of them, moved right across to the other side, to the corner that was farthest away from me.*

Earlier that day, Isaac Goodman, crime and court reporter for the *Rand Daily Mail*, had made his routine enquiries from the CID. Acting on what little information he was able to glean, he paid a visit to 19 Isipingo Street with a staff photographer. Later, *Rand Daily Mail* readers read all about the event thereafter referred to as the 'Bellevue Tragedy'. Across two columns was spread a photograph of the house and above it a series of staccato journalese phrases clamoured: 'MAN SHOT IN HIS BEDROOM ... STEPBROTHER DETAINED BY THE POLICE ... CRIES IN THE NIGHT ... DIFFERENCE OVER LOVE AFFAIR ALLEGED.'

Information – some of it speculative and inaccurate – found its way into the report. With the reader's permission, I'd like to quote it at length:

*Rifle shots and wild screaming heralded the discovery, during the early hours of yesterday morning, of a sensational tragedy in a house in Bellevue East. The parties concerned were a young man, David Russell (23), who was found dead in his pyjamas on his bedroom floor with a bullet wound through the heart, and his stepbrother, Henry Bosman (21), who was subsequently detained by the police.*

*The affair took place at the residence of the dead man's father, Mr William Russell, in Isipingo Street. Neighbours were awakened shortly after one o'clock by the sounds of two rifle shots in quick succession, and the crash of broken glass. Almost immediately someone was heard screaming wildly, and a voice cried out: 'Oh God! Oh God!'*

*It is not certain whether the two stepbrothers were alone or whether there was anyone else in the room with them. According to the version of the affair current among the residents in the vicinity, a quarrel was proceeding.*

*It is said that there had been an unpleasantness in the family over a love affair of one of the brothers. The girl to whom he wished to become engaged was not quite in favour with the rest of the family.*

*The difference of yesterday morning may possibly have been the upshot, though this side of the affair is at the moment wrapped in close secrecy.*

*After the shots had been fired, David Russell was picked up bleeding by his father from the floor of his bedroom. The bullet had pierced his arm and entered the chest, striking the heart with an effect which was instantaneously fatal. A service rifle with several cartridges in the magazine was discovered in the room.*

*The police were sent for, and in the meantime Bosman seems to have left the house. Police officers, CID men and a doctor were soon on the scene, and a few minutes after their arrival Bosman came back to the house again. He was at once apprehended, removed to Marshall Square, and placed in the cells pending full inquiry into the several aspects of the affair which are at present not clear.*

*A window-pane was shattered in the room where the firing took place, and it is understood that yesterday morning a spent bullet was discovered on an open space across the street in direct line with the window. This was taken possession of by the police.*

*David Russell was born in Kinrosshire, Scotland, and came out to South Africa with his parents. He was an engineer, twenty-three years of age, and was single. His mother died and about two years ago his father married a Mrs Bosman, who had a son named Henry.*

*The two stepbrothers, Henry Bosman and David Russell, lived with their parents at the house in Bellevue East. Bosman was a teacher. The family is in good circumstances financially and is very well connected.*

The 'very well connected' comment was probably a reference to his uncles Charles and Victor's legal connections.

This account of the shooting makes no mention either of Pierre or of Herman's fainting fit, and consistently refers to Herman as Henry. It did allude to the Russells' disapproval of Vera as a possible contributing factor to the highly explosive emotional climate in 19 Isipingo Street. However, the Russells were certainly unaware that she was Herman's wife at that stage. Neither did the press allude to this.

The report carried by *The Star* of the 'Bellevue Tragedy' was less sensational, and a shade more accurate. The headlines announced: 'ARGUMENT ENDS IN DISASTER ... A FATAL SHOT ... LIGHT ON SHOOTING AFFAIR'.

*David Russell, a motor engineer, aged twenty-three, was shot in his bedroom at 19 Isipingo Street at one o'clock yesterday morning. His stepbrother, Herman Bosman, aged 21, a teacher at Marico, who was spending his holidays at home, appeared in the Magistrate's Court today at a preparatory examination on allegation of murder. He was remanded until July 28. No evidence was called.*

*Russell and Bosman, who have been stepbrothers only for 12 months, shared a bedroom. The cause of the tragedy is said to have been nothing more important than an argument as to whether the window should be open or shut. Whether this argument was playful, and the tragedy in the nature of an accident, has yet to be investigated. The account of the affair given today to a representative of* The Star *was that the two men had an argument about the window. One shut it and the other opened it, and in the upshot Bosman appeared in the doorway with his rifle. A bullet was discharged. It struck Russell in the shoulder, passed through his heart and his body and sped on its way through the window-pane. The shot awakened Russell's father, who rushed into the bedroom to find his son sliding from the bed to the floor. He was beyond all aid and died a minute later.*

*In the meantime Bosman, overcome by what had happened, rushed through the house with the rifle in his hand. His demeanour suggested that he was about to shoot himself and with this thought, his younger brother Pierre wrenched the rifle from him. Pierre fired the rifle again, his intention being to empty the chamber. When the rifle was examined five bullets were found in the magazine. The top one had been cut, thus converting it into a dumdum, the inference being that the rifle had last been loaded when game shooting ...*

*David Russell was very well known among motoring bodies in Johannesburg, and extremely popular with all with whom he came in contact. He was a prominent member of the Harley-Davidson Motor Cycle Club, and in all social functions by that body he took a leading part. His funeral will be attended by members of the club.*

*Herman Charles Bosman made a brief appearance before Mr S. Ellman in the Magistrate's Court, when he was remanded to July 28. He is to undergo a preparatory examination on the allegation that he murdered David Russell by firing a rifle at him.*

*Bosman is a tall, sturdily built, clean-shaven young man of 21 years of age.*

The preliminary hearing on 28 July 1926 was the prelude to the trial that took place four months later. A number of female university students (decorously dressed in black) were in court.

In mid-November, almost two years after Herman had first met Vera, the Johannesburg public was getting ready for another festive season. There was a Mary Pickford film at the Bijou cinema, a Rudolph Valentino at the Standard Theatre, and the *Rand Daily Mail* was sponsoring a charleston competition at St James with prizes totalling £35. Across town from 11 to 15 November, the final chapters of the 'Bellevue Tragedy' were being played out in the Rand Criminal Court. Justice Gey van Pittius presided with two assessors, Messrs J Young and Hull.

According to the court record, the prosecutor, Mr Jarvis, introduced the testimony of the government astronomer, suggesting that at 1 am on the night of the shooting a full moon penetrated the west window of David Russell's otherwise unlit room, and despite the closed curtains shed, in his estimation, sufficient light for the accused to distinguish clearly between the two men locked in physical combat. Mr Jarvis also read in court a manuscript story that Bosman had written shortly before, dealing with a murder and the dismembering of the victim's body. He presented as an exhibit the bloodied pyjamas that had been removed from the body of the victim.

Bosman's counsel, Advocate J G van Soelen, based his defence unswervingly on his contention that the shooting was an accident. Bosman claimed that he had rushed into the room fearing an intruder, had let the gun slip and, in catching it again, had inadvertently fired a shot. Improbable as this hypothesis was, in view of the force required to release the 5½-lb safety-catch of a hunting rifle, he stuck to it, thereby excluding any suggestion of a motive.

The prosecutor's line of questioning hinged inflexibly on the significance of the fact that Bosman had not *said* it had been an accident, to which charge he quite reasonably replied: 'I could see that any explanation of mine would not affect them at the time; they were all so hopelessly distressed.'

Page after page of reporters' notebooks were filled with observations such as:

*His face looked sallow and drawn with anxiety ... he frequently ran his hand through his fair hair.*

*Tense stillness held the crowded court as Mr Justice Gey van Pittius put some vital questions to Bosman concerning the condition of the light in the room.*

*Before giving his verdict Mr Justice Gey van Pittius referred to the case as a particularly sad and pathetic one. He could not see his way clear to reduce the charge to one of manslaughter.*

He intoned, 'The sentence of the court is that you be returned to custody and from there you shall be taken to the place of execution, and at a date and place to be fixed by His Excellency the Governor General, you shall be hanged by the neck until you be dead.'

*As he pronounced the death sentence only a high flush and a nerve flickering spasmodically in the accused's cheek betrayed his otherwise iron self-control.*

The report continued:

> *He was about to turn and descend the stairs that led to the cells when he changed his mind and asked the judge if he might make a statement. The ticking of the clock could be heard as Bosman leaned forward towards the bench and spoke:*
>
> *'My lord, in this strange world of laughter and sighs, I am in my predicament strengthened by the knowledge that there are those whom I love and who love me and who still have faith in me. In that tragic moment, the happenings of which are still not quite clear to me, I was impelled by some wild and chaotic impulse, in which there was no suggestion of malice or premeditation.'*
>
> *He concluded by paying tribute to his family's support.*
>
> *The Judge, much moved, said that his words would be noted and forwarded to His Excellency, the Governor-General.*
>
> *The whole speech was made in a clear cultured voice with only a break of emotion where reference was made to his 'loved ones'. His attitude was one of fortitude and not bravado.*
>
> *As he moved towards the stairs, his eyes searched the court; they rested on his brother who stood red-eyed nearby. The condemned youth's lips framed a message of encouragement to his brother, and he walked steadily down the stairs.*

William Russell was in the well of the court. So was Advocate Fred Malan and he telephoned the news through to his brother Charles in Potchefstroom.

Bosman's bride Vera had stayed away at his request; but the trial must have been semipublic knowledge because her mother was there. She went to Vera's employer and asked him to break the news to Vera in her presence. The press never commented.

Vera, whose love of her life had begun so light-heartedly that Christmas eve, accepted her destiny with fortitude. She had probably never consummated her marriage but would care for Herman Bosman all her life. She insisted that she divorced Bosman for publicity reasons. As Benny Sachs put it so well, for a little while she had touched the knee of a prince.

# 6

## The citadel

*But Oh! dear God the tears that flow,*
*The anguished grief, the bitter woe,*
*In that stone-builded citadel:*
*The hearts that break ... my heart as well.*
*HERMAN BOSMAN*
  *The Sjambok* – Pretoria Central Prison 1929

After the death sentence was pronounced, Bosman was led through the loose knot of spectators and left court in a Black Maria (slang for a police van). The doors slammed shut, the engine revved and the van moved off.

He was brought from Johannesburg under police escort by train to Pretoria Central Prison. The 'stone-builded citadel' of his poem, (Judge Gey van Pittius's 'place of execution') is a great red-brick building near the railway bridge on the Johannesburg road, on Potgieter Street. Once his escort had delivered him to the Pretoria Central Prison authorities, he was photographed, finger-printed, and booked – like all other prisoners. He was allocated the same regulation uniform and equipment, and was assigned a cell.

At this point the regulations that treat all prisoners with uniform impartiality diverge: a new set is introduced which applies only to the élite few condemned to death. The unblinking eye of an electric light, never to be extinguished for the duration of his detention, inspects the prisoner's every move. Surveillance is kept around the clock by a series of warders who relieve one another at four-hourly intervals. His first night there Bosman lay sleepless, waiting for the 5 am rising bell.

The sharp focus of time that distinguishes day from night is blurred and reshaped, encompassing both day and night without particularly delineating either. Sixty minutes may still make an hour, and 24 hours a day, but apart from the punctuation points of mealtimes, exercise hours and change of warders, for the man condemned to die time moves to its own strange rhythms, to be measured in moments or nothing at all. In this way he passes into a twilight existence that serves to prepare him for the ultimate test as though he were an athlete going into training.

There are certain privileges accorded the condemned prisoner. He is excused from haircuts. He may smoke freely. He has, of course, no duties, but if he had and failed to carry them out satisfactorily, he would naturally be exempted from the usual disciplinary measures. In his prison memoir, *Cold Stone Jug*, in which he chronicled his experiences in prison, Bosman wrote how as a condemned prisoner he had envied a regular convict whom a warder had been obliged to hit over the head with a baton:

> *How infinitely privileged I felt he was to be able to be regarded by a warder as a live person, as somebody that could be hit over the head. For no warder would dream of hitting a condemned man with a baton. To a warder a condemned man was something already dead.*

In the weeks that followed, Bosman had ample time to contemplate his circumstances. According to his closest friends, he never discussed what it felt like to have become one of that minority of untouchables who have committed murder, but his vivid descriptions of it must be amongst the most telling in English literature:

> *In prison, the murderer, unlike the blue-coat, does not wear a distinctive garb. He is not dressed by the authorities in a way to single him out from the other convicts – bank-robbers, forgers, illicit gold-buyers, rapists and the rest. There is no need for men to put any distinguishing marks on the murderer's clothes. Cain's mark is there for all to read. Murder is a doomed sign to wear on your brow.*

Within the walls of Pretoria Central Prison the imminence of execution was closing in on Bosman. Outside, during those first few days, his family and friends worked tirelessly for his reprieve.

His uncle, Advocate Fred Malan, approached the Minister of Justice, Tielman Roos, to intercede on his nephew's behalf. Bernard Sachs and Fred Zwarenstein unceasingly gathered signatures among their fellow students of the previous year for a petition urging leniency. A journalist, Terence Clarkson, had a personal interview with Tielman Roos. And Harry Rajak, his old school friend from Jeppe High School whom he had never seen since, privately wrote a letter pleading for mitigation on the grounds that his behaviour patterns had always seemed eccentric, suggesting a nervous structure subject to attacks of diminished responsibility.

Fred Zwarenstein visited him in prison. 'We're planning to get you out of here soon,' he told Bosman on one occasion with a bravado he did not feel. 'What will you do then?'

'Get a job as a shooting instructor.'

Bosman might still have been heckling him on the City Hall steps.

There was one other prisoner in the condemned cells when Bosman arrived, a man for whom he would later choose the name 'Stoffels' in his prison memoir, *Cold Stone Jug*. Their teasing of a particular night warder and their uproarious laughter one night brought a visit from the head night warder:

> '*You condemned men mustn't laugh so loud,*' *he said.* '*The hard labour convicts got to sleep. They got to work all day. You two don't do nothing but smoke cigarettes all day long and crack jokes. You'll get yourselves in serious trouble if the Governor finds out you keep the whole prison awake night after night, romping about and laughing in the condemned cells.*'
>
> *I wondered, vaguely, what more serious trouble we could get into than we were already in.*

He was right, of course, certainly as far as Stoffels was concerned:

> *For early that morning two warders came and fetched me out of my own cell and locked me in a cell two doors away ... And from the sounds I heard later on, when the hangman came to perform his office, it sounded as though everything went off very efficiently. There was the tramping of feet on the iron stairs and the sound of doors being locked and unlocked, and no sound of voices. No orders had to be given. Each man knew what was expected of him, even Stoffels, who played his part tolerably well, considering the fact that he was not rehearsed in it and was getting no pay for it.*
>
> *I heard what sounded like a quick scuffle, then many footfalls. And then a muffled noise in which I recognized Stoffels's voice, but with difficulty, for only part of that noise seemed to come out of his throat. The rest of it seemed to have come out of his belly. More heavy footfalls and doors creaking on hinges. And still no rapped-out words of command. Then a mighty slam that shook the whole building, rattling the pannikin on the floor of the cell in which I was. And it was all over. I looked at the warder guarding me on the other side of the grille. His face was a greenish-white.*

From 14 June 1929 there began to appear in *The Sjambok*, a bi-monthly Johannesburg periodical, a serial purportedly by fellow-inmate-broadcaster, Lago Clifford. Allegedly sourced from the cleaners, it featured a detailed sketch of the gallows, the trap-door mechanism, and expressed a fascination – almost an intimacy – with the whole hanging process.

In the 12 July 1929 issue of *The Sjambok* readers read:

*A few minutes later I was released from my cell at 7.15 and at 7.15 passed the mortuary where I knew the body was lying with the spinal cord broken and the head hanging limp ...*

*Not only does the drop cause the knot in the rope to fracture the thin bone behind the left ear at the base of the skull, but it severs the spinal column. Death by hanging therefore is instantaneous and physically painless.*

The article might be attributed to Lago Clifford, but in it I sense Bosman's urgency to communicate and report his personal experience to the outside world, written scarcely a year before his release. There seems just too much in the turn of phrase, the gallows humour and the echoes of Edgar Allan Poe for it not to be Bosman's work.

After Stoffels's execution Bosman was left alone in the condemned cell, his existence dominated by the gallows chamber, knowing that soon he, too, would have to face one of two alternatives. Either the sheriff would appear with a document on which black lettering would spell out 'Greetings' and he would be notified that his execution had been ordered for the morning after the next; or the governor and the chief warder would arrive and, although they would not be bearing a document with 'Greetings' on it, the prisoner would know that because it was not the sheriff, his sentence had been commuted.

According to the Department of Prisons, he had been in the death cell from 15 November to 24 November 1926. Nine days. His sentence was commuted to ten years' imprisonment with hard labour.

The following lines so closely resemble Bosman's style one can't help questioning their source:

*A thing that struck me forcibly was that murderers were mostly in the First Offenders' Section. There men had committed one crime only and that crime was the last.*

This is a vivid comment on what murder is and how it comes about. The series continued:

*One of the wrongs of the death sentence under the British code is that no distinction is made between a crime that has been premeditated and carefully thought out (such a crime as the Crippen murders) and a crime which is the impulse of a moment such as that of the student of whom I wrote last week.*

*In the Latin countries – France, Spain, Portugal and Italy – these two classes of crime are very emphatically separate, 'le crime intentionnel' and 'le crime passionel'.*

*The first is murder in the strictest sense and the second is invariably homicide. The French always understand and forgive crimes of impulse and passion but never forgive mercenary crime, a sordid murder for gain. The English, on the other hand, seem more ready to forgive murder for gain than murder for passion. But I shall always think mercy should be extended to him whose uncontrollable impulse of a moment caused him to kill.*

Further observations on death row suggest a certain intimacy with the gallows:

*The body is allowed to hang for, I think, seven to ten minutes and then the doctor goes below and pronounces life extinct. The hangman cuts the body down and it is taken through a door at the back of the room (through which we pass every day) into a mortuary, where a post-mortem is held. Later on the death cart comes and the body, sewn in a blanket, is shoved into this cart and driven off – all along our shops – as it were.*

*It was a ghastly sight, especially when the six were hanged, for it was difficult to get all the bodies in, and these had to be packed in like bales of merchandise. Whether it were imagination or truth, yet it seemed to me that the fourth man's head was turned right round and hanging very horribly and actually wobbling.*

*The bodies after execution are buried in quicklime.*

These lines may be attributed to Lago Clifford, but ever since Bosman's contributions to the Jeppe High magazine, his mule-kick endings had become a signature. The description of Clifford's meeting with a fellow convict (who must be Herman Bosman) reads:

*The most interesting and intellectual man I met at the Central Prison was a young student – refined, creative, poetical. He is serving a sentence of ten years hard labour having been convicted of murder and reprieved. He is highly read and possesses a most fascinating personality.*

*The poor young student I speak of is an Afrikander and educated wholly in South Africa. But he has no trace whatever of any Colonial accent. His aspect is a bright and cheerful one; he has clear blue vital eyes. He was convicted of having shot and killed in a fit of ungovernable rage and jealousy. There was not any suggestion of a premeditated crime; it was wholly a crime of passion and impulse. The law recognized this when it reprieved him; but ten years is a cruel sentence. The young man has undoubtedly great literary gifts, some think genius. And there he lies wasting his life and abilities, which could be used in service of his beloved South Africa.*

59

The 'Bosmanisms' resemble far too closely the style he would later adopt as a journalist on his release, and if there were an opportunity, his puckish humour would be unable to resist writing Lago Clifford's impressions of himself, himself.

This article quoted a poem written by the 'student' and titled 'Perhaps Some Day', the last stanza of which reads:

*Though my heart is bruised and riven,*
*Though my soul is scathed with scars,*
*Yet I've touched the fringe of heaven,*
*Yet I've lived among the stars.*

The poem wasn't consistent with the potential he was later to justify, but the last two lines contain an image that would appear in Bosman's later writings as consistently as a signature.

Before we leave his prison poetry, I'd like to share a poem sent me long ago by a 'fellow prisoner':

*WHERE THE FLOWERS GROW*
*Once I saw the lilies fair*
*and the purple daisies grow,*
*Which I wreathed in her hair –*
*Ah, it seems so long ago.*

*Poppies filled the garden wide,*
*And my heart was free from care,*
*With Irene by my side.*

*T'was when all the roses died,*
*When that garden wide was bare,*
*That Irene left my side.*
*Season sad beyond compare.*

*In that time when blossoms fade,*
*Thou, Irene, fragile fair,*
*Like a flower, to rest was laid.*

*Once again the lilies bloom,*
*With the purple daisies fair,*
*But my thoughts are steeped in gloom,*
*And my heart is in despair.*

15a—7/7/26—250.                                      U.D.J. 412.

# DEATH SENTENCE-PARDON OR REPRIEVE

## MINISTER'S NOTICE TO SHERIFF.

**To the Sheriff of** TRANSVAAL

### or his Lawful Deputy.

WHEREAS by Section 341 (2) of Act No. 31 of 1917 it is provided that the Sheriff or his Deputy shall not execute the Judge's warrant for the carrying out of a sentence of death, if at any time the Minister by written notice under his own hand to the Sheriff or Deputy-Sheriff intimates that the Governor-General has decided to grant a pardon or reprieve to the person so sentenced, or otherwise to exercise the Royal prerogative of mercy with regard to him.

THEREFORE I do hereby give you notice that in respect of the sentence of death passed upon

HERMAN CHARLES BOSMAN

by the WITWATERSRAND LOCAL DIVISION OF THE SUPREME COURT OF SOUTH AFRICA holden at Johannesburg

on the 15th day of November 19 26

for the crime of MURDER

the Governor-General has decided to commute the sentence of death to one of imprisonment with hard labour for

ten years

Given under my hand at *Cape Town*

this 10th day of *January*

19 2 7

*[signature]*

**Minister of** Justice.

*[initials]*

(SEE OVER)

*Bosman's reprieve signed by the Minister of Justice, Tielman Roos, 10 January 1927*

*Scarlet threads the poppies wave,*
*God, to think they should grow there,*
*O'er Irene's lonely grave.*

Even in prison the themes of death, poetry and Edgar Allan Poe were Bosman's constants. And somehow – like his humour – they must have been his lifeline.

Bosman's first job in prison was actually in the printing shop, where he served an apprenticeship beginning with elementary tasks like sorting paper, and progressing to hand-setting type and printing anything from government forms to hymn books – experience that came in handy later when he published his own poetry and periodicals.

Bosman also worked in the stone yard and the carpentry shop, and what he learned there enabled him to hold down a job on a construction site many years later. In fact, he told Benny Sachs that forever afterwards, when picking up a fountain pen, he had to think twice to stop himself from first spitting on his hands.

Pretoria Central Prison was, it seemed, as good a place as any to learn the ropes. Here, a young man of 21 could broaden his horizons in more ways than one. Dagga-smoking was a forbidden experience eagerly anticipated and secretly indulged in. For Herman it was invested with all the glamour of absinthe and suggested a private membership of the school of decadents. More than the actual experience was the idea that he had indulged in it. He later wrote: 'I am so peculiar and my thought so erratic that it is difficult for people to believe that I am not under the influence of dagga half the time.' This was absolutely true. In fact, his friends have often described him as getting high on his own thoughts.

An experience that pierced Bosman's sensibilities far more deeply occurred during a period when he seriously suspected himself to be close to the verge of insanity:

> *During this time I found out what insanity was. I found it out through my own symptoms. I realised that insanity had nothing to do with the brain. The ancient Greeks were right. The seat of insanity was the stomach. When I got those mad feelings coming over me, at night, when I was locked up in my cage, and I could see those grotesque figures etched in black against the blackness of the steel walls, then I knew that my insanity wasn't coming out of my brain at all. Because my brain was working reasonably and logically, and I could think clearly. But that purple lunacy, that was like a handful of some slippery substance, was coming out of my stomach. That was where I was going mad; not in my head but in my stomach ...*

*What I dreaded above all: the moment when a fellow-convict would detect that wild gleam that I was convinced shone in my eye; and he would say nothing, but he would sort of turn pale and walk away from me ...*

The following passage reflects Bosman's fear of procreation and the demons that haunted him:

*One evening as we were marching back to the section, I overheard one convict ask of another why mules were sterile. And the other convict said, well, there had to be order in nature. You couldn't have too much bastardization, or where would the world be? A human male and a female baboon could have intercourse, he explained ('Talking from experience?' – I wondered, idly, because my brain was sick), but they couldn't have any progeny. Otherwise it would be an impossible world, he said. What sort of a monstrous thing, for instance, wouldn't the progeny of a pig and a rooster be, he said, by way of example.*

*By the time I got back to the cell, after having overheard that last remark, my mind was in a state of fever. I was locked into my cage, and my mind revolved, over and over again, the import of that dreadful picture. A pig and a rooster would have sexual intercourse: and the offspring they would produce would be half pig, half rooster. A snout and a comb, and a curly tail and feathers. And pig's trotters with spurs. And it wasn't so much a thought as a sensation. I could feel all this madness oozing up out of my belly. It was stomach insanity. All chaos had been let loose in my belly, and was seeping through into my brain.*

*And this half rooster and half pig monstrosity – what if it went and mated with something else? With the progeny of the mating of an elephant and a frog, for instance, or the mating of a railway engine with my jacket – my prison jacket, with the number on, and all? Part frog and part jacket and part elephant's trunk and the tusks of a railway engine, and part – I was going mad. I tried to control my feelings. It was useless. My mind was in a whirl of horror and chaos. A frenzied world in which no single thing would have a brother or a sister or a father or a mother, because there would be nobody to look like him. And if a snake's tail hung down from where my head should be, and there were pieces of fish-scale and red brick in place of my hand, and I walked on one foot and two sticks and one wheel, what in the world would there be, in animate creation or in the inanimate realm, that I could fall in love with? What female would there be even remotely in my image?*

*These things were not so much thoughts as feelings. Horrible black feelings working their way up into my consciousness. I wanted to scream. I knew I was going to scream. But what was the use of screaming? It was very late at night. Nobody would hear me. Or the whole prison would hear me. The warders would come and lock me up next to Krouse. The terror mounted. I walked round and round my cage. It was even narrower, in the dark, here, in my state of dread, than it was in daylight ...*

Finally, when he could bear it no longer, quite oblivious of what he was doing, he took the lid of his urine pail and began pounding at the steel door of his cage until one of the warders came. As a result he spent about three months under observation in the hospital.

*Sometimes I was in the observation cell, and at other times I was allowed to wander about the wards, helping to attend to the patients. But I had learnt one thing. And that was that I was mad, stone mad. And that all the other people in the world were mad, also. And I learnt that what I had to do was to play-act sane. And I am still doing the same thing. I am still play-acting sane: it has come easy to me with the years.*

Early in Herman's fourth year he took to writing petitions for remission of sentence on behalf of various prisoners. Several times he succeeded in getting a man's sentence cut in half. It was only when he became impressed with his growing success in this endeavour that it occurred to him that he might attempt a petition on his own behalf.

Finally, the chief warder sent for him to advise him that his petition had succeeded and that on instructions from head office his sentence had been reduced by half.

Although the letter I have from the Commissioner of Prisons (Captain Delport, 3 March 1973) states on 15 August 1930 he was released on parole until 14 September 1931, I believe this to be a misprint. (In 1929 he would already be out of prison and contributing to a literary magazine, *The Touleier*.) In the event he served three years and nine months.

And so the young man who at the age of 21 had entered Pretoria Central Prison condemned to die, returned to the world to live. Of those he left behind he wrote:

*I think of the long prison years in front of them and behind them. I see them hemmed in by brown walls and brown years. I think of these men leading their silent lives. And I hope that God will go with them, through all those years.*

And to that slice of his life that had slipped by while other young men were doing the charleston, cheering for Willie Smith in the boxing ring, betting on the horses or falling in love, Herman Bosman wrote:

*This is really a love story – a story of adolescent love, my first love ... Her eyes were heavily fringed with dark lashes, like barred windows. Her bosom was hard and pure and cold – like a cement floor. And it was a faithful and chaste love. During all those years of my young manhood, in whose arms did I sleep each night, but in hers?*

These would become the concluding lines of the prison memoir Bosman would publish in January 1949, *Cold Stone Jug.*

*Bosman in the rebel press days of the early 1930s, using the name Herman Malan*

# 7

## Rehabilitation and Herman Malan

After Bosman's release from prison there was naturally no question of his returning to the Russell household – nor any suggestion of his setting up house with Vera. So Elisa arranged with her brothers that he should have a period of rehabilitation in the country: first with Charles in Potchefstroom, then with Victor on his farm, *Tweefontein*, in the Bronkhorstspruit area.

He would be accommodated in a guest rondavel not far from the main house and the neighbours should be kept in ignorance of his immediate past. Accordingly, he arrived at the rural railway station with a suitcase, some boxes crammed with books and a dilapidated old typewriter.

Herman's prison experience had given him an adequate grounding, so he was assigned the erecting and maintenance of uncomplicated structures such as fowl runs. He was also charged with a few general farm chores such as feeding the pigs and poultry, collecting eggs, and the care and clearing of the incubators. He learned to milk the cows and feed the calves – all therapeutic for his unstrung nervous system.

His aunt pampered him and cooked his favourite dishes to compensate for the hair-raising prison rations that he had described to her. His little cousin Zita worshipped and adored him. As soon as she had completed her school lessons, she would join him. She was his constant companion and assistant in all his chores.

He encouraged Zita to write and gave her an exercise book that he expected her to fill with stories or poetry, but which she used as a drawing book instead.

In his free time at night, Herman could be heard rattling away at his typewriter, and for a while all went according to plan. He took to visiting the neighbouring farmers on foot and secretly making their acquaintance. He kept his part of the bargain by maintaining secrecy about his past. Because his studies of the Bible during his incarceration had made him something of an authority on the subject, the farmers mistook him for some kind of preacher and were tremendously honoured by his association with them.

One morning Herman was asked to attend to the repair of some window frames. Instead, in a ferment of inspiration, he closeted himself with his typewriter in his rondavel. His uncle was irritated by his lack of responsibility,

*Aegidius Jean Blignaut, Bosman's friend and colleague, during the rebel press years*

and Herman resentful of a regime that was daily becoming more irksome. The whole point of rehabilitation is that it is meant as a bridgeway back to life. Herman's aunt and uncle appreciated this point of view, but his little cousin Zita was desolate at the prospect of losing her hero.

Bosman stood on the country station platform with his suitcase, his carton of books and his typewriter, just as he had done some weeks before. The train arrived. He said his goodbyes, climbed aboard and, as the train started with an almighty lurch, he braced himself to retain his balance. He leaned out of the window and waved until the little family became remote, doll-like figures no longer distinguishable from one another.

He decided to stay a while with his grandparents, then living in Boksburg, some miles from Johannesburg. From there he could stage his advance on the big city.

While Herman had been in prison, his brother Pierre had also studied English. The first issue of a new Johannesburg literary monthly, *The Touleier*, was due to appear in December 1930 with the first instalment of Pierre's serial, 'The Children of the Desolate'.

Johannesburg had grown four years older; the charleston and the black bottom were no longer the rage. The whole of Joubert Park had broken out with ballroom dancing studios and all of them advertised in one of Johannesburg's early literary magazines, *The Touleier*. And the editor, Aegidius Jean Blignaut, wanted to meet Herman Malan.

Herman Bosman had, in fact, first met Jean Blignaut at a literary soirée during his first year at university, but they had lost track of each other until Pierre Bosman asked if he could bring Herman to *The Touleier* offices.

Jean Blignaut was a spectacular personality in his own right. Cast in the hybrid image of a hero such as Rhett Butler, with both Ronald Coleman's moustache and his elegance of speech, he simply could not miss. Tall, with smiling brown eyes, he had the sort of engaging personality that made him intriguing to men, devastating to women and irresistible to people of any age.

By the time Bosman arrived in Boksburg, Blignaut had formed a company with some friends to launch a literary monthly called *The Touleier*. As executive director and future editor, Jean owned one-third of the shares. Another one-third of the capital was subscribed by John Webb, who was to be mostly in charge of the business side of the venture. The remaining shares were held by a sleeping partner by the name of Mulligan. The total of £200 raised sufficed for a month's rental for five offices, the first instalment on the furniture, the cost of stationery and the salary of two typists.

On 24 November 1930, shortly after Bosman's arrival in Boksburg, the *Sunday Times* carried an article signed 'Herman Malan'. Jean noticed it and began to wonder about the identity of the writer. Somehow he seemed to recognise the style of a student against whom he had once competed. He was still wondering when a few days later Pierre brought Herman to the offices of *The Touleier* in Goodman's Building.

*The cover of the first issue of* The Touleier

# THE TOULEIER

## A Monthly Magazine

Volume 1.        DECEMBER, 1930.        Number 1.

Head Office: 23, 24-26 Goodman's Buildings, Commissioner Street, Johannesburg. P.O. Box 5020.

Subscription Rates: 10/6 per year, post free; 5/6 per half--year, post free. Overseas: 11/6 per year, post free; 6/- per half-year, post free. 1/- per copy. Procurable from any branch of the Central News Agency, Limited.

Inquiries about advertisement space must be directed to the Advertisement Manager.

Unsolicited Mss must be accompanied by stamped addressed envelopes, otherwise they will not be returned, nor will the Editor enter into correspondence about them.

General Manager: John Webb.        Editor: Aegidius Jean Blignaut.

Contributing Editor: Herman Malan.

### LITERARY COMPETITION.

The results of The Touleier Short Story Competition will be published in the January issue. Entries will be received up to January 4, 1931.

The names used in this magazine are entirely fictitious and no reflection on any living person is intended.

*The table of contents of the first issue of* The Touleier

This was the beginning of a working relationship in which Jean might have been editor, but it was his immediate appointment of Herman Malan as literary editor that would make history.

Jean showed Herman some of the 'Ruiter' stories he had written but not yet published. Ruiter was a simple but wily Hottentot who had unstrung his bow and become a raconteur. Bosman was so intrigued with the stories that he and Jean talked far into the night – so late, in fact, that there was no train or bus to take Bosman home to Boksburg. So he spent the night with Jean and returned the following day.

Bosman was justly intrigued. He had found in Jean's Ruiter stories a formula for all the Bushveld stories he had been writing in his head since he left the Marico. The missing ingredient had been his equivalent of Ruiter. With Jean's blessing, Bosman promptly appropriated a minor character in one of Blignaut's Ruiter stories – Oom Schalk Lourens.

A sometimes wise, but mostly bigoted Boer War veteran, who frequently appears to miss the point, Oom Schalk spins a yarn where he uses this 'missing the point' to create his unexpected double-thrust ending. Bosman had not only encountered a gold seam he would mine all his life, but his destiny.

Bosman's lightness of touch has been compared to that of the French Impressionists. Prose poems etched in wisp-like lines, in which he barely touches the earth. And the humanity that he had not been able to direct into society now flowed in marvellous profusion into the short stories he began signing as Herman Malan.

In a playful piece of autobiography he would describe how he found the Marico a cornucopia of riches:

*I was a schoolteacher, many years ago at a little school in the Marico bushveld, near the border of the Bechuanaland Protectorate. The Transvaal Education Department expected me to visit the parents of the school-children in the area at intervals. But even if this huisbesoek was not part of my school duties, I would have gone and visited the parents in any case. And when I discovered after one or two casual calls, that the older parents were a fund of first-class story material, that they could hold the listener enthralled with tales of the past, with embroidered reminiscences of Transvaal life in the old days, then I became very conscientious about huisbesoek.*

*'What happened after that, Oom?' I would say calling on a parent for about the third week in succession, 'when you were trekking through the kloof that night, I mean, and you had muzzled both the black calf with the dappled belly and your daughter, so that Mojaja's kafirs would not be able to hear anything?'*

*And so the Oom would knock out his pipe on his veldskoen and he would proceed to relate – his words a slow and steady rumble and with the red dust of the road in their sound, almost – a tale of terror or of high romance or of soft laughter.*

Nearly 20 years later Herman's disciple, Gordon Vorster, would say that the wonder of Bosman is that he 'wrote in Afrikaans in the English language'. And 70 years later, scholar and Bosman aficionado Craig MacKenzie would write of his remarkable ability to render the Afrikaans experience in English. In MacKenzie's *The Oral-Style South African Short Story in English* (1999, Rodopi, Amsterdam), Bosman takes centre stage as 'The Oral-Stylist *par excellence*'. But this was still 1929 and Jean Blignaut was the very first Bosmanophile.

During that night Bosman and Blignaut had spent talking, it was arranged that Bosman would move to Johannesburg, share digs in Rosalind House and join the staff of *The Touleier*. Within a day or so of their reunion, Jean received a preface Bosman had written for the Ruiter stories:

*In a few whimsical flashes he reveals the sycophancies and frailties underlying the characters of the people with whom he comes into contact ... and through it all his words remain untinged with bitterness or venom; through it all there remains a twinkle in his eyes, and on his aged and swarthy visage there lurks a smile. For he has lived long enough to look very deeply into life, and through the understanding that he has gathered with the years he displays an enduring tenderness towards human weaknesses ...*

*It is not enough to say that Ruiter is typical of the Hottentot nation. He is also typical of the human race ... Ruiter is not only the primitive son of an African tribe ... He is also the son of Adam and the son of God. And this is the character whom the author has created as a medium for relating the stories ...*

*Perhaps their most striking feature is their humour ... This is genuine humour. It is great humour. It is that humour that lies so very close to tears.*

In his covering letter Bosman said these stories had inspired one of his own. Typically, when he came to stay in Johannesburg, he left his story behind in Boksburg. He was unconcerned and quite prepared to write another, and had Jean not insisted that they return to retrieve it, 'Makapan's Caves' might have been lost, instead of making literary history in the first issue of *The Touleier* in December 1930.

# Makapan's Caves

## By HERMAN MALAN.

"KAFIRS?" said Oom Schalk Lourens. "Yes, I know them. And they're all the same. I fear the Almighty, and I respect His works, but I could never understand why He made the kafir and the rinderpest. The Hottentot is a little better. The Hottentot will only steal the biltong hanging out on the line to dry. He won't steal the line as well. That is where the kafir is different.

"Still, sometimes you come across a good kafir, who is faithful and upright and a true Christian and doesn't let the wild-dogs catch the sheep. I always think that it isn't right to kill that kind of kafir.

"I remember about one kafir we had, by the name of Nongaas. How we got him was after this fashion. It was in the year of the big drought, when there was no grass, and the water in the pan had dried up. Our cattle died like flies. It was terrible. Every day ten or twelve or twenty died. So my father said we must pack everything on the wagons and trek up to the Dwarsberge, where he heard there had been good rains. I was six years old, then, the youngest in the family. Most of the time I sat in the back of the wagon, with my mother and my two sisters. My brother Hendrik was seventeen, and helped my father and the kafirs to drive on our cattle. That was how we trekked. Many more of our cattle died along the way, but after about two months we got into the Lowveld and my father said that God had been good to us. For the grass was green along the Dwarsberge.

"One morning we came to some kafir huts, where my father bartered two sacks of mealies for a roll of tobacco. A picannin of about my own age was standing in front of a hut, and he looked at us all the time and grinned. But mostly he looked at my brother Hendrik. And that was not a wonder, either. Even in those days my brother Hendrik was careful about his appearance, and he always tried to be fashionably dressed. On Sundays he even wore socks. When we had loaded up the mealies, my father cut off a plug of Boer tobacco and gave it to the picannin, who grinned still more, so that we saw every one of his teeth, which were very white.

He put the plug in his mouth and bit it. Then we all laughed. The picannin looked just like a puppy that has swallowed a piece of meat, and turns his head sideways, to see how it tastes.

"That was in the morning. We went right on until the afternoon, for my father wanted to reach Tweekoppiesfontein, where we were going to stand with our cattle for some time. It was late in the afternoon when we got there, and we started to outspan. Just as I was

---

### WHISPERS IN A FOREST.
*Anonymous.*

The stately trees, in row on row,
    With moss about their knees:
I daily strive and pray to grow
    As steadfast as are these.

They rest a bird on every twig
    And freely give to bees:
I ever strive to be as big
    And kindly as the trees.

When comes the time, they pay the price,
    And human needs appease:
I long each day to sacrifice
    As quietly as these.

There, with death in their sides, they
        swing
    And dance in every breeze—
Oh, to live and suffer and sing
    As bravely as the trees!

---

*Bosman's first Oom Schalk Lourens story, 'Makapan's Caves', as it appeared in the first issue of* The Touleier

74

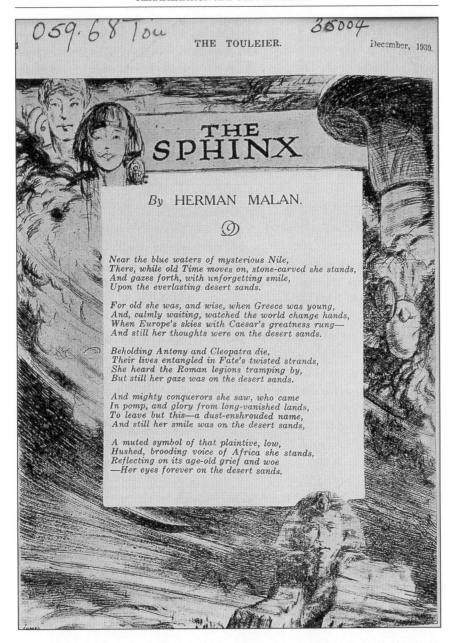

THE TOULEIER.                                    December, 1930.

# THE SPHINX

### By HERMAN MALAN.

Near the blue waters of mysterious Nile,
There, while old Time moves on, stone-carved she stands,
And gazes forth, with unforgetting smile,
Upon the everlasting desert sands.

For old she was, and wise, when Greece was young,
And, calmly waiting, watched the world change hands,
When Europe's skies with Caesar's greatness rung—
And still her thoughts were on the desert sands.

Beholding Antony and Cleopatra die,
Their lives entangled in Fate's twisted strands,
She heard the Roman legions tramping by,
But still her gaze was on the desert sands.

And mighty conquerors she saw, who came
In pomp, and glory from long-vanished lands,
To leave but this—a dust-enshrouded name,
And still her smile was on the desert sands,

A muted symbol of that plaintive, low,
Hushed, brooding voice of Africa she stands,
Reflecting on its age-old grief and woe
—Her eyes forever on the desert sands.

*Bosman's poem, 'The Sphinx', which appeared in the first issue of* The Touleier

In 'Makapan's Caves' Herman Malan sets us up by having Oom Schalk Lourens begin his story with a racist statement, and then turns the tables on us with a story that turns out to be one of the most powerful antiracist statements in South African literature:

> Kafirs? (said Oom Schalk Lourens). Yes, I know them, and they're all the same. I fear the Almighty, and I respect his works, but I could never understand why He made the kafir and the rinderpest. The Hottentot is a little better. The Hottentot will only steal the biltong hanging on the line to dry. He won't steal the line as well. That is where the kafir is different.

During the telling of the story, he relates another incident, in which Oom Schalk Lourens does his characteristic trick of apparently missing the point:

> They also said after killing him, the kafirs stripped off old Potgieter's skin and made wallets out of it in which to carry their dagga. It was very wicked of the kafirs to have done that, especially as dagga makes you mad, and it is a sin to smoke it.

'Makapan's Caves' is the story of a friendship between Schalk's older brother Hendrik and his black friend, Nongaas, where the latter rescues Hendrik, who is besieged in one of Makapan's caves, but at the cost of his own life.

> 'You know,' he [Hendrik] whispered, 'Nongaas was crying when he found me. He thought I was dead. He has been very good to me – so very good. Do you remember that day when he followed behind our wagons? He looked so very trustful and so little, and yet I – I threw stones at him. I wish I did not do that. I only hope that he comes back safe. He was crying and stroking my hair.'
>
> As I said, my brother Hendrik was feverish.
>
> 'Of course he will come back,' I answered him. But this time I knew that I lied. For as I came through the mouth of the cave I kicked against the kafir I had shot there. The body sagged over to one side and I saw the face.

Bosman's mule-kick ending leaves us winded and guilt-ridden.

The first issue of *The Touleier* duly appeared in December. The printing costs of 5 000 copies were borne by the CNA, eventually to be deducted from future profits. Herman and Jean had also been advanced £100 to help launch the first two issues, until advertising revenue began to flow in, and arrangements had been made for a bank overdraft of £50 in case they ran short.

The day Herman and Jean carried their advance copy home from the printing press, Jean said Herman was delirious with joy.

> *On our way to the office, he laid it on the pavement and, stepping
> back a yard to improve the perspective, said: 'Yes, Jean, it looks good
> outside too.' That was an allusion to our contributions inside, for
> amongst the pages lay his Makapan's Caves like a jewel.*

In an introductory passage, Jean Blignaut explained the objectives of *The
Touleier* and the origin of its name:

> *When the Voortrekkers turned their faces towards the dark interior of
> Africa, they placed their faith in their God and the little leader, the ragged
> barefoot Touleier ... Always it was the Touleier who tugged at the riem –
> and moved on. He was the herald of the coming civilisation, he blazed the
> trail for our culture.*

In the few months the periodical survived, there appeared in its pages the first
of the 'Oom Schalk Lourens' stories by Herman Malan, as well as Pierre's
serial, titled 'The Children of the Desolate', and Blignaut's Ruiter stories,
under the title 'The Hottentot's God'. Other contributors included Hedley
Chilvers, Max Drennan and Guy Gardner, as well as two of Herman's fellow
writers on *The Umpa* magazine during his student days, William Waldman and
A D Hatfield.

The second edition of *The Touleier* combined a January-February issue in
one. In it was one of Jean Blignaut's stories from 'The Hottentot's God'
collection, titled 'That Was All', and one of Herman Malan's longer stories,
'The Rooinek', spread over the January-February 1931 issue and then
continued in March. It begins with an incident during the Boer War:

> *Rooineks, said Oom Schalk Lourens, are queer. For instance, there was
> that day when my nephew Hannes and I had dealings with a couple
> of Englishmen near Dewetsdorp. It was shortly after Sanna's Post, and
> Hannes and I were lying behind a rock watching the road. Hannes
> spent odd moments like that in what he called a useful way. He would
> file the points of his Mauser cartridge on a piece of flat stone until
> the lead showed through the steel, in that way making them into dum-
> dum bullets.*
>
> *I often spoke to my nephew Hannes about that.*
>
> *'Hannes,' I used to say. 'That is a sin. The Lord is watching you.'*
>
> *'That's all right,' Hannes replied. 'The Lord knows that this is the
> Boer War, and in war-time He will always forgive a little foolishness like
> this, especially as the English are so many.'*
>
> *Anyway, as we lay behind the rock, we saw, far down the road, two
> horsemen come galloping up. We remained perfectly still and let them*

*approach to within four hundred paces. They were English officers. They were mounted on first-rate horses and their uniforms looked very fine and smart. They were the most stylish-looking men I had seen for some time, and I felt quite ashamed of my own ragged trousers and veldskoens. I was glad that I was behind a rock and they couldn't see me. Especially as my jacket was also torn all the way down the back, as a result of my having had, three days before, to get through a barbed-wire fence rather quickly. The veld-kornet, who was a fat man and couldn't run so fast, was about twenty yards behind me. And he remained on the wire with a bullet through him. All through the Boer War I was pleased that I was thin and never troubled with corns.*

Schalk and Hannes fire at the same time, hitting one of the officers. The other officer then gets off his horse, goes to his friend's aid and hoists him across his saddle. Schalk and Hannes watch, momentarily astonished at his coolness.

*... But when he waved his hand I thrust another cartridge into the breach of my Martini and aimed. At that distance I couldn't miss. I aimed very carefully and was just on the point of pulling the trigger when Hannes put his hand on the barrel and pushed up my rifle.*

*'Don't shoot, Oom Schalk,' he said. 'That's a brave man.'*

*I looked at Hannes in surprise. His face was very white. I said nothing, and allowed my rifle to sink to the grass, but I couldn't understand what had come over my nephew. It seemed that not only was that Englishman queer, but that Hannes was also queer. That's all nonsense not killing a man because he's brave. If he's a brave man and he's fighting on the wrong side, that's all the more reason to shoot him.*

*I was with my nephew Hannes for another few months after that. Then one day, in a skirmish near the Vaal River, Hannes with a few dozen other burghers was cut off from the commando and had to surrender. That was the last I ever saw of him. I heard later on that, after taking him prisoner, the English searched Hannes and found dum-dum bullets in his possession. They shot him for that. I was very much grieved when I heard of Hannes's death. He had always been so full of life and high spirits. Perhaps Hannes was right when he said that the Lord did not mind about a little foolishness like dum-dum bullets. But the mistake he made was in forgetting that the English did mind.*

'The Rooinek' contains a most moving passage written on the Boer War:

*I was in the veld until they made peace. Then we laid down our rifles and went home. What I knew my farm by was the hole under the koppie where I quarried slate-stones for the threshing-floor. That was about all that remained as I left it. Everything else was gone. My home was burnt down. My land was laid waste. My cattle and sheep were slaughtered. Even the stones I had piled for the kraals were pulled down. My wife came out of the concentration camp, and we went together to look at our old farm. My wife had gone into the concentration camp with our two children, but she came out alone. And when I saw her again and noticed the way she had changed, I knew that I, who had been through all the fighting, had not seen the Boer War.*

The April 1931 issue of *The Touleier* contained 'The Man-eater', a story about cannibalism drawn from the darker recesses of Bosman's imagination. It was followed by 'Veld Fire', also in April, in a different magazine, *The New L.S.D. The Touleier* had fallen on hard times, and the May issue carried Bosman's last Schalk Lourens story to appear in the magazine, 'The Gramophone'.

'Francina Malherbe' appeared on 5 May in *The New L.S.D.* followed by 'The Ramoutsa Road', on 11 May. After this Bosman's writing in South Africa shows a gap not easily explained in this chapter, so I'm going to ask my readers to bear with me through this cliffhanger until we reach 'The missing years' in chapter 11.

Meanwhile, to return to the Bosman-Blignaut collaboration, Jean Blignaut described in a taped interview in London (circa 1973) how he and Bosman shared a similarity in incident and anecdote. He described an incident that later appeared in Bosman's story 'Dopper and Papist', in which the driver of a cart constantly has to swallow a swig of brandy to breathe into his horse's nostrils to prevent the horse from growing tired. This episode first appeared in Blignaut's 'The Wayside Remedy', and later propagated as one would a plant cutting.

In this, no suspicion of plagiarism is implied. Rather there existed between Bosman and Bilgnaut a generous hospitality that not only permitted the one to wander in the regions of the other's ideas, but also to be welcomed there. In this way, each enriched the fabric of the other's thinking. Such was the empathy between them that no particular character or idea was the exclusive property of either.

During the Bosman-Blignaut collaboration they shared more than their sleeping accommodation, their meals and their money or lack of it. They also shared their ideas, images and attitudes and in the totality of their association the whole by far exceeded the sum of the parts. They believed there was an alchemy between them that illumined their words respectively and collectively. Like little boys playing with folded paper boats, they would toss their ideas into the swift-flowing current of their imagination and watch them vaulting obstacles and riding rapids. Impelled on an adventurous course that would lead them to undreamed-of shores, they carried in their wake a wealth of free associations that would launch a fresh fleet on even wilder journeys.

There could be no possibility of one interrupting the other's train of thought. With each constantly receptive to the vibrations of the other, they were capable of having a multilevel conversation in which two or more thought processes could be juggled and all kept in play at the same time.

Little by little, this comradeship began to thaw the frigid introspection that had held Bosman in limbo. The long years of suppression had infected even his writing with a sort of paralysis, but the undreamed-of communication he found with Jean Blignaut acted on his inertia. Gradually he began to write more and more, until a feverish compulsion drove him to waking early in the mornings to work on a new short story, to open the floodgates of an extraordinary wealth of imagery spilling out in a myriad fantasies in his poetry.

While talking to Jean about layout, Herman would suddenly grab a pencil and jot down a few lines - the germ of an idea that was to become another poem when the pressure of going to press was off. Afterwards, Herman would fling himself on his bed to write until Jean eventually came to find him, his pencil reduced to a stub and his poem complete. Because he was long-sighted, Herman would position the sheet of paper on the floor and, propped on one elbow, would read it aloud while Jean listened attentively. That was how he wrote most of his poems.

In the January-February issue of *The Touleier*, Bosman also paid tribute to Tielman Roos, the maverick Minister of Justice at the end of 1926 when Bosman's fate hung in the balance:

> *Some heard him talk and thought he was a mountebank; they heard his laughter and accused him of levity ...*
>
> *When he walked it was always in the limelight. But then he, above all other men, could appear to advantage in the limelight, for beside him, others seemed puny men, whom the crowd, with the crowd's insight, set down as puppets. Tielman Roos flung Titanic things about them, and the mob bowed and scraped; he laughed at them and it was laughter that had in it always a sadness of a divine sort, and the mob idolised him. Afterwards, they found they loved him ...*
>
> *We could speak about Tielman Roos's work. But that does not matter. With all of us who have lingered on the earth a little while, indulging in the earth's futilities, the least about us is what we have done. The most important part of Tielman Roos is the fact that he lives.*

This last paragraph reveals one of Bosman's basic credos. He believed a person's acts – even acts of creation that could be called poetry – are significant only in that they are an integral part of their creator's existence. This remained one of the central pillars of his thinking, applied consistently as a litmus-paper test of his own values.

Bosman believed himself to be a poet (calling himself 'a poi-et'), and thought that the gift of the poet was a divine form of madness granted only to the élite few, and certainly beyond the comprehension of the mob.

He loved the fruitfulness of sumptuous words and learned Francis Thompson's 'Hound of Heaven' by heart, simply for the sensuous joy it gave him to speak the lines. He could get high on words, in the same way that other people might get high on drugs. When Jean was translating 'Le Chanson d'Automne', he compelled Jean to read it to him repeatedly so that he could absorb the musical quality of the sounds, despite the fact that he had no knowledge of French.

When he was particularly entranced with a poem, he subconsciously held the sheet of paper as though to feel the words and at the same time shelter their delicate vibrations, that were for him more fragile than a blossom.

Even in those days, Jean felt that he ought to keep Herman's pictures, books and records, because he knew, instinctively, that these would one day be valuable Africana. Herman concurred. Only, in the rapture of the moment, they were quite unmethodical about it.

For him the act of creation was the supreme moment. He believed one should write poetry in the sand and let the elements claim it for their own. When a poem had been written, the responsibility for it passed from the poet to the historian, and he was concerned only with his destiny as a poet. Accordingly, he would as readily let his manuscripts find their way into the wastepaper basket as into print. His ideas on art were equally radical:

> *If an artist does that thing, daubing paint on to a canvas, he creates, in no matter how few strokes, a master-piece. But if a man who is not an artist sets out to achieve the same effect, the result is, of necessity, impudence.*

Their lifestyle was suitably colourful. Herman and Jean both took to wearing felt hats. Jean's was narrow-brimmed and worn at a neat angle that added a touch of elegance to his Ronald Coleman image. Herman's had a broader brim and was the first of a whole succession of hats that he wore with the flourish of Frans Hals's laughing cavalier. To this he added much later the embellishment of two-toned shoes, which he hoped would create the effect of a Portuguese gangster.

But whilst shoe styles were to come and go in Bosman's life, his magnificent Borsalinos, cocked with such inimitable style over one eyebrow, were to become as much a part of his personality as his extraordinarily luminous blue eyes and ready laughter.

Jean acquired an imported red Salmson motorcar, whose previous owner had established records for hill-climbing, and would become a celebrity in a court case they would report. Shortly afterwards, Bosman and Blignaut moved from Rosalind House to Berea, where the ground offered more scope for hill-climbing. But the only way they could coax the Salmson up Harrow Hill was ... backwards. At certain stages of their stay in Berea, they had four cars parked outside – a Buick, a Hudson and then a Moon, which followed the red Salmson. This extravagance scandalised their cook Rosie, especially when the estate agent cut off their water for not paying the rent.

When Jean visited his sister in Potchefstroom, Herman would take off alone for the home of his Uncle Charles. Charles had meanwhile married and become the father of two little boys, but his door was always open to Herman, who regarded his uncle's house as home. Herman would invariably sleep there and receive free legal opinion when necessary.

Charles was a frequent visitor to the little cottage in Boksburg where his parents, Piet and Bettie Malan, had chosen to end their days. Herman invariably tried to time his visits to his grandparents' home to coincide with Charles's, and then the trinity across the generations that had originated in Herman's Potchefstroom childhood would be revived as Bettie and her son and grandson would fall into those animated discussions of ideas to which only 'great minds' had access.

Although it had a certain Bohemian appeal, Berea without light and water became quite impractical, despite its procession of cars, and so Jean and Herman moved back to Rosalind House at 259 Bree Street. Their first apartment had been in the back, where an electric light burned all night to light their way past one building into another. Now their accommodation faced onto the street. It was more cramped, in that there was only one double bed, one wardrobe, one chest of drawers, one bookcase, and a bath and shower next door.

Rosalind House was a single-storey building and, as such, may have lacked the garret where poets are expected to write. But because he never was a literal person, this suited Herman Malan just fine.

# 8

## The Blue Princess

In the second issue of the *The Touleier* there appeared a poem of exceptional tenderness. It was written by someone called Ellie Beemer (pictured here).

*L'Ingénue*
*You danced. Your feet were bare.*
*You stole the strong white magic of the moon*
*To bind your golden hair.*
*You laughed, and tore the wonder from the moon*
*To talk of craters there.*

*We watched the stars.*
*I told you their sweet names –*
*Nihal and Mizar, Maia, Gienaars;*
*You laughed, made them the frames*
*For measurings. The Stars!*

*I knelt, and worshipping I kissed your feet*
*(They gleamed moon-white and fair).*
*Cruel! you laughed. 'Why does your child's heart beat?'*
*Your goblin soul mocked at my wild despair,*
*And then you cried because I stroked your hair ...*

Herman first met Ellie after she had submitted three untitled poems and 'L'Ingénue' for publication in *The Touleier*. Jean was intrigued by the poem and asked her to call at the office. She was enthusiastic about *The Touleier*, keen to be associated with it, and he forthwith invited her to become both a contributor and his secretary.

As editor, Jean might have done the hiring, but Ellie captured both the editor's and the literary editor's hearts, and during the magazine's short life she played a more significant role than her own contributions suggested. She was Herman's inspiration for his first published volume of poetry, *The Blue Princess*, which he began shortly after their first meeting. According to the poetry, she was his first experience of truly erotic love. She *was* his Blue Princess.

Ellie Beemer was an olive-skinned brunette with a small but voluptuous figure. She was lovely in an unconventional way, with an attractive way of expressing herself that somehow managed to be both sensuous and refined. It made her irresistible to the coterie of admirers she had gathered at university and afterwards, even when she was married and hopelessly out of reach.

She came from an upper-middle-class Jewish family in the fashionable suburb of Parktown. Her father had earned this prosperous lifestyle as a successful import-export merchant. It was a lifestyle based on a series of 'thou shalt nots', with an occasional 'thou shalt, if thou possibly canst' thrown in. The former specifically excluded marriage out of the faith, association with ex-convicts, and fraternising with murderers, even if they had been pardoned.

Hers was a society obedient to the tacitly understood dealings of a simple marriage market, where professional men were the most sought-after husbands, with medical doctors the ultimate in prizes. All Jewish mothers of the period tried their best to nurture in their daughters a desire for members of the medical profession. Consequently, most Jewish girls were vaguely aware that somewhere there was another commandment urging them, if at all possible, to marry a Jewish doctor. Like David Klugman.

Herman Bosman was at quite the wrong extreme of the spectrum of desirability and never featured at all. He was an Afrikaner of no particular church, an ex-convict with the stain of murder on his soul, who had the bad taste to be called to the vocation of a poet.

Yet, those two spirits inhabiting regions that had nothing to do with Parktown or Bellevue recognised something in each other, and they fell hopelessly in love. By heritage and environment their love was doomed from the start, and the inevitability of its conclusion had about it all the finality of the condemned cell.

The current that flowed between Herman and Ellie was based on communication on all levels, but their love was as ill-starred as Romeo and Juliet's. All of this found expression in the poems with which, at first, they made love to each other and afterwards they used with equal efficacy to savage each other. One can trace the convolutions of their love story through the things they wrote to each other and, eventually, of each other.

Curiously, in Ellie's poem 'L'Ingénue' are the very images that filled a little notebook Herman had begun to keep. Like Herman, Ellie was a voyager among the stars, one of the elite bewitched by 'the white magic of the moon'.

Granted, such images are the popular currency of all poets, but the observant will find clues to a secret dialogue in which Herman and Ellie seemed more intent on communicating with each other than with those who were to read their poems in print.

In the preface to *The Blue Princess* Herman asserted with a godlike arrogance:

*The mob will not understand these verses. It would be an insult to me if they pretended that they did. A little sane logical man understanding the mad glories of a poet with his head in the stars and his feet on the white sand.*

The second poem in *The Blue Princess* for me has great tenderness, and I somehow think it alludes to one of the many kinds of defloration there can be in the sexual act. And yet I cannot tell you why.

*And He said unto Thomas, 'Behold these hands'"*
*Sister, there is blood upon the dusk –*
*Cold blood on the red petals*
*Of the Spring.*
*Trembling,*
*A hand put forth to pluck*
*The flowers that bleed beneath the grass.*
*His touch lies on all life*
*Who tears*
*The purple petals of the rose's lips.*
*A man no longer*
*But a God*
*With bleeding hands.*

By this time Herman Malan's poetry had developed both passion and rich erotic symbolism. He used a colour code with myriad suggestions not directly related to literal meanings. At a time when mixed media were the revolutionary tools of a more sophisticated art milieu in Europe, Herman Malan was – maybe not even consciously – 'painting' his poems as much as he was writing them. And can there be many lines in love poetry that express the poet's sexual fantasy more vividly than these?

*A long time he lingered in a strange ecstasy;*
*And then he went in*
*Deeply.*
*A star-flung mansion decked with pearls*
*And fringed with draperies,*
*Scarlet with purple.*

One of Ellie Beemer's own poems read in part:

*Cool room – you nod –*
*Your face against the window pane.*

*You see ... the rind*
*Of the world. You child!*
*And the man at the window*
*Turned from the glass-cool pane*
*And smiled.*
*His eyes were blind.*

The motifs of 'blindness' and 'the rind of the world' are the coinage of both Ellie's and Herman's poetry, and were minted in the imagination of both. In addition, the themes of lack of communication and disillusionment had begun to haunt the verses of both alike. They both adopted the short line at about the same time. With all this, their poems took on a likeness to each other's until they could be interpreted not only as a dialogue between two people, but also as variations on a single theme. Herman first used this technique in the poem 'Only'.

*You whom I called my princess,*
*I did not know*
*That you*
*Were only*
*A woman.*
*I called you princess, my princess;*
*In the eagle's loneliness, princess I called*
*But you*
*Were only*
*A queen.*
*The rose,*
*Whose petals I felt with the strange touch*
*Of fingers that had broken the rind of the yellow fruit – I did not know*
*That the dark rose*
*Would one day*
*Open.*
*I did not know these things,*
*Until I saw*
*That the grass was white*
*And that my verses*
*Were only*
*Torn paper.*

One of Ellie's poems bore such a resemblance to Herman's work that, if by some mistake it had found its way into *The Blue Princess* collection, it might easily have been ascribed to Herman Malan, and no-one would have been any the wiser. Ellie made a bid for Herman's understanding when she said: 'We live in different worlds.'

Herman was intractable and replied: 'Yes, from mine I can spit on yours.'

The demise of *The Touleier* coincided with that of the two poets' love. By this time Ellie and Herman's love story was being played out in stolen moments in *The Touleier* offices, or in secluded spots under an open sky, causing Herman forever after to think of grass as 'the natural bed'. The requiem for their love was a forbidden correspondence, like that of most ordinary ill-starred lovers, left under an even more ordinary stone at the bottom of the Beemers' garden.

In the preface to *The Blue Princess* his words were scorching:

*Mostly these verses are about a princess to whom I gave millions of blue jewels that were real because I made them so. But I lost this princess. You see, she didn't want jewels; she wanted jewelry.*

*I have made these verses by living them; and where they are not true is where I have lived lies. But the verses remain true poetry.*

*But what is strange about it all is that in losing my princess she remains mine for always.*

Even though marriage might not have been Herman's objective at this point, he felt that in conforming to her environmental conditioning, by giving herself in matrimony to a Jewish doctor, Ellie was betraying the 'jewelled firmament' he had offered. He wrote a poem titled 'The Poet Gets The Boot':

*In losing me,*
*You who were my princess,*
*You remain*
*A princess still.*

But he seemed to be writing something like a curse into the last lines, where he charges her with wantonness:

*You have lost all these.*
*Your possessions,*
*Shrunk to nothingness, have left you*
*Bare.*
*A pauper princess.*
*And yet,*
*I fear you, princess,*
*In your poverty finer than Sheba's splendour –*
*with your cold hands*
*To fling a god away.*

Herman Malan hadn't finished with his Blue Princess who had spurned his 'blue jewels' for jewelry:

> *It is queer that people should go to the trouble of having themselves bound by empty social vows, when even a dud poet can break them with laughter that also holds passion.*
>
> *A marriage made by a priest can be broken and leave nothing behind, except, maybe, a beast pain of a torn body, like piles. A poet's marriage can never be broken as long as there is grass.*

Ellie had rejected his 'blue jewels'. Their love affair had flowered with poetry and it had withered with letters. There was only one way it could end: with words.

Herman evidently felt Ellie's story called for his having the last word. When it came, it was in two instalments in the July and August issues of the *The New Sjambok*. It wasn't a Schalk Lourens story. It wasn't even a veld story. It was a story about a wedding in Parktown, and it showed a strange sense of menace and a viciousness unknown in Bosman's other writings. The first part, 'Rita's Marriage', was published in July and August 1931.

The second story appeared on 14 September of the same year. Titled 'Heloise's Teeth', it tells the story of a man who was murdered in a lift. It so happens that a short while before the story was published, Ellie Beemer's uncle fell to his death down a lift shaft. He was the man who finally forbade Herman to continue to see Ellie.

# 9

## The gutter-press

The end of Herman Malan's and Ellie Beemer's love story synchronised with that of *The Touleier*. As early as the third issue, in March 1931, it had become clear that if *The Touleier* were to remain afloat, it would require much more revenue from advertisements. Herman Bosman's business acumen had not been unduly taxed since the Floydd B Warrington escapades at school, and now he rose to the occasion.

John Webb's policy was to seduce prospective advertisers with offers of a double exposure – once in the advertising for which they paid, and once in an editorial by the poet Herman Malan. Accordingly in March 1931 *The Touleier* featured a new column titled 'By the Kerb-side', the author's name tantalisingly represented by a series of dots. But even from the opening paragraph, anyone familiar with Herman Malan's work could have spotted his identity. It read:

> *The other night I strolled through town in a leisurely manner. There seemed to be a certain freshness about the evening; the air held a fragrance that you don't often find about the Johannesburg streets. I noticed that there were other people, also, who obtained profound spiritual gratification just from breathing the city air. One man even sat down on the pavement, so that he could breathe the air in better, I suppose. When I passed again, two hours later, he was still sitting there. By that time he was asleep.*

In the course of this new column, a benign limelight focused in turn on the Herbert Evans Paint Shop and Art Gallery, the Stephanie Hotel, the Bar-Lock Typewriter and Mackay's Music Saloon, all of which soon found themselves ranking as status symbols essential to the lifestyle of Johannesburg in the early 1930s.

However, this was still not enough to save *The Touleier*. By mid-year, after five issues, the writing was on the wall. Jean agreed that *The Touleier* be taken over and published by African Publications under the name of *African Magazine*. It ran for one issue, which contained two of Blignaut's Ruiter stories, one Schalk Lourens story by Herman Malan and a contribution by

Vol I. No. 1.      JOHANNESBURG, SATURDAY, JULY, 18. 1931.      PRICE 3d.

# Editorial.

Four months ago an unobtrusive paragraph in a local newspaper announced that "The Sjambok" had stopped publication. There were those who felt it was malice that had induced the Big-Sheet Press to be so ostentatiously reticent about a matter of the utmost public interest, there were others who held it for a feeble effort at showing contempt for a paper that had become a power in the Union ; but the regular readers of " The Sjambok " knew it for what it was without casting about. They knew that the gutter newspapers stood in such awe of " The Sjambok " that they feared it might come to life again. if they seemed to be taken with what was going forward. As the little boy becomes scared of the silence in a wood through which he is passing and whistles timidly to reassure himself, so these newspapers whispered " ' The Sjambok,' a Johannesburg publication, will cease publication." This was a compliment to " The Sjambok "

When certain lawyers and parsons and Salvation Army " Officers " and other lovers of the dark read the announcement, they locked themselves away and said, " Thank God." These people detested and feared " The Sjambok." While it held sway they went in fear and trembling, doing their evil deeds in hidden places. And so it was easy to understand that they were filled with joy when the grotesque libel laws by which we are all led to the slaughter relieved them of anxiety on the score of their iniquities by making it temporarily impossible for " The Sjambok " to continue. They rejoiced in their hearts and nothing but the fear of laying themselves open to a charge of having something to conceal kept them from calling for a public holiday.

They rejoiced but their happiness was short-lived, for the spirit of healthy criticism that had animated " The Sjambok " came to life again in " The New £ s. d."—a gallant little paper this that filled the breach till " The New Sjambok " had had time to gather itself for action. " The New £ s. d." should be commended for the spirit of sacrifice in the public weal that moved it to make way for us. We feel that our readers will continue to support it wholeheartedly where it appears within a short period as a critical sporting weekly. The thousands of readers of " The New £ s. d." know us of old, and theer is no need for us to take the oath of allegiance : they know we shall at all times be fearless in our fight for justice. We are the defender of the poor and the despised and the downtrodden, we are the joy of the honest and the just. They know in whom they have placed their trust.

### And, of course, the great thing is—we are back again.

*The editorial page from* The New Sjambok, *18 July 1931*

*A page from an early issue of* The New L.S.D.

Ellie Beemer acting as ballast through its stormy passage. Lack of funds had made it far too buoyant for the high seas, and in June 1931 it had capsized and plunged to its end.

Almost simultaneously, the demise in March 1931 of a Johannesburg scandal sheet, *The Sjambok*, edited by Stephen Black, left a yawning hole in the market. When the last issue of *The Sjambok* appeared, Bosman's and Blignaut's appetite for journalism had been sufficiently whetted for them to start a rebel paper of their own.

The first issue of *The New L.S.D.* appeared on the streets in the same month – March 1931. 'L.S.D.' stood for 'Life, Sport and Drama'. It was timed to hit the newsstands on 7 May 1931, the day the next issue of *The Sjambok* would have appeared.

Jean Blignaut claimed it ran for two years, but I make it a scant six weeks. It was mainly dedicated to attacks on the penal system, attributed to ex-inmate Lago Clifford, but more likely ghostwritten by Herman Malan. Part of its brief success was that people believed that scandal-sheet editor, Stephen Black, still had a hand in it.

It also featured Herman Malan's veld stories, 'Veld Fire' on 2 April 1931, 'Francina Malherbe' on 5 May, and 'Ramoutsa Road' on 16 May, after which it died. It was replaced by *The New Sjambok* which ran from 10 August until 12 October 1931. Jean Blignaut would later revive it in 1939. According to Blignaut, 'As far as general content was concerned, there was a distinction between the two papers. Both were used for crusades and sensational stories, but at least some pages of *The New Sjambok* were devoted to literature and could be described as a continuation of *The Touleier*.'

In fact, almost concurrently, Herman Malan's 'The Man-eater' appeared on April Fools' day that year in *The Touleier* and two days later 'Veld Fire' launched *The New L.S.D.*

May was a busy month for Herman Malan. *The Touleier* celebrated May Day by featuring 'The Gramophone'; *The New L.S.D.* did so with 'Francina Malherbe' on 5 May and 'Ramoutsa Road' on 16 May. Three months later *The New Sjambok* replaced it, and ran for five months. It featured two essays that I believe made literary history. One was Herman Malan's assessment of poetry, 'A Few Words in the Sand' (31 August 1931). On 12 October 1931, it published his (and Jean's) hilarious, 'The Day the Gutter-press was Scared' – one of the funniest pieces I've ever read.

According to Jean Blignaut, 'their circulation was remarkably high for their time, and twenty thousand copies of both papers were sold weekly throughout South Africa.' Credit for their 'success' must go to their fearless journalism, their crusades, their jibes at the 'big-sheet press', and their knack for upsetting almost every section of the establishment. Countless times they ended up in court on charges of libel, *crimen injuria*, publishing obscene or objectionable material, and even blasphemy.

Like *The Touleier*, these papers were first printed by Technical Press of Johannesburg. Later, Bosman and Blignaut acquired a run-down old printing press of their own at 67 Simmonds Street in Fordsburg, where they printed the two rebel sheets for a while. When the dilapidated old machinery could no longer turn out a combined print order of 40 000 copies a week, Blignaut arranged with another printer, Brill Brothers in Fordsburg, to print the papers on the understanding that it would be exonerated from responsibility for the contents.

In the early 1930s, when the papers were launched, South Africa was gripped by the worst depression in its history. Hundreds of garment workers were laid off work and unemployment threatened the victims with starvation. But no situation was ever so black that Herman could not make everyone see the funny side. Laughter was probably the rarest commodity of all during those days, and the humour that glowed within the stone-cold walls of their offices warmed the spirits of all who came there.

Enoch, the African tea-server, also infected by the prevailing sense of loyalty, kept two photographs prominently displayed – one of Herman and one of Jean. Enoch had a built-in smile on his face, but it was never broader than the day his photograph appeared in *The New L.S.D.* The caption read: 'Mr Mtushwa Fish, representative of Messrs Malan and Blignaut.'

By the middle of 1931 the course and pace had become severely taxing. In addition to the two weekly papers, they published several pamphlets. So Bosman and Blignaut changed gears and pedalled even harder. They could – and often did – bring a paper out in one night. On such occasions they would dictate right through the night – as fast as the copy-holder could handle their output.

Blignaut recalled how Bosman could write any of the Schalk Lourens stories in a couple of hours, his speed being governed only by his mechanical ability to record his thought. 'I witnessed many a feat that proved his facility with words; no matter how fast he wrote, his felicity of diction was unaffected by what ordinary authors would regard as haste.'

On Fridays, when the paper had been put to bed, they would emerge into the dawn and restore their failing energies with meat pies and tea from the all-night cafe in Harrison Street, not far from the location of the Traffic Department's headquarters today. And on many occasions, when the cook Rosie appeared to dust the Berea house sitting room, she found the two literary gentlemen out for the count on the lionskin rug.

In *The New L.S.D.* Bosman and Blignaut also revived a column titled 'Women, lovely women, by One of em'. Ellie Beemer was the 'One of em' trying wistfully to fit into the mould for which she had never really been made. Unable to continue for both professional and personal reasons, sadly, her resignation from the column was recorded:

> *'The above feature is missing from this column. The one of em who used to contribute got off with the office boy. The boss wouldn't fall.'*

In October 1931 *The New L.S.D.* carried an article titled 'What the best man did to the bride for the last time'. In reading it one has the suspicion that the authors were settling an old score with the Beemer family. They said:

> *It is disgraceful to contemplate a situation in which 'pot-gutted' Philistines spend hundreds and even thousands of pounds on celebrating shabby marriages de convenance, while poets, who have found the real beauty of life, have to starve on the streets. We should like to know what proportion of marriages taking place in Parktown are inspired by no loftier considerations than animal lust and a disgusting greed for money.*

The article earned them a conviction and a fine of £3 in the Magistrate's Court. They appealed, but the conviction was upheld. This was just the beginning of a series of tussles with the law where 'The gutter press' – as they now called themselves – got the worst of it.

When it came to writers, George Bernard Shaw was dismissed as an intellectual poseur. For Herman Charles Bosman the intellect counted for very little:

> *Bernard Shaw started well enough. He wore one suit eight years, and until the age of thirty he lived like a king, which is the only way a real artist can live – that is, he lived by bumming off Philistines who were yet great enough to see the mark of the gods on the brow of the man whose feet were in the gutter. But of course, the Philistines were mistaken about Bernard Shaw ... Shaw is completely sane. No God touched his forehead with the madness that changes blood into red wine ...*
>
> *Genius needs no defense ... there is no need for a clown with a painted nose to come along and say that the mad dreams of the genius are all right after all.*

Of Roy Campbell: Art, Herman Malan said, was a divine way of getting God's words mixed up. This had not yet been learned by Roy Campbell, who was wasting his time on the high seas writing so-called satire.

*I would advise the captain of the next boat Roy Campbell works on to boot this young man up the hatchway as soon as he tries to borrow a fountain-pen off the bo'sun. We don't need any more of Campbell's sterile wit ...*

Interestingly, Roy Campbell never retaliated and among the published assessments by other authors of Bosman's writing, his still ranks among the highest.

Of writers, Sarah Gertrude Millin was the most frequent victim of Bosman's invective, but not the only one. He was equally derisive of William Plomer, Oscar Wilde and even Shakespeare. Herman Malan said of Shakespeare in *The New L.S.D.* on 10 June 1932 that he failed to measure up to the poet's madness when he 'made Othello murder Desdemona because he thought she was carrying on with another man'.

In an article in *The New L.S.D.* on 10 June 1932 Herman Malan wrote:

*You degraded it into a sordid squabble in a bedroom in Stratford-on-Avon. I can see the soiled counterpane on your second-best bed. I can hear Anne Hathaway's voice declaring that the butcher didn't have his arm round her.*

*How much finer it would have been had Othello strangled Desdemona for no reason in particular – merely because he loved her, or simply because he wanted to, or just for fun. Othello is the tragedy of a man who is bigger than his creator. I feel that Othello could have murdered Desdemona for nothing.*

Anyone who ever saw Hitler on a 1930s newsreel will understand my wanting to share Herman Malan's impressions as a 1930s patron at the Bijou theatre:

*What I saw of Hitler on the screen merely confirms me in my belief that Hitler is being directed by some man with great creative genius. There is an opening in Germany for a dictator. Somebody has seen that opening – some man who has not the organising ability to carry out the scheme – and has asked Herr Hitler to take it on.*

*I don't know who that man is, the man behind Hitler, but I suspect it is Einstein.*

*Anyway, Hitler's oratory is not impressive. He doesn't speak with force in the way that Mussolini does: he only shouts out words loudly in an obvious attempt at copying Mussolini. Hitler seems to think that Mussolini has merely folded his arms and shouted his way to the position of Dictator. Hitler has imitated everything of Mussolini except his soul.*

*In one respect Hitler is delightfully original ...*

*When Hitler gets stuck for a word he turns about face with a smart click of his heels – and stands immersed in thought with his back to the audience. Then, when he remembers the rest of his speech he turns round briskly and shouts out more words. But they are only words. I am satisfied that Hitler will never get anywhere at this rate.*

Seven years and many newsreels later Herman Malan – as Herman Bosman – would observe Hitler's style from just across the English Channel.

In August 1931 Bosman published in *The New L.S.D.* his significant early statement on art and poetry mentioned earlier, 'A Few Words in the Sand'. He believed art and poetry to be the dominion of an élite whom God had invested with a certain type of madness.

*The first poet was a magician. His verses were incantations; they were magic blood things which the mob could not understand; but there was a power in the words that held the mob spellbound. Whether the poet himself knew the meaning of what he was trying to say only God can tell. And God knows that it does not matter. The first poet was a mad man.*

*Thereafter, other men who were not mad started to imitate the poet – without success. They wrote about 'small sane things' which small men could grasp with their intellects.*

*It is the artist who is great, not his works ... An artist to live for an eternity has only to live once. And he will need to do no more than just live.*

*The plodder, dazzled by the idea that God should have gifted him even to the small extent that he has, hoards up his small change like a miser, and puts everything he knows on paper, deathly afraid of losing a mite ... (After all he hasn't much to lose.)*

*The artist is a millionaire with great treasures of blazing jewels that he thinks nothing of, for he knows that they are his to throw away ...*

If art was Herman Malan's major inspiration, capital punishment was his major crusade. His incarceration had inflicted on him wounds that ached on grey days ... and dark nightmares that would engulf him for the rest of his life.

Describing prison conditions, he wrote that the inmates led a kind of life from which the soul of things had fled:

*Even the imagination was caged. Self-expression was strangled. Sleep was mostly a nightmare in which I was a hunted animal fighting for freedom. Occasionally a poor brute raised his voice in a desire to break the stillness of the night. The only echo to his wail was a combination of foul curses mingled with the scream of derision from creatures that had once been men.*

From its very first issue in June 1931, *The Sjambok* attacked the prison system through 'Lago Clifford's' impressions:

> *Before a convict can respect himself he has first got to learn to respect other people. He learns very quickly. There is no man doing twelve months or over who hasn't got a deep respect for the oldest safe-blower in the place and for those consistent boys who are doing their third and fourth long stretch. Some of them have even got respect for the warders. But maybe this is carrying a good thing somewhat too far.*

According to Jean Blignaut, in 1932 when Daisy de Melker was condemned to death on three counts of murder, Herman Malan wrote two pamphlets. The first was titled *The Life Story of Mrs De Melker*. Blignaut reported that within a week of its appearance it had become a bestseller, and eventually 200 000 copies were snatched up throughout South Africa, becoming collectors' pieces.

But would Jean Blignaut have had access to this information? He was still in Pretoria Central Prison and this would have had to be hearsay evidence. Herman Malan, on the other hand, was no longer incarcerated, and was in a position to report:

> *More than one wardress set about improving her table-manners, trying to drink her tea in the refined and genteel way she had seen Mrs De Melker do it. A wardress was afraid to indulge in the usual coarse abuse of prisoners in case Mrs De Melker should overhear it and think her unladylike. Even the speech of the wardresses altered. From the loud crudities and solecisms of slum parlance they modulated their voices to what they regarded as Mrs De Melker's aristocratic tones. One or two of them started talking with an Oxford accent.*

He recalled the condemned cell:

> *These stories of the gallows – these half-laughs with the hangman – will terrify Mrs De Melker long before they come to take her weight in order to calculate the height she has to drop, long before they measure the circumference of her neck in order to work out the size of the noose.*

Eventually, once Bosman had declined to plead for a reprieve for Daisy de Melker, it became simply a matter of how the gutter-press might outdo the big-sheet press in reporting her execution. Knowing that the big-sheet press would come out with something imaginative like 'Mrs De Melker Executed', Herman Malan decided on the title 'How Mrs De Melker was Hanged'.

Using his own intimacy with the condemned cell, Herman Malan prepared his copy in advance. On the Friday morning of the execution, a gutter-press stalwart telephoned the Superintendent of Pretoria Central Prison. Posing as the editor of *The Star*, he asked whether Mrs De Melker had been hanged. The Superintendent confirmed that she had, at eight o'clock that morning. The team sprang into action. Their posters were on the street in time for late breakfast. Macabre? I have to admit it. But their scoop was a sell-out.

Naturally, at times, too, these papers served as a vehicle for the Malan-Blignaut mutual admiration club. Herman Malan reviewed Blignaut's Ruiter stories ('The Hottentot's God'), in *The New L.S.D.* of 5 February 1932:

> *It's all right, Sarah, you needn't be jealous. Aegidius Jean Blignaut is not going to compete with you. He is not going to do you out of a job. Pauline Smith is there for that purpose. Aegidius Jean Blignaut wrote those stories for the only reason an artist does anything at all. He wrote them because he liked doing it. That is why his stories will live, and people will laugh and sigh and wonder over them long after your* Men on a Voyage *has been forgotten. I know that the Hottentot Ruiter series will go well in England and America. These stories will be acknowledged immediately as masterpieces. Even in South Africa Aegidius Jean Blignaut is not altogether without an audience. For one thing, he has me for an audience. And I am a hell of an audience ...*
>
> *Aegidius Jean Blignaut is the greatest short-story writer since Edgar Allan Poe.*

Jean then allegedly returned the compliment with his praise for *The Blue Princess*. (I have to say 'allegedly', because I suspect Bosman of having written the whole thing himself, and attributing it to Blignaut.)

> *In this little volume of poems the author who is South Africa's most brilliant poet has recaptured the spirit of the greatest Hebrew poets. The word has power in Herman Malan's mouth.*

This accolade was then trumped by Herman Malan as himself:

> *Mine is the finest poetry since Keats.*

I, personally, suspect Herman Malan of having been the sole author of the entire dialogue. Either way, Bosman's games with identities were intended to be both extravagant and funny. And they were.

*The New Sjambok* of 12 October 1932 featured a report of yet another court appearance by Bosman and Blignaut, this time on a charge of not having paid for a secondhand motorcar. Jean maintained that it was defective. It was one of the most hilarious reports of *The New Sjambok*. Hannah Greenberg and Bertha Solomon appeared for the Automobile Exchange, while Bosman and

Blignaut, though represented by a certain Mr Patel, mostly conducted their own defence. One exchange went like this:

*Bertha Solomon: Were you the editor of* The Touleier, *a literary magazine?*

*Jean Blignaut: You ought to know. You unsuccessfully tried to write for it.*

*Bertha Solomon: Why didn't you look under the bonnet?*

*Jean Blignaut: I wasn't interested. I know she had belonged to somebody else before. Besides, it wasn't dark enough.*

*Bertha Solomon (to Herman Malan, the next witness): What was wrong with the car?*

*Herman Malan: It was only a five-seater.*

*Bertha Solomon: What has that to do with the case?*

*Herman Malan: It required eight people to push it.*

*Bertha Solomon: Why didn't you walk instead of travelling in that car?*

*Herman Malan: Madam, I never once travelled in that car. I travelled behind it.*

*Bertha Solomon: You say you are a poet. As a man in the street, what is your opinion of that car?*

*Herman Malan: I can't speak as a man in the street. I can speak only as an artist ... As an artist I should define that car as a poseur.*

*Bertha Solomon: Your Worship, with your indulgence, I shall ask Mr Malan, as a matter of general interest, to explain himself.*

*Herman Malan: The difference between that car and a real car is the difference between Sarah Gertrude Millin and myself. Sarah Gertrude Millin has to be pushed from behind. Of late the* Rand Daily Mail *seems to have grown tired of pushing her.*

*At this stage Hannah Greenberg, convulsed with laughter, had to leave the courtroom hurriedly.*

*(In a letter criticising his work Sarah Gertrude Millin speaks of Herman Malan as having his head in the stars and his feet in the gutter. He wishes us to state that she is quite correct. His feet were in the gutter, all right – when he was pushing that car.)*

The gutter-press's skirmishes with the law were to be their undoing. Sometimes the prosecutors won; at other times Herman Malan and Jean Blignaut did. These skirmishes started towards the end of 1931 and continued intermittently up to 1933, when Bosman left for London.

Looking back on their story, October 1931 was a very busy month for Bosman and Blignaut. On 9 October Blignaut appeared in court charged simultaneously with having employed unqualified men as journeymen, and with contravening another regulation by failing to pay these same journeymen (now qualified) the going rate. Blignaut was acquitted because he successfully argued that the two charges were mutually exclusive. At one stage Jean was rebuked by a judge for his record of convictions. He conceded the point, but reminded the court that he had also had seven acquittals.

The 'big-sheet press' focused public attention on them like two flies in a bottle. Far from squirming, they actually enjoyed it, and played to the public gallery like seasoned troupers. The dailies never passed up an opportunity to report on the editor and proprietor of *The New L.S.D.* and *The New Sjambok* who, in turn, never hesitated to insult them.

In November 1932 *The New L.S.D.* announced that the Courier News Agency Limited of Empire House, Queen Victoria Street, London, was negotiating for Blignaut's Ruiter stories. Several had appeared in *Empire* (John Webb's monthly) and were being 'translated into five European languages'. They did appear nearly 50 years later (in Lionel Abrahams's 1980 edition *Dead End Road*), but I am still looking for evidence that they got off the ground at that point in time.

Jean Blignaut was the product of a distinguished legal family, and relished nothing more than a legal skirmish. He conducted his own defence whenever he could with elegance and wit, and was as handy with his law books as he was with his typewriter. Their finances eventually came under scrutiny when Jean Blignaut admitted that he received a salary of £85 a month, out of which he had to remunerate himself and his staff. He explained that his staff consisted of two sub-editors, Pierre Bosman and Willie Charmers, and a literary editor, Herman Malan. They were paid £20, £10 and £25 respectively.

Prosecuting counsel, again Hannah Greenberg, latched onto this like a terrier onto a bone: 'You mention two men, Malan and Bosman. What is Bosman's real name? Are Malan and Bosman not one and the same person?'

Imperturbable, Jean replied: 'No, I can produce Bosman in five minutes' (Pierre). In the end Blignaut was fined, but the gutter-press team had had their money's worth in fun.

By the end of the first quarter of 1932, between the time a misdemeanour was filed and the time it came to court, several others had been committed – rather like an energetic game of leapfrog. In fact, on Friday, 26 February 1932, *The New L.S.D.* nearly failed to appear at all, owing to the absence at His Majesty's pleasure of the editor and his assistant, Herman Malan.

But the intrepid sub-editor Pierre Bosman brought the paper out with the banner headline, 'Arrest of our Editor', filling most of the front page. An explanation followed:

> *Aegidius Jean Blignaut and Herman Malan were arrested yesterday, no charge being framed definitely. They appeared in court, when the case*

*was remanded until March 3. No evidence was led, but bail was allowed in the sum of £150 each. No opportunity was offered to our editor to refute the vague charges laid. It is understood that Mr. Blignaut and Mr. Malan are to be tried for alleged criminal libel. Details and particulars will be given in next week's issue of* The New L.S.D. *Look out for next week's edition: startling revelations will be made.*

The headline and report took care of much of the front page. Pierre then cast about frantically for suitable copy to fill the rest of the paper. Nearly one whole column of the back page was devoted to selections for the following week's races, the rest of the page being taken up by a parcel of Herman's poems that Pierre begged from a certain Mrs Neppe, with whom they had been left for safekeeping.

The poems were not necessarily intended for publication. In fact they were perhaps not intended to be poems at all – unless one accepts Bosman's definition that poetry is *anything* a poet writes. These pieces included a couple of casual references to God.

*'Hold out your hands,' God said, 'here are a few loose jewels I didn't want to waste by making stars out of.'*

*'But they are my jewels, God,' I said, 'I don't know where you got them from.'*

*God sighed.*

*'Ah well, I must have been drunk again,' God said.*

These poems led to yet another appearance in court – this time on a charge of blasphemy. Herman Malan contended that since he had never intended the poems for publication, he was, in fact, the injured party. He complained that the act of putting them in *The New L.S.D.* was like trampling on beautiful flowers.

When asked which God he referred to, Bosman replied: 'I regard myself as the final product of evolution ... The only way I could explain it would be to write another poem.'

The arrest and proceedings that so very nearly caused the non-appearance of *The New L.S.D.* on 26 February were the result of an article in its Christmas number of 1931, which had been advertised with large posters proclaiming: 'Joh'burg girls stuffed ... more than one way'.

When Bosman and Blignaut duly appeared in court on 3 March, they found they were facing 13 charges of publishing indecent material. This was too good to miss. The Magistrate's Court was packed. Mr W C Lawrence presided, while the principal witnesses for the Crown were custodians of public morals of the standing of the Bishop of Johannesburg and Mrs I L Salamon, president of the Johannesburg Branch of the National Council of Women. This all-star cast was supported by a galaxy of legal personalities. Mr V Rosenstein appeared for the defence and Mr L Venables for the prosecution.

Since communication is not a precise science, the meanings of words and their connotations arbitrary, the Bench agreed to several witnesses being invited to offer their personal interpretation of the offending words. The first witness was Detective-Sergeant Lionel Carter, who had snatched the posters from black newspaper vendors. He said that in army slang the word 'stuffed' referred to copulation. In the sense in which it had been used in the article, however, he thought it might mean 'fooled' or 'humbugged'.

The Bishop, the Right Revd Dr Karney, had never been in the army. He said that although the posters shocked and disgusted him, this particular one conveyed nothing to him. Although he was not at all certain about what the poster was meant to communicate, he was certain about other foul aspects of the case, and he felt that such a poster was meant to sell the paper for low and unworthy motives. He also said that while he would be inclined to consider worthy the motive of drawing public attention to certain undesirable practices, he nevertheless felt that the editors of the paper were going the wrong way about doing the right thing.

The Bishop further objected to the posters on the grounds that they were designed to attract young people to buying the paper for something spicy and filthy. He admitted that although he had never taken issue with questionable passages in Chaucer, Shakespeare or even the Bible, which supposedly addressed an even wider public, he somehow did not feel the same indulgence could be extended to *The New L.S.D.* Come to think of it, even certain passages of the Bible might be considered a bit risqué for young people.

The outcome was no laughing matter, though. Bosman and Blignaut were convicted on several of the charges. Jean called for his law books and lodged an appeal. On 9 May 1932 the entire cast was back for an encore performance – in the Supreme Court. The case also involved a tangle of affidavits by Bosman and Blignaut either assuming or denying responsibility for these scurrilous allegations. Jean stoutly insisted that the responsibility had to be his in his various capacities as editor, managing director and proprietor. There seems to have been some confusion regarding the latter, because at one stage Herman Malan had also been designated proprietor. When Jean insisted on taking the responsibility, Herman amiably concurred, telling the court:

> *He (Jean) is the L.S.D. I am the spirit of the L.S.D. By that I mean that I painted the curve of her smile ... The influence that made it beautiful is mine. I am responsible for the part of the L.S.D. that makes it literature.*

In spite of Jean's efforts to shield Herman and take the rap himself, Herman Malan was fined £25 or three months' hard labour. According to Jean Blignaut, he was fined £75 or eight months with hard labour. Both were stone-broke and so, for a while at least, the two literary gentlemen became the guests of His Majesty.

Bosman wrote to Jean's parents from prison asking them to forward money to pay his fine. 'I am dying,' he said.

When Jean later reprimanded him for this, Herman replied: 'But I was dying ... To get out.'

Jean Blignaut attributed the latter witticism to Herman, and Benny Sachs attributed it to Jean, so just to be on the safe side I'm quoting both.

In 1972 while I was researching the Malan-Blignaut court cases in the semi-basement reading room of the Johannesburg Public Library, I came across a newspaper account that Jean Blignaut would be detained until 1939 on 11 counts of fraud. This meant that Bosman and Blignaut were never to meet again.

*Sketch of Pierre Bosman by Helena Lake*

# 10

## Pierre, George and Ellaleen

We can't leave the 1930s without meeting three other members of the supporting cast of Bosman's private life. The first was Ellaleen Manson, Bosman's second wife, the second his brother Pierre, and the third was George Howard, a man touched by that divine madness that admitted him to the élite permitted to understand Bosman's poetry.

While Herman was still in prison for murder, his brother Pierre quit his job as a customs clerk, studied English and decided that he, too, wanted to write. In an effort to shed the image of a civil servant, he went to sea, journeyed to the United States, where he became 'drenched in American literature', and then on to Britain. Although he never got as far as the shadow of the gallows, he did manage to get himself arrested in a dockyard brawl in Liverpool.

After Pierre returned to South Africa, he befriended Jean Blignaut, who was about to launch *The Touleier*, and another wanderer, George Howard, also of a literary turn of mind but no fixed occupation. It was only a matter of time before Pierre introduced George to Herman. The date was 1929; the venue, the Johannesburg City Hall steps, where Bosman and Blignaut were involved in many battles. According to essayist A B Hughes, the City Hall steps were the recognised rioting place, as is Trafalgar Square, London. There was no nonsense about pansy beds: steps and forecourt were kept clear for baton charges.

In his memoir George recalls Bosman at that time as 'tallish, broad, blue-eyed, with a high forehead and thinning, wild fair hair, knitted tie and wide black leather belt, high merry laugh, large actor's hands and a wide-brimmed hat worn like a ship with a heavy list'.

George himself was a little younger than Herman and Jean, a brown-eyed young man of medium height with a distinctly Irish flourish to his almost oratorical manner of speech, and a sense of humour that functioned on the same level as Bosman's. He had a magic in his mode of expression that Bosman recognised and valued like a rare collector's piece.

I have George to thank for the following extract from an unidentified newspaper in 1932, which I used in *Uncollected Essays* in 1982. Actors Patrick Mynhardt and David Butler have both immortalised it further in their one-man stage shows. He sets the scene with these wry words:

*I know that the world will one day know me as a poet when it comes to an understanding of what poetry means. Yet life has given me a raw deal, I am twenty-seven now and I look over forty. And I look so lugubrious that only the other day when I was leaning against a wall of Hobkirk's Funeral Parlour waiting for the arrival of a friend, a passer-by mistook me for the chief embalmer of the establishment.*

*But all this is nothing. It is the fate of the poet to be wounded while he lives, perhaps to die from his hurts in order that his songs may live.*

Herman and George took to wandering about Johannesburg at night, in the fashion Bosman would later describe in one of his essays in 'Talk of the Town', now also in the collection *A Cask of Jerepigo*. George remembers how they would speak of Garbo or Chaplin:

*How he would have loved this Johannesburg of ours; what a world he would have made of our Jeppe, our Vrededorp dreams.*

*And Garbo, queen of sorrow, knew all about the broken heart in love. What a pair of lovers they would have made – Charlie Chaplin playing the fiddle on the cold lonely moon to tell of their love threaded through with the secrets of poetry.*

Often they would wander in a westerly direction, to continue their discussion at the municipal tram sheds. With the permission of the cleaners on duty, they once chose a comfortable seat on the upper deck of an old bone-shaker whose indicator read 'Zoo'.

On another nocturnal perambulation they found themselves near the Old End Street Convent and Herman invited George to follow him over the wall. George was reluctant, fearing that the nuns might call the police if they spied two strangers in the grounds at that hour of the night. Herman reassured him. 'I like to sit under that old oak tree. It was planted in the first year of Johannesburg's mining-camp life. I often sit there and call up the spirits of those days for my comfort. A priest came here by ox-wagon. He was in Bordeaux when his bishop gave him the chance to come to Africa. He brought some acorns from his native village to plant here in End Street, and now that tree stands dreaming high in the Johannesburg night, a leafy house of ghosts.

'Little girls who are now grandmothers did their homework under that tree and others hid from their teachers or watched the swanky parades of early Doornfontein from those very branches.

'I like to think that the priest who planted these acorns that grew this marvellous tree had something of the visions of the French poets moving in him. Perhaps Charles Baudelaire is up there, even now, listening to us,'

Herman whispered. The next moment he bellowed: 'Are you there, Charles? Can you hear us, Charles? Speak to us, Charles?'

They did not wait to see whether they had woken up the nuns. They fled for the safety of Doornfontein railway station.

George said that Herman always associated a Harley-Davidson motorcycle with the police and could never hear its roar without turning white with panic. One day George happened to mention to Herman that the sound of a Harley-Davidson engine being revved could strike terror into his soul. Herman clutched George's sleeve at what he considered proof of another cosmic truth between them and whispered: 'How did you know?'

I, personally, don't think it was the police Harley-Davidson Herman feared. It was more likely the ghostly image of David Russell's (his accidentally murdered stepbrother's) Harley-Davidson that haunted him.

Pierre Bosman and George Howard were so poor they had nowhere to sleep. So, in a gesture of largesse Bosman offered them the only hospitality he could – permission to sleep on the premises of the printing press. 'You can sleep here at night,' he told George, 'but see that you are out of here in the morning before the printers come on duty. Printers are very strait-laced people, you know, and the sight of your poverty might distress them. That would have a deleterious effect on their output,' warned Herman. 'Can't have that.'

After Herman and Jean were evicted from Berea for non-payment of the rent, they moved to Rosalind House. There were no spare beds available, so they offered Pierre and George accommodation on the floor, where George made himself comfortable by sewing two sugar sacks together. Herman, comparing these with his own conventional bedclothes, wondered uneasily whether George's style was not perhaps the more poetic.

Herman was slightly disillusioned when George remarked later that he was considering getting another sugar sack. Suspiciously Herman asked why, and George mentioned vaguely that he might want to get married. Only then was he fully reinstated in Herman's estimation.

On his travels Pierre had absorbed a great deal of Jack London and adopted a Eugene O'Neill manner of speech that could be understood by no-one except George. Herman once remarked to George: 'I believe my brother does not speak English any more. If you can get him to give up attempting to write English as well, I would be in your debt.'

Herman would say to George: 'Pierre is a realist. Who wants realism? It is only poetry that counts. Pierre's writing is just so much bricklaying.'

The only compliment Herman ever paid his brother was at the expense of the much-maligned Sarah Gertrude Millin: 'Even Pierre writes better than you, Sarah.'

*Bosman with a friend (left)
and second wife Ella
Manson, Pietersburg, 1943*

From time to time it fell to George to negotiate the catering arrangements with Lucas's Place, the cafe across the road where for two shillings and sixpence he could procure a five-course meal. Carefully shared, this would keep them going for the whole day. Lucas also had rooms to let and whenever anyone of them wished to entertain a lady in private, George would also be charged with arranging suitable accommodation.

On one such special occasion George had to arrange a room for Herman. There was no money to pay the rent, so George was given Herman's overcoat to pawn. In the threadbare '30s a man did not lightly pawn his overcoat. The lady in question was Ellaleen Manson, who was to become his second wife.

According to Gordon Vorster some time later, Herman met Ella when she was a librarian in the Johannesburg Public Reference Library and he asked her for a copy of Baudelaire's poems. When they subsequently discovered their mutual delight in Baudelaire, the next logical step seemed simply to marry and to go to Brussels, to live, if possible, in the house where Baudelaire had lived. All this did happen, and Herman and Ella did actually rent the premises in Brussels once occupied by Baudelaire.

Gordon Vorster explained that there was about a six-year gap between the day they planned this in the reference library and the time it came to pass, but that was of no consequence to Bosman. He described their action as spontaneous and immediate – and in terms of artistic truth, it was. And so Gordon naturally believed it too.

We owe much of our knowledge of Ella to Bosman's own view of her. Accordingly, I would place *his* fantasy of *her* above the amazingly few facts I have managed to accumulate. Ella Manson came into Bosman's life a few months after Ellie Beemer had gone out of it, somewhere between mid-1931 and mid-1932. Ella was the youngest of the three children of journeyman Magnus Manson: Harley, Magnus junior and Ellaleen.

Both Ellaleen's brothers qualified as electrical engineers from the School of Mines and later carved distinguished careers for themselves in their chosen fields. Thus Ellaleen Junior, or Ella as she was called, grew up in a family of achievers. She was an extraordinarily gifted pianist, and all who heard her play recall it as an exalting experience.

She must have had a high IQ, for she grew up testing other people's judgements against her own. This independence of spirit came at the price of a certain degree of solitude, but that day Bosman met her in the library he recognised her to be apart from the 'mob' – one of the élite with whom he could communicate.

Ella was a tall, large-boned woman with rebellious blonde hair and the round-shouldered carriage of people who do not quite know how to come to terms with their height. She was a contradiction in mannerisms. She dropped her chin when she spoke, and she had a wide, splay-toothed smile. Among her friends at the library she was admired for her strange, oblique intelligence and talent, and loved for her kindness and impetuous generosity.

Soon Ella worshipped Herman and could not bear to be deprived of his presence. When she was not playing the piano for him, she sat at his feet or hovered about him with little gestures of attention. Multifaceted both, they delighted in exploring each other's territory. Ella taught Herman to play a Chopin sonata, while she began writing poetry and later even started a biography of him.

They would go up on to the minedumps and scrawl their poems in the sand and then laugh when the wind blew them away. George Howard recalls that Herman and Ella found a fascination in those goldmine hills that told of the romance of Johannesburg's yesterdays. George says:

*Three volumes of verse produced by Bosman in the early 1930s.* Mara *was a play in which the 'Ellaleen' collection of poems appeared as an addendum*

*There they both wrote poems on the backs of cigarette boxes, on the blank spaces in summonses that came their way or any old scrap of paper handy. Then, from their high places they threw their love manifestos to the winds. Indeed, some of those poems may still be buried in the yellow sandy slopes.*

Not surprisingly, only a small number of Ella's poems survived, and even those had to be gathered from various sources for publication after her death. The following is a poem written by Ella for Herman:

*Your canvasses*
*Are the forgotten*
*Dews*
*Of man's tremblings.*
*Go lightly in your ways, youth of stars and dreams.*
*My dreams have folded protectingly over your cherished head.*
*My hands shall smooth away the tempest which comes unbidden*
*To the flowered walls of your imagination.*
*Oh youth eternal*
*Oh eternal flower*
*Eternal is the spirit commanded to speak*
*From out this earth's riches.*
*Your hand laid innocently on the world's heart*
*Makes audible life's message.*

Ella was convinced of Bosman's personal destiny, and pledged herself to safeguard it. There never was a moment when she did not live by this credo; and there never was a doubt that she would die for it, if necessary.

On 7 October 1932, when they were both 27 years of age, Ellaleen Sinclair Manson and Herman Malan (his name for this occasion) were married in the Magistrate's Court in Johannesburg. The library staff made a collection and presented the couple with a set of crockery. But the concert platforms of Europe awaited Ella and it was time for their long-planned meeting with the shade of Baudelaire.

If Ellie Beemer had been Herman Malan's 'Blue Princess', Ella Manson inspired the group of eight poems that made up the poem 'Ellaleen'. Here, I wish another Bosmanophile could help me. In the *Mara* collection, in the poem 'Ellaleen' there is a review passage attributed to Edgar Bernstein. I would ask this other Bosmanophile why the following lines seem so suspiciously like Herman Malan's?

> *I don't think any Christian has understood the message of Christ more than he has done ... Herman Malan has been pilloried all over South Africa. In years to come generations yet unborn – descendants of the very people who now vilify him – will acclaim his as the greatest poet South Africa has produced ... This is no extravagant boast. It is prophecy.*

In the preface to *Mara* Herman Malan (as himself) said:

> *I have written this play* Mara *and the succeeding poems for the fine, beautiful people of the world. The rest doesn't matter; the nearest they can come to an understanding of genius is to hurt it. I am glad that the rest have never mattered in the scheme of God.*

Now it becomes confusing, because I need to date the sequence of his post-Ella poetry. While he dedicated the whole *Mara* collection to Ella as follows:

> *To Ella*
> *who helped me believe again in all the sad-browed Christs on earth.*

He dedicated the poem 'Ellaleen':

> *To Aegidius Jean Blignaut who recognised me ten years ago – in spite of what the mob said.*

The earliest Jean could have 'recognised' Herman was when he was a student at Wits at a literary soirée in 1923. This dates the whole *Mara* collection by Herman Malan 1933, when Jean Blignaut was incarcerated (as it turned out, for a very long time).

*Mara*, priced at five shillings, was published by African Publications Johannesburg and Courier News Agency Ltd, Empire House, Wardrobe Court, 146 Queen Victoria Street, London ECI.

Personally, I have only ever seen one copy of *Mara*, and believe Bosman was constructing a smokescreen preparatory to changing his entire lifestyle and place of abode. And his last months in South Africa were a preparation for changing Herman Malan back to Herman Bosman in England. (Throughout the '30s and, in fact, well into the '40s, Herman Malan/Bosman/and a number of other aliases would play complicated games with his identity.)

The 'Ellaleen' collection contained one of the few poems Bosman wrote in Afrikaans – 'Oorlog', dedicated to Tielman Roos. Another poem, 'Africa', was dedicated to Fred Zwarenstein 'for keeping me awake during university lectures'.

Bosman as Herman Malan also attributed the foreword to colleague Edgar Bernstein of *The Rolling Stone* magazine, but by now Bosmanophiles must have caught on.

But back to 'Ellaleen'. Gordon Vorster used to say that the following lines are some of the most resoundingly beautiful in South African poetry:

> *I sing of the morning, I who have seen*
> *Only the afternoons.*
> *My westering heart is sunset-stained,*
> *But white where the languorous lips had been*
> *of Ellaleen.*

In the play, *Mara*, Bosman places incest, like genius, on a pedestal to be worshipped. He berates Byron for regretting his incestuous relationship with his half-sister Augusta:

> *That was the flaw in Byron – that he regretted what he had done. Genius does not regret.*
>
> *Incest is a word that has been invented by unclean men who have defiled love. When the puny Davids can't understand a giant's love because it is too large for them, they call it silly names.*

For Bosman, incest was a coveted state for the super-privileged. And the word itself had 'a deep florid sound, like murder or heaven ...'

Whilst I (personally) don't consider the play *Mara* significant in terms of literature, I do consider it significant as a 'theme' in Bosman's life. And I'd like to share my reasons why. The play *Mara* not only dramatises the incestuous relationship between a brother and sister, it vindicates it.

In the second year of my research into Bosman's life, when I told Bosman's old school friend, Robbie McKibbin, that I was going to Potchefstroom for

Bosman's old school records, he suggested I look for a 'Charles' in academic circles who might have fathered him. I drew a blank with the school principal of Potchefstroom College: no resemblance. At the end of a discouraging day of more blanks I was on the point of telling one of Elisa's ex-pupils, Mr Weeks, so, when he volunteered that he had served on the same school committee as Charles Malan. He asked whether I would care to see a photograph.

As I looked at it, there was Bertha McKibbin's Charles – 'the brilliant man in academic circles to whom Herman bore a strong physical resemblance but whom Elisa could never marry'.

Initially, I was in denial and didn't want to confront this. I first consulted Lex Malan (Charles's son), who was not at all surprised at the inference; this would make Herman his half-brother. Robbie McKibbin simply said, 'That explains things, doesn't it?' And I had the eerie feeling that I wasn't really surprising either of them, but simply confirming a feeling each man had confronted long ago.

Interestingly, incest also played a part in Ella's life. I have no idea whether it was with her father or one of her brothers. Nor do I know whether it was forced on her or if she was a willing participant. I only feel it was somehow a common bond that united them.

In 1932 Bosman also published two other poems – a longish poem called 'Rust', and 'Jesus, an Ode and Other Poems'. The poem 'Rust' was published in June 1932 by African Publications. It was printed in a small format, 11 x 7 cm, a stanza to a page, and sold at two shillings a copy. The publisher's address was given as 88 Polly Street, the Bosmans' residential address.

The shadowy images of these stanzas harbour thoughts of strange portent. Like many of Herman Malan's other poems, 'Rust' is open to various interpretations. The second-last stanza, perhaps the most obscure and disturbing of all, reads:

*'Oh, Earth,' the new moon sang, 'My sister Earth,*
*'Oh, wherefore do you mourn*
*'With the clumsy-moving lives that grow*
*'Within you? Huddled in a heap of birth,*
*'My sister with your head bent low,*
*'Why must you brood*
*'That fleshly shapes be born?*
*'– Changing grey shadows into blood?'*

In this stanza Bosman laments the fact that he could never risk having children. Painter-poet Gordon Vorster, Bosman's friend during the last five years of his life, believed Bosman's fear of having children had nothing to do with a reluctance to assume ordinary material responsibility for a child. He thought the terror was rooted in the thought of monsters lurking in his semen.

*A mother who knows that the first-generation love-child was physically normal only through luck, but who lived through his upbringing and strange, wild maturing, culminating in murder, must, when he marries, warn him and tell him why it is dangerous for him to have children. This could tear the balls out of any man.*

At no stage in his life was Bosman prepared to have children. I think this is the same terror of madness and also of breeding monsters that he would later describe so graphically in his autobiographical novel *Cold Stone Jug*. Whatever it was, it very nearly destroyed his manhood during the middle years of his life. One day, quite soon after Bosman's marriage to Ella, she became pregnant. Before long, Ella had arranged with a midwife to terminate the unwanted pregnancy.

Like Bosman's lost loves and the gravestones with their half-obliterated names of his stories, abortions were to become a recurring theme in Bosman's life. And Ella Manson would one day play the ultimate price.

# 11

## The missing years

As far as I'm concerned, 1933 really *is* missing, disappeared. According to my records, after the gutter press's last court case in 1932 Bosman and Blignaut dropped clear out of sight.

Benny Sachs says in his biography, *Herman Charles Bosman as I Knew Him* (1974), they were detained at His Majesty's pleasure for an indefinite period, and Bosman preceded Blignaut to England when he got out.

My last documented traces of Herman and Ella in Johannesburg are when they married on 7 October 1932. A month later, the November issue banner headlines in *The New L.S.D.* announced 'Fame for Our Editor' by the Literary Editor. The Courier News Agency, Limited, of Empire House Queen Victoria Street, London (John Webb's paper *Empire*) also reported that Jean had received offers to translate the Ruiter stories into seven European languages. However, despite the advance publicity, I can find no trace of the Ruiter stories for about 20 years, and can't help wondering if this wasn't a smokescreen for the gutter press while Bosman and Blignaut were in detention, because simultaneously *Empire* magazine published a review of random Herman Malan stories by 'Princess Zulia'. Then nothing.

There were the two Daisy de Melker pamphlets, of this murky period. Jean Blignaut was understandably sensitive about this period and I respected his need for privacy.

In one respect I regret that all this only occurred to me too late to confirm with John Webb or Benny Sachs, when it was still possible. And in another way I'm relieved to pass the baton to the next Bosman biographer. So for his or her information:

– 1931: with no magazine publishing to guide me, the poetry is even more difficult to date. *The Blue Princess* would be historically first, about the same time as his story 'Rita's Marriage'.

– 1931: with pretty much the same anger, the new love he now writes of with yellow hair must be Ella.

– 1932: *Mara* (poems and a play): African Publications, PO Box 3947, Johannesburg, and a dual address, Courier News Agency Ltd, Empire House, Wardrobe Court, 146 Queen Victoria Street, London E. C. S. I suspect the latter to be bogus, never having seen a second copy different from the one with the grim reaper on the cover. Moreover, Edgar Bernstein allegedly wrote the preface, although in Herman Malan's style. Further still, if the poem 'Ellaleen' is dedicated to 'Jean Blignaut who recognised him ten years ago in spite of what the mob said', where was Jean that he was unavailable to write the preface in 1932? Next comes *Rust* (African Publications, this time at 88 Polly Street) simply because *The Blue Princess* and *Mara* are already printed, reviewed and advertised in this little volume.

– 1933: the cover of *Jesus, an Ode and Other Poems* published by Brill Brothers.

Gordon Vorster assured me Bosman's future biographer would love his subject and treat this information gently. I hope this is helpful.

We interrupted our storyline to flesh out Bosman's poetry of the 1930s. Now we pick it up again where Bosman's old friend John Webb had been watching the 'gutter press' fortunes from London with growing alarm. He predicted disaster for them in Johannesburg's 'lynch-mob' climate, and urged them to join him and make a fresh start.

Herman and Ella had also dreamed about her becoming a concert pianist at the Albert Hall, while Fleet Street awaited him. And then there was also that fantasy world inhabited by the shades of Oscar Wilde, François Villon and the impatient Baudelaire. Bosman wrote a farewell article titled 'The Poet Gets The Boot', featuring a photograph of the broadly smiling Herman Malan, and they packed and left.

My sources for this period were mainly John Webb, who knew Bosman almost throughout this interval until 1938, and George Howard, who met him quite by chance in London six months prior to his and Ella's return to South Africa. Of the entire period of about six years the Bosmans spent in Europe until the outbreak of World War II, astonishingly few traces remain.

In attempting to follow Bosman through those years, the feeling that strikes me most is not so much his inability to relate to Europe, but his intense awareness of his absence from South Africa. Rather than providing him with the stimulus of a fresh environment, it seems to have confirmed his attachment to his old one.

The most telling testimony of all is that only a small body of writing was salvaged from that period. We can partly ascribe this to his using pseudonyms unknown to us, so that this material is untraceable. Then, too, a whole pile of abandoned manuscripts was apparently destroyed during the Battle of Britain. But one central fact emerges by Bosman's own admission: he himself did not feel deeply enough about his unpublished writing in London to consider it a loss.

According to John Webb, the Bosmans first holidayed in Madeira, and arrived in London in March 1934. Herman telephoned John Webb from Waterloo Station and they met at the restaurant in Barker's department store in Kensington High Street.

Webb had invited his old *Touleier* colleagues, Herman and Jean, to join him in London, so he was understandably dismayed to find no Jean, but Ella instead. Until they were settled, the Webbs invited the Bosmans to be house guests at 45 Emperor's Gate, a house belonging to a wealthy patron of the Empire Movement. Bosman soon immersed himself in the activities of the Empire Movement – a powerful force in pre-war British politics. The movement ran a number of publications, such as *The Empire Movement Annual* and *The News Digest*.

Later, in 1936 Webb launched *The Sunday Critic*, with Bosman as both deputy editor and contributor where he wrote a few episodes of 'Claude Satang's Prison Experiences' as Herman Malan. Through John Webb and the Empire Movement, Bosman met people like H G Wells, Aldous Huxley, Lord Beaverbrook, Lord Nuffield, William Joyce, W W Jacobs and Oliver Onions. Regrettably, I was unable to source any interviews with them in *The Sunday Critic* by Herman Malan. There was not even one with Herman Bosman.

Bosman's pen names are worthy of a story in their own right. After the newsworthy Bellevue tragedy and his subsequent imprisonment, Bosman had adopted Herman Malan as his pen name. By the time he reached England Herman Malan now bore the stigma of the scandal sheets and prison and he reverted to Bosman.

Meanwhile, in November 1934, almost a year after the Bosmans' departure from South Africa, his old school friend, Benny Sachs, launched *The South African Opinion*, a literary magazine comparable to *The Touleier* and the political material of which made it one of the most significant Johannesburg periodicals of the time. The first issue was very much in the nature of a reunion, for all four participants in the famous poster-pasting caper – Benny Sachs, Raymond Lake, Eddie Roux and Herman Malan – were represented. The second issue carried four contributions by Bosman: three poems and a short story, under three different pseudonyms. The poem, 'Reveille', bore the initials H C B, as did the poem 'Carthaginian Sandals' in the January edition. In both, the poet sang of fleshly loves, but with sadness. The short story, 'Veld Maiden', today one of the best-loved of Bosman's stories, was attributed to P de Beer, who has never been heard of since.

Practically every subsequent issue contained a new Schalk Lourens story – 'Yellow Moepels', 'The Love Potion', 'In the Withaak's Shade', 'The Widow', 'Brown Mamba', 'Willem Prinsloo's Peach Brandy', 'Ox-wagons on Trek', 'The

Music Maker', 'Drieka and the Moon', 'The Mafeking Road', 'Marico Scandal', 'Bechuana Interlude' – and the authorship of all these was ascribed finally and boldly to H C Bosman. In fact, some of his most memorable Bushveld stories flowed from his pen in exile.

'In the Withaak's Shade' is beloved by grandparents reading to grandchildren for lines such as:

*... whatever kind of leopard it is that you come across in this way, you only do one kind of running. And that is the fastest kind.*

and:

*Every big-game hunter I have come across has told me the same story about how, at one time or another, he has owed his escape from lions and other wild animals to his cunning in lying down and pretending to be dead ... Now, as I lay there on the grass, with the leopard trying to make up his mind about me, I understood why, in such a situation, the hunter doesn't move. It's simply that he can't move. That all. It's not his cunning that keeps him down. It's his legs.*

And there was 'Willem Prinsloo's Peach Brandy', celebrating Grieta Prinsloo's return from finishing school in Zeerust where she went to learn English manners and dictation, and other high-class subjects.

*'Go right through, kêrels,' he [Willem Prinsloo] said, 'the dancing is in the voorhuis. The peach brandy is in the kitchen.'*

*Although the voorhuis was big it was so crowded as to make it almost impossible to dance. But it was not as crowded as the kitchen. Nor was the music in the voorhuis – which was provided by a number of men and guitars and concertinas – as loud as the music in the kitchen, where there was no band, but each man sang for himself.*

*We knew from these signs that the party was a success.*

*When I had been in the kitchen for about half an hour I decided to go into the voorhuis. It seemed a long way, now, from the kitchen to the voorhuis, and I had to lean against the wall several times to think. I passed a number of other men who were also leaning against the wall like that, thinking. One man even found that he could think best by sitting on the floor with his head in his arms.*

*You could see that Willem Prinsloo made good peach brandy.*

In 'Mafeking Road' Bosman actually shared with the reader some of his secrets to storytelling:

*When people ask me – as they often do – how it is that I can tell the best stories of anybody in the Transvaal (Oom Schalk Lourens said,*

118

*modestly), then I explain to them that I just learn through observing*
*way that the world has with men and women. When I say this they noa*
*their heads wisely, and say that they understand, and I nod my head*
*wisely also, and that seems to satisfy them. But the thing I say to them is*
*a lie, of course.*

*For it is not the story that counts. What matters is the way you tell it.*
*The important thing is to know just at what moment you must knock*
*out your pipe on your veldskoen, and at what stage of the story you must*
*start talking about the School Committee at Drogevlei. Another*
*necessary thing is to know what part of the story to leave out.*

That passage was meant to be used as the introduction to a television series
that was never made. And these are pearls of wisdom he is passing on to
aspiring storytellers.

Sometimes Bosman contributed to *The South African Opinion* essays on his
impressions of Europe. 'Royal Processions' described how he waited in the
crowd for the procession of the Duke of Kent and his bride Princess Marina of
Greece to Westminster Abbey for the marriage ceremony. What Bosman
admired most about royal processions were the men in the street, preferably
those on pavement level.

On this occasion he observed one man passing the long hours of waiting by
reading a library book by the light of a candle. Shortly after four in the
morning the crowd began to cheer and someone explained to Bosman that the
English dawn had come.

*I wondered how they found out. This is one of the major difficulties which*
*the English winter presents to a man used to blue skies. It is always a*
*problem to distinguish between the kind of darkness they call night-time,*
*and the other kind of darkness that they call day-time. To the uninitiated,*
*all darkness looks about the same.*

*When he was told that the dawn had come, the man with the library*
*book blew out what was left of his candle, and went on reading in the dark.*

He continues:

*I obtained a good view of General Hertzog. That was because he held his*
*head very high. Yet there was a strained look on his face. Perhaps he was*
*trying to remember whether it was the Crown Colonies that J H Tomas*
*had promised to hand over, or whether it was the Crown Jewels.*

And here, I believe, Bosman waxes homesick. Never mind the punchline. In
the paragraph just before it, you can *feel* his *eina*.

*Perhaps General Hertzog was only home-sick.*

*And I recalled another South African, who drove through London when Victoria was Queen. They still talk about him here. What did he think, I wonder, when his carriage swung into St James Street? About a Bushveld farm, maybe, and the sun lying yellow on white-washed walls, and big tree by the dam. And yet I hardly think so. I think it more reasonable to think that Paul Kruger was pardonably vain about his triumph. And what he really thought was: 'If only the boys in the Rustenburg district could see me now.'*

A fortnight later, in his essay 'This is London' for *The South African Opinion*, Bosman wrote:

*When you have been suitably impressed by the hushed solemnity of the past, you discover that in London there is something older than her monuments, something more venerable than her tombs. I refer to the jokes that are classified generally as Cockney wit.*

Of Fleet Street he said:

*I once wrote a couple of articles for a newspaper foretelling the downfall of civilization. That was almost two years ago [1934]. A few weeks back the editor asked me for another article along those lines. 'Write me some more of that coming doom of civilization dope,' he requested elegantly.*

*But I told him it was too late, then. 'The doom,' I said, 'has already happened.'*

*The journalists of Fleet Street ... accept life simply here. They feel no things deeply. You may call it civilization, if you like; more probably you will call it decadence. And yet I think it is better so. I think it is better when the hearts of men are free from the turmoil of aspirations, from wayward dreams, and old and far off longings, and wistful things, and they seek no more. It is as though hope has cast away her burden, in the way that a prisoner, summoned for release from a weary sentence, flings down his hammer by the stone-pile. Or on a warder's foot.*

In one of his contributions he slated T S Eliot's *Murder in the Cathedral*, which was then playing in a small theatre in Nottinghill Gate. Bosman was ever ready to share his thoughts on poetry:

*Poetry – particularly English poetry – is a very proud and mighty force. It has never been led astray. And it never will be. I realise that other critics have contented themselves with writing a lot of harmless clap-trap about* Murder in the Cathedral, *mentioning the medieval spirit and so*

120

*forth. Wiser than I am, maybe, they have written playfully, secure in the knowledge that posterity will put it all right.*

*But I feel that ultimately mine is a more kindly attitude than theirs: it lets Mr Eliot know right away where he stands.*

Even after two years of exposure to London's elite society, Herman Malan was still very much a *Sjambok* man.

Throughout 1936 Bosman, as Herman Malan, regularly contributed articles to *The Sunday Critic*, as well as a serial on the prison experiences of one Claude Satang. In it he recalled the night in 1914 when the notorious Foster Gang (South Africa's Bonny and Clyde) were caught in a shoot-out near Germiston. Quite coincidently, Boer War hero General Koos de la Rey was caught in a road block that night and accidentally shot to death.

But history aside, mainly when Herman Malan was taking the mickey out of Claude Satang's prison experiences, he was replaying his own 'Lago Clifford' stories written for Stephen Black's *The Sjambok* in 1929.

*The Sunday Critic* cast included such *Sjambok* stalwarts as 'Beauty Bell' and 'Taffy Long', whom Bosman must have met in prison and who would also populate the pages of the prison memoir he would publish in 1949: *Cold Stone Jug*.

This was far from a new book, but rather the continuation of an old one he had been researching all his life, and publishing in instalments in *The Sjambok*, *The Sunday Critic* and now *Cold Stone Jug*. On 12 July 1936 the Claude Satang serial was abruptly terminated after about thirteen instalments and readers' complaints about the manner in which a convict ate a portion of a live cell-mate (another of Herman Malan's recurring themes).

*The Sunday Critic* had ceased publication after about a year and early in 1939 attempts would be made to revive *Piccadilly*, a class magazine of the early 1930s. Spencer Allberry, former editor of *The Bystander*, was appointed editor and Herman Malan associate editor. They even produced a splendid dummy copy with which to impress prospective advertisers, but the plan died in embryo.

As part of Bosman's London experience I'd like to share the way street processions always had an irresistible fascination for him. Although actually published much later, it is just so relevant:

*When I see a long line of people marching through the streets – the longer the line, the better I like it – something primordial gets stirred inside me and I am overtaken by the urge to fall in also, and take my place somewhere near the end of the procession. I have no doubt that the reason why, many years ago – before Communism had the social standing and prestige which it enjoys today – the reason why in my youth I joined the Young Communist League in Johannesburg was because that part of Socialist ideology which consisted of organising processions through the streets, holding up the traffic and all that sort of thing, made a very profound appeal to my ethical sense.*

*And it has been like that all my life.*

*There is something about the sight and the thought of a long line of men marching through the streets of a city that fills me with an awe that I can't define very easily. And it has got to be through a city. A procession through a village or just over the veld just isn't the same thing. The people taking part in it should be mostly men. One or two women are all right, perhaps. But there shouldn't be too many of them. Banners are optional. And while I am not too keen on a band, I can overlook its presence.*

*The ideal conditions for a procession are grey skies and wet streets. And there should be a drizzle. My tastes don't run to the extremes of a blizzard or a tropical downpour. Thunder and lightning effects are out of place. All you want is a steady drip-drip of fine rain that makes everything look bleak and dismal, without the comfortable abandonment of desolation. Then through these drab streets there must come trailing a long line of humanity, walking three or four abreast, their boots muddy and their clothes (by preference) shabby and shapeless in the rain, and their faces a grey pallor. They can sing a little, too, if they like, to try and cheer themselves up – without ever succeeding, of course ...*

*... And I find myself, contrary to all promptings, of good sense and reason, yielding to the urge to try and find a place for myself somewhere near the tail end of the procession.*

*I get gripped with an intense feeling of being one with stupid, struggling, rotten, heroic humanity ...*

*Similarly, I have, at different times, marched through the streets of London with Communists, Mosleyites, Scotchmen on their way to the Cup Tie, unemployed Welsh miners and the Peace Pledge Union.*

The literary section of *The South African Opinion* of 31 October 1936 carried an article on Bosman's impressions of Paris. Bosmanophile Lionel Abrahams still regards it as one of his best essays.It began:

*In the spring I went and stayed for a while in Paris, a city of which I had heard.*

This line reveals two significant facts about Bosman. In spite of churning out so much sensationalism in the cause of Claude Satang in *The Sunday Critic*, he had not mislaid his delightful talent for the throw-away line. Secondly, the Bosmans must have been in France some time between April and June of 1936. Spring comes reluctantly to Paris. The nodules on the willows lining the Seine swell so imperceptibly that they seem suspended in a state of non-growth for weeks, so that May and even June may still be springtime in Paris.

What Bosman observed of Paris had little to do with the Eiffel Tower, the Arc de Triomphe and the Madeleine, but much to do with those regions where the shades of her writers still lingered. This is true of his responses to all the old cities of Europe: he loved them for their role in the lives of the people he cared about, rather than for themselves.

*The Paris that Villon knew is still there. The Paris of Baudelaire and Verlaine. It is all still there. It lives on, that wayward spirit animating the visionary and the past, arraying the half-god in sudden jewels and startling sublimities, and then putting him again in the gutter to wonder vaguely, without splendour and without laughter.*

*It is this thing that is in the soul of Paris. And it is changeless. And it is this thing that has lured the world's strange men to Paris ... men whose hearts have been turbulent with dreams and wine, and bitter with immortalities.*

*In the cemetery of Père Lachaise I saw a number of men standing before the grave of Oscar Wilde. One by one they took off their hats, half diffidently, as though they had been caught in the act of shame. I went up to the tomb, then, and stood there, and took off my hat also, diffidently.*

*And then I laughed. For this seemed to be the perfect way of saluting the memory of Oscar Wilde. Saluting his memory as you would salute the man. Doffing your hat in tribute to his genius, but half afraid, also, that people might know you are acquainted with him. It was a fitting and a noble greeting. And I felt that nobody would have appreciated it better than Oscar Wilde himself.*

*I looked out of a window in Paris, one night. The streets were silent. Pieces of torn paper fluttered in the chill wind. And I sensed – with a strange and sure sort of emotion – that there was something different about these fragments of torn paper merely because the night wind was blowing them through a Paris street.*

*The city in which a genius has lived becomes recreated into something that is more than the inanimate background to his sorrows. The streets through which he has walked much. The scenes amid which the*

*incomparable patterns of his life unfolded. Above all, the places where*
*sublime inspiration came to him. It doesn't matter what happens to such*
*a place afterwards. That spot on the earth's surface remains*
*impregnated with a spirit of beauty that is forever rich and rare. Take*
*a stroll through the streets of Brussels and you will see what I mean ...*

*The South African Opinion* closed down in 1937, *The Sunday Critic* followed suit in 1939, and the Bosmans were strapped for cash.

Soon afterwards a curious message reached Bosman's family in South Africa that he had died of exposure abroad. Herman's brother Pierre cabled Reuters for confirmation and in reply received some garbled information to the effect that, as far as could be established, Herman Bosman could be presumed dead. The cable also implied that Ella was destitute and could not afford the expenses of a funeral. The family were deeply shocked and Herman's mother Elisa immediately sent money to pay for the funeral.

Bosman's uncle, Charles Malan, was sceptical that the message was from Reuters. It seemed to him that the police, not a news agency, would have been the logical source of information. Nevertheless, he fretted that he might not see Herman again.

Bosman's first wife Vera mourned Herman, as did his little cousin Zita, with whom he had spent the happier hours of his stay in Bronkhorstspruit. Jean Blignaut recalled that when he heard the news, he wrote a note for his brother, thinking of Shelley, who after the death of Keats had gone out and carved on a stone somewhere: 'Keats is dead'.

Benny Sachs heard the rumour and dismissed it as one of 'Bozzie's jokes' – like the time Bosman had said he was going to Lourenço Marques and thought he would take a short cut through the Union Grounds.

During Bosman's fictitious death his Uncle Charles, who had moved to Johannesburg, and was ailing after a fall, did die in August 1938 without knowing whether his doubts about Herman's death were justified. Shortly afterwards, Herman's mother Elisa visited London and the Fleet Street office in which her late son had worked. She was shown into a room where it seemed that he was still working – and in excellent health.

For Elisa, suffering two bereavements – Charles's real death, and Herman's fictitious one – the reunion may have been solace initially. But their entire relationship bore ancient wounds that still festered. Soon they were at loggerheads. And Ella – never daughter-in-law material – exacerbated matters.

The news of Herman's 'resurrection' had not yet reached George Howard when he visited London, and he was still under the impression that Bosman was dead. Shortly after his arrival, he and his friend Gwen Davies were passing the British Museum when they virtually bumped into the Bosmans, and they went off to celebrate with cider at a High Holborn pub.

'Did anyone write a poem about me, in requiem, when they heard I had died?' Herman asked George. 'It would have brought me nearer to Baudelaire.' (When Baudelaire was falsely reported dead in Brussels, Swinburne had hastily penned a requiem poem.)

There were to be many more meetings at that Holborn pub 'catching up'. George had yet to learn that the Bosmans had fallen on hard times, and happened to speak in praise of the beauty of snow. Herman exploded: 'Don't talk such rubbish to me. There is nothing beautiful in walking about Brussels in slush in the kind of shoes I could afford to wear. I tell you, snow is hell.'

Ella's brother and sister-in-law also visited the Bosmans during those years and found them in unbelievably straitened circumstances. On several occasions they took them baskets of fruit and food. Via a colleague of the rebel press days came the rumour that Bosman had been a door-to-door salesman, and after the war he told Gordon Vorster that he had also been a polisher of London steps. Apparently he took great pride in the latter job, for he spoke about it with relish and nostalgia.

On 3 September 1939 Britain declared war on Nazi Germany. It was an Indian summer day tempered by the approach of the September equinox. The sun shone and the blue sky was dotted with barrage balloons, which had already become a feature of the London scene. Protective sandbag walls were beginning to appear and familiar landmarks disappeared overnight.

An air-raid siren howled and people disappeared in an orderly manner into the underground shelters to emerge after the 'all clear'. Together Herman and George repaired to a pub on Lambs Conduit Street, from where they emerged whenever they heard the newspaper sellers announcing the arrival of fresh bulletins. Their mood was one of interest in the people around them and their hushed response to impending doom, rather than a personal identification with the war. They were witnesses of, rather than participants in, the events taking place. As they ambled down the street they were finally confronted by indisputable evidence of war – an army column marching down the street. Herman and George watched their approach in silence. The column turned into a nearby Lyons Corner House teashop.

'Well, an army marches on its stomach,' George observed and the two continued on their way through a London that had become faceless.

During the weeks that followed, there was some talk of evacuating children. Black-out restrictions were enforced and a series of air-raid drills took place during which civilians disappeared like obedient ants into the London underground stations. Gas masks were issued. George and his friend Gwen collected theirs first from the distribution centre at Holborn. Their spirit of levity prevailed until the moment Gwen tried on her mask.

The first time Herman saw this he recoiled in horror, but it was a horror that probably had very little to do with war. From the farthest reaches of an imagination peopled by monsters and fiends was conjured up an image that struck terror into his soul as no concrete thing ever could. Eight years later he was to describe this fear of monsters in his prison memoir *Cold Stone Jug*.

They all parted company shortly afterwards. George and Gwen went to Dublin prior to their repatriation to South Africa. The sparse information on the Bosmans from the outbreak of war until they arrived back in South Africa in January 1940 seems to hide more than it reveals.

After *The Sunday Critic* and *The Bystander* had left Bosman jobless, he and Ella had started a publishing venture that Kelly's Post Office Directory for 1939-40 listed as occupying premises at 249 Shaftesbury Avenue, on the corner of New Oxford Street. It was called the Arden Godbold Press, apparently after Herman's pseudonym of this period, when Ella called herself Eleanor Roosevelt Godbold.

Kelly's Post Office Directory is as far as they got. Neither the University of Warwick nor the University of Manchester, both of which have compiled comprehensive historical source material on publishing in England, has any records relating to the Arden Godbold Press.

After his return to South Africa, Bosman would describe their entry into the publishing world as a 'highly successful' venture. He told of sumptuously furnished offices and how Ella had bought chandeliers and antiques and all the things she had always wanted but never could afford. Herman advertised in the press inviting would-be authors to submit their manuscripts for publication. Then, instead of awaiting results in London, Ella talked him into going to Paris. When they returned, they would find the offices flooded with manuscripts. Although they claim this is what happened, documentary evidence suggests otherwise.

Then there is also Bosman's own account much later when he was grieving and didn't have the heart for any tall stories. It was probably just after that jaunt to the Continent that the Bosmans one day found themselves in front of the Fulham Road post office – penniless, jobless and homeless, and facing another London winter. Bosman recounts how he suddenly began to reproach Ella for having persuaded him to give up his newspaper job to take a holiday in Europe, thereby landing them in the gutter.

Ella took the blame readily. 'Yes, that's exactly what I've done. You told me you were a poet, didn't you? That's where a poet's place is. How can you expect to write at all if you haven't been in the gutter?'

The success of the Arden Godbold Press strikes me as pure myth. Lionel Abrahams once said, 'regarding history, Bosman put the poet's embroidered lie above the carefully authenticated fact. He was not only readier to hear it, but readier to believe it.' And I think the Arden Godbold story was one of those. So now when I read fellow-author Laurens van der Post's autobiography, I think of Bosman giving him a wink like Krisjan Lemmer gives Oom Schalk Lourens in 'In the Withaak's Shade', to let him know there was a new understanding between them, and that they could now talk as one Marico liar to another.

What *really* happened is they were evicted, and the premises ransacked. In the end their personal effects were auctioned for one pound ten shillings, the locks were changed, and the file closed. The Bosmans had abandoned a pile of manuscripts on top of a wardrobe and then left. In true poetic style, without payment of the rent.

After October 1939 a stranger began to call regularly at the Arden Godbold premises in an effort to locate the tenants. It was Jean Blignaut travelling under the name of 'Mr Rousseau', according to an interview we taped in London in 1973.

Following enquiries, Jean had received the information that Herman lived at 49 Shaftesbury Avenue as Arden Godbold, with his wife, Eleanor Roosevelt Godbold. Jean was instructed to ask for Herman Bosman or Arden Godbold.

This was just the latest in Bosman's long-running game with names and identities. My impression is that, when Herman Malan left South Africa, he really wanted to kill off the Herman Malan of the scandal sheets. Hence his reversion to Herman Charles Bosman. And then, destitute in London (circa 1939), he staged a fictitious death to bring in some money for funeral expenses, and thereafter adopted the name Arden Godbold as cover.

Once, before the premises were ransacked, Jean Blignaut told me, he had called and actually gained access. When he saw all the mail and manuscripts lying about on the floor, he wondered vaguely whether he should take these away with him for safekeeping, but since the state in which he found the quarters seemed to indicate that the tenants would be back, he left everything as it was.

He did have a brief conversation with a Miss Nugent, however. He sympathised when she complained to him about their pictures of Hitler on the landing, and the Godbolds' eccentric behaviour. Then he asked Miss Nugent to be good enough to tell the Godbolds that he had called. His name was Aegidius Jean Blignaut. He must have missed Bosman by days.

In fact, they probably crossed in mid-ocean. For, Bosman, broke and out of a job, had no intention of remaining in London. For him the war with its promise of aid for repatriation to South Africa was a godsend. By birth and upbringing he was quite alienated from Britain's war. Besides, the material he had been sending back for *The South African Opinion*, like his 'Royal Processions' with its insight into Paul Kruger's *oulaas*, could never have been written with such feeling if he himself weren't achingly homesick.

He applied to the authorities at South Africa House for repatriation. It was time to return home.

# 12

## Return to Africa

Herman and Ella had left for Europe in 1932 during the rise of Nazi Germany. People were reading Aldous Huxley's *Brave New World*, and going to Shirley Temple movies to beat the depression. They returned to a South Africa gearing up for the war effort, *The Grapes of Wrath* was book of the year, and Charlie Chaplin was working on his film *The Great Dictator*.

The Bosmans' homecoming in January 1940 was sad for several reasons. For two years Bosman had been quite unaware of his Uncle Charles's death. His brother, Pierre – breaking the news to him shortly after his arrival – would recall Herman's grief, which was in sharp contrast to his callous acceptance of Jacobus Bosman's death. Bosman's bereavement was further compounded by the struggle to survive. Repayment of the war loan acquired through South Africa House now put a huge strain on his and Ella's ailing budget.

He had also been looking forward to seeing Jean Blignaut again, only to find he was now in London. He dashed him off a letter dated 31 January asking him to return at once. 'I wrote numerous letters enquiring about you, as I was in a position to pay your fare over to London' – another Krisjan Lemmer tall story in view of their finances, 'Don't let them get you down. We'll be ruling the world yet.'

It was one of life's ironies that, after seven years, Bosman and Blignaut should set out across the hemispheres from opposite ends of the compass for a reunion, only to miss each other altogether, never to meet again.

Ella and Herman became George Howard's unofficial guests in Wroxham House, near the Union Grounds, until the landlady found out and had them all evicted. If the Bosmans were 'Bohemian' in their London lifestyle, they were frankly weird in Johannesburg, and not ideal 'rented-room' material.

Friends like John Webb's brother, Clewin, rallied round and gave them free accommodation in Ascot Road, Judith's Paarl. George Howard recalls that Herman had retained his boisterous sense of humour, but there was a flint-like quality to his mirth, as if desperate for every spark he could ignite to stave off the dark.

They now found life in South Africa as tough as it had been in London. Everything was being geared to the war effort, with austerity tightening its grip over the land. With newsprint severely rationed, jobs in journalism were scarce. Conditions did not allow for such luxuries as *The Touleier* or *The New L.S.D.* of the pre-war years.

Benny Sachs gamely tried to launch *The South African Spectator*, a literary-political magazine along the lines of *The South African Opinion*. It ran for only three issues from the end of 1940. Bosman contributed to it, but there was no question of permanent employment, and he had to fall back on sundry pursuits to earn a living. Edgar Bernstein later recalled a chance meeting with him, when he had told him he was employed as a blacksmith – a skill he'd learned on Oom Jim Flattery's farm.

Pretoria Central Prison had also qualified him to work as a builder's assistant, and he found further employment on a building site on Hospital Hill. He soon grew proud of the gnarled look his hands assumed through doing heavy manual labour. George Howard told of biting winter days when Ella 'was conspicuous at the building site, at lunch time, carrying plates of steaming food and soup up Hospital Hill from their Rissik Street flat'.

Bosman's first contribution to *The South African Spectator* appeared in January of 1941. It was titled 'Art Notes on Charlie Chaplin' and clearly showed that, whatever hardships he was suffering in earning a living, his notions on art and the artist remained true to his credo of the early 1930s. Yet one cannot fail to notice some reference, however indirect, to his own situation:

> *As an artist, Charlie Chaplin can be classed with the greatest American geniuses of all time ... To say that Charlie Chaplin wasn't born in America doesn't affect the issue. For that matter Hitler wasn't born in Germany.*
>
> *With the release of the film* The Great Dictator, *there has been a mild revival of the old Charlie Chaplin-Adolf Hitler controversy as to who imitated who. But on this standpoint Hitler is quite clear. He says that he grew his moustache that way long before he heard of Charlie Chaplin. As for the walk, he has walked that way all his life, Hitler says.*
>
> *It is characteristic of distinguished people that when they come to write down their thoughts for public consumption they pointedly ignore all references to those personages who have most profoundly influenced them. Thus in Bernard Shaw's work an important feature is the hiatuses in regard to Oscar Wilde. And there is little direct reference to Charlie Chaplin in the pages of* Mein Kampf ...
>
> *It is assumed that the highest form of genius is of such a sort, with its scarlet flames and ruinous flowers, that it renders the possessor incapable of adapting himself to the practical demands which the world makes. This view appears to be incorrect.*

*All the facts show that the artist is essentially practical, that he has got all his wits about him, that he is gifted above his fellows, and that when he applies his gifts and intuitions in a straight line he can and does achieve immediate success. There is nothing surprising in the fact that Rimbaud became a successful slave-dealer. If he had turned out an unsuccessful slave-dealer – that only would have been a cause for surprise ...*

*Art is at once the glory and the disaster of the human race. And the life pattern of the artist is but an expression of this deathless sublimity, and of this drunkenness ill-starred ...*

*It is this same quality of sadness that is the most profound characteristic of Charlie Chaplin's films. This sadness is an inseparable part of all great artistic achievement. It haunts the background of music. It enters the poet's brain as a fragrance and remains as a phantom by his poem. It glides gracefully but unbidden between the painter and his easel, and will not go away ...*

*Charlie Chaplin makes use of this sadness with unerring skill. He handles it like a master. He pushes it around like a tangible and concrete commodity. He manipulates this quality earthily in the way that Turner paints water as though it is a solid.*

In the February issue of *The South African Spectator* his subject was Napoleon, whom he termed an artist and a genius.

*Mussolini is, like Napoleon, an Italian. Both are masters of the penetrative phrase.*

*Napoleon said, 'An army marches on its stomach.' (Everybody knows what Pitt said after Austerlitz.) And after Bardia Mussolini said, 'That's only Caporetta stuff.'*

*I have no direct associations with Mussolini. But once, in the absence of the uniformed attendant, I climbed the barrier and seated myself on the gilt and magenta throne formerly occupied by Napoleon. I did not find that throne very comfortable to sit on. And, of course, Napoleon didn't either – as it turned out ...*

*Perhaps the vital clue to the Napoleonic legend is the habit he had of standing with his feet apart, with his shoulders slightly forward, and with one hand behind his back and the other thrust in his waistcoat. It is very difficult to stand like this and not feel Napoleonic.*

*There have been conquerors since Napoleon, but what each of them has grown to realise, each in turn wistfully, is that victories are but empty things without the accolade of St. Helena.*

*Napoleon did nothing new to triumph. Triumph is an old thing in the world; triumph was already tarnished before he found it and embraced it. But Napoleon immortalised defeat ...*

*Nevertheless of Napoleon's imitators there seems one who is well on the way to achieving the final flourish that transmutes into gloomy grandeur the trappings of worldly pomp. That man is Benito Mussolini. He seems pretty solidly destined for St. Helena. And to judge by recent events, he seems determined to get there quickly ...*

*Napoleon is an artist and he has made this tremendous contribution to art: he has proved to the world that it is almost permissible to be a genius. The lunatic and his blood-brother the man of genius, together behold in Bonaparte a fellow-spirit who nearly got away with it ...*

*The artist does not expect appreciation for the things he has created, the world being what it is. And, if, from the way he walked on the playing-fields of the Military Academy, his professors could not see the glory of the First Empire they could at least see St. Helena sticking out a mile.*

On 28 April 1941, shortly after this article appeared, Herman's mother Elisa Russell died of arteriosclerosis and myocardial failure. Again Herman only learnt this a few weeks later.

Ever since Herman had shot his stepbrother David Russell in 1926, there had been an estrangement between mother and son, mostly dictated by other members of the family. After Herman's release from prison, Elisa could not be too overt in her affection for the son she had always idolised for fear of offending the Russells. Moreover, Herman's fictitious London 'death' further compounded matters.

And then there was Ella, of whom Elisa had never approved, and who reciprocated by maintaining that Elisa was instrumental in creating the atmosphere that had led to the 'Bellevue tragedy'.

After Herman's return from London in 1940, Elisa would have welcomed a rapprochement, particularly after William Russell's death. But Ella wasn't even neutral, she was a formidable foe, and prevented it.

Thus it came to pass that Robbie McKibbin, Herman's old school friend and one-time neighbour, met Herman in the newspaper room of the Johannesburg public library some time after Elisa Russell's death. Herman spoke disparagingly of her, and only when Robbie rebuked him for his callousness did he realise that she had died. There is the sadness of Bosman's poetry in Elise's story – she who had worshipped her love child was scarcely to see him after she married William Russell.

The price of allowing Ella to prejudice him was high. Elisa Russell – as she had prophesied long ago – had inherited some money from her husband and at her death her own estate was comparatively large. Herman's brother Pierre was the sole beneficiary.

In the course of the following year or two Bosman contributed articles to two other magazines published at the time – *The South African Democrat* and *Common Sense*. In August 1942 he published in the former an article titled 'The Artist in South Africa', the first of a series he was to write on this subject over the next few years. In these articles would appear some of the most penetrating and often controversial comments on this subject. The theme of the article was what Bosman believed to be the emergence of 'a true South African culture', and in the course of it he had some strange if not hilarious things to say:

*The person who knows least about the earth he walks is the farmer who grows mealies on it.*

*It is for the poet and the artist to tell us about the real Africa. Instead, this office is being usurped by the economist, the archeologist, the historian, the man of religion, the ethnologist – in fact, by everybody except the poet and the painter.*

*In this respect, Africa is suffering the same tragic fate which has to a large extent befallen the ancient world. Rome and Greece have been ruined by the researches and interpretations of scholarship ... The spirit of Rome and Greece has always been alive and warm – hysterical even. The museum-pieces have been the professors ...*

*Africa is the genius among the continents, untamed and old in civilization as is all genius. To talk of Johannesburg as a new city, as a mushroom growth, is to be almost unpardonably superficial ... Johannesburg is as startling and yet as intelligible an African whim as is the Kalahari. If the buildings in Eloff Street appear, at first sight, to deny this truth, the mine-dumps do not bother to deny anything. The mine-dumps are no less authentic an expression of Africa than are the Pyramids, and they are more of a mystery than the Pyramids. The mine-dumps have no entrance ...*

*During the past three centuries South Africa has been extensively settled by foreigners from Europe. But this circumstance should not be given undue importance. Africa has had barbarians before. What is of significance is that we can all learn. And Africa has much to teach us – of thought that it is created in sand and ceremony and that life is an ancient ritual.*

The *Common Sense* issue of December 1942 carried a critique by Herman Malan (once again) of an exhibition of Irma Stern's Congo paintings. He used the exhibition as a peg on which to hang wider and deeper comments. As usual, they concerned universalities rather than the contents of one exhibition. Once again he used the opportunity to explain whatever a true artist did was art.

*It is the supreme achievement of modern art that it has given the artist back his ancient freedom. Not the freedom to paint because this is of questionable value, anyway – but the freedom to do what he likes, and it remains art: and only then is it art. Modern art has made the artist lord again over his brush; it has re-established the age-old truth that an artist is a person who does something or nothing, and that these created or uncreated things exist in the world because of the artist ...*

*Africa is pure art. The continent itself is the expression of a complete fantasy ... It seems better to me that Africa should express her art in magic – in dancing and in music, in painting and in blood, and in nothing – and that African art should continue in its purest forms, the blossomings of witchery, rather than that it should be given expression in the form of cities and roads and industries ...*

*I am personally grateful to Irma Stern for having thrust before the world, in so bold and uncompromising a fashion, the only things in life that matter. She has created a wide and unsentimental world, brilliant with the raw colours of feeling, where the spirit is a woven mantle, and the earth is pageantry, and hope is a cereal, and things change before the eyes, with nearness, and chains are only made of steel.*

And then there is an entrancing piece, 'Rock Paintings of the Bushman', written in this period that I included in the *Uncollected Essays* I collected for Timmins Publishers in 1981.

*They came as immigrants, and in the to them whimsically-foreign country of South Africa they proceeded to paint pictures. Because they were Bushmen, they were concerned only with the deeper realities of life. There was not the frivolity of later immigrants, whose lack of reverence for the veld led them to cut it into pieces of their personal property, or in a naïve Philistinism to erect headgears and smoke-stacks among the koppies.*

*Because they were Bushmen, they had a serious understanding of the purpose of man, and of his high destiny, and when they passed by, what they left behind them, on krantzes and in caves, was beauty. When we grow discouraged at the tawdry manifestations we discover in regard to the low state of development of the human mind today, it is as well to reflect on the exalted achievements of a people who saw life truly, and who knew better than to regard a stone merely in the light of potential mineral wealth.*

*To investigate the gold or iron content of a rock is to exercise a superficial cunning that is far beyond the Bushman's comprehension – that Bushman who could turn that same rock to an elevated use as a canvas on which to paint a hippopotamus's portrait. For the Bushman knew the hippopotamus's little vanities so well: he knew the hippopotamus liked having his picture done. He also knew that the hippopotamus had good reason to be proud of his appearance, for he has in his countenance and body that nobility and luxury of line which Africa lavishes on all her creatures.*

*I can only hope that it is of some satisfaction to the departed Bushmen to realise that they did not do so badly. When we speak of his projects and colossal undertakings, let us not forget the vastest conception of all, that it was the Bushman who conceived of an entire continent in terms of an open-air art gallery. And, on the whole, this does not appear to be inferior to the idea of turning the continent into a battlefield. And what is most unpleasant about a battle, of course, is what happens immediately after it: I refer to the unhappy zeal invariably displayed by the losing side in searching for scapegoats.*

*The best reason for painting a picture is, of course, when it is done for no reason at all. This is true of every kind of creative effort. But it would seem that the Bushman painted for magical reasons, and in this way conformed to what is but inherently part of a wayward and wistful fantasy of the soul of Africa, which dreamt of the crocodile. The Bushman sought for the magic with which to paint, and he found it, in Africa, in a strange rapture, sombre in its power, stirring, heavy with the colour of life.*

*I have noticed that when a nation is intimately associated with art, when painting lies close to its spirit, it uses everyday commonplace words to describe the appurtenances of the painter's trade. It should therefore come as no surprise to learn that in the Netherlands the artist refers to his canvas as a 'doek'. After this there is no need to question the status of Dutch painting. The implication is that to the Hollander painting is a simple and natural accomplishment, as homely as stirring the porridge in the pot.*

*For this reason I am not so much interested as to the way the Bushman ground and mixed his colours, and how he made his brushes, and what he used for a palette. What does interest me is the words he employed for the tools with which he turned out his pictures. They must have been very ordinary words, stark metonymies, raw and bloody out of the earth, and therefore having in them the very spirit of great cultural achievement. I wonder what was the word he used for paintbrush, this artist who spoke in clicks.*

*As there is a war on today, it is perhaps not inappropriate to utter a few well chosen remarks on patriotism. When we speak of South Africa we seem to forget that we really are dealing with some part of the actual continent of Africa. Our patriotism, at its strongest, is an emotional attachment to some section or other of the inhabitants of a certain expanse of terra firma. But it is patriotism that is little disturbed by an African consciousness. Our patriotism is hardly more native of the soil than is our culture; they are both exclusive, and the part they exclude is Africa.*

*For this reason nearly all South African art and literature is, culturally, thin. To describe or depict Africa is not to convey her message. Similarly, our patriotism would be greatly strengthened if it were to undergo a genuinely African orientation; if we grew to accept the fact that Africa is different, and that we are part of her wonders.*

*Cleopatra was an African. The strategist of Cannae, who employed the flank attack, and the pincers movement, and broke a Roman army, was an African. As South Africans, such thoughts should move us. And if we accept Piet Retief as a national hero, a true sense of South African patriotism would not allow us to exclude Dingaan.*

*And in the cultural sphere we should take a personal and intimate pride in the artistic achievements of a vanished race.*

*For that painter of another time, who tarried here a while, and then passed on, has bequeathed a splendid heritage to the South African painter of today. He strove to marvellous avail.*

*That Old Master, who knew, in his living and his work, the inspiration of Africa, has built up a tradition. He has left behind an unidentified bequest. A faith as firm as the rocks on which he painted. He was an artist. He was a Bushman.*

But enriching as Bosman's essays were to read, he struggled to earn a living. In late 1942 Bosman's friend Arthur Markowitz introduced him to Mikel Goldin, a Jewish merchant who claimed to be a deep thinker and who was looking for a literary gentleman to ghostwrite a book on his philosophy. Bosman, still struggling to make ends meet and glad of anything that would bring in some money, agreed to do it. It duly appeared under the title *One Only*. The foreword explained:

H.C. Bosman                January 31. 1940.
                          No. 25 Park House
                          295 Bree Street,
                          JOHANNESBURG.

My Dear Jean,
            Have just arrived and
heard about you. Could you come
back at once? I am worried at
the thought of your being there, as
I am certain it is going to be
terrible.
            Why didn't you write to me in
England? I wrote numerous letters
enquiring about you, as I was in a
position to pay your fare over to
London.
            Don't let them get you down.
We'll be ruling the world yet.
                    Best wishes. Herman Bosman

*A letter Bosman wrote on his return from Europe at the outbreak of World War II*
*to Jean Blignaut*

*My reason for calling this book 'One Only' is this: when I have discussed*
*my views with various people they have at first been unable to*
*understand me; but after I have got them to see my way of looking at the*
*situation, they have invariably declared that I am the only one from*
*whom they have heard these views.*

If there was a Bosman smile between those lines, it was the only one in the book. Tedium got the better of him, and there was not even a glimmer of another smile in the rest of the book.

It must have been during this period when Bosman was strapped for cash and in need of a steady job that he resorted to writing a 32-page pamphlet on Anti-Semitism for £100, and sending it to prominent members of the Jewish community. It was a misguided caper, and its aftershock would follow him to his next job in Pietersburg.

Early in 1943 a man by the name of Gleisner took up a position with the Jewish Board of Deputies in Johannesburg, thereby vacating his post as editor of the *Zoutpansberg Review and Mining Journal* in Pietersburg. The paper was a United Party-orientated bi-weekly owned by Solly Marcus. Bosman heard of the vacancy through some Jewish friends and applied for the job.

Solly Marcus sought a reference from Ehrhardt Planjé, a colleague of Bosman's from the *The Sjambok* days, and Bosman was appointed to his first steady job in journalism in years.

# 13

## An oracle in Pietersburg

Bosman's first steady job in South Africa was at the editor's desk of the *Zoutpansberg Review and Mining Journal*. As editor of a bi-weekly United Party paper in a Nationalist stronghold, he was expected to be the voice of confrontation. On the other hand, Pietersburg owes its origin and name to that hardy stock of pioneers whose wagons creaked their way across the plains in the 1830s. Their descendants were still fired with Boer War ideologies against Britain and her allies.

In the midst of this political vortex, the new editor couldn't align himself with either side. He was a confirmed pacifist, and it was with a measure of consternation that platteland readers read:

*Words are the most powerful instruments that life holds, and since poetry expresses itself through the medium of these tools, it is inevitable that the poet must exercise a stronger influence than a general or a statesman.*

Readers accustomed to letters on the merits of corundum deposits, the farmers' co-op and a new local cinema were startled by the explosion of poetic flights. Pietersburg was confronted with the peculiar lunacies of a poet in their midst.

War was still in progress and the *Review* policy supported the war effort. Conversely, the people of Pietersburg were mostly Afrikaners and anti this Englishmen's war. The children and grandchildren of the Boer War *bitter-einders*, they were sworn to fight the English to the bitter end and, in fact, many of them belonged to the anti-war Ossewa-Brandwag. Its anti-war activities were confined to underground resistance. Members were divided into cells and meetings held in secret, but if a message had to be relayed, each link in the chain functioned with speed and precision.

The young men wore beards in proud identification with their Voortrekker forebears and confirmation of their national identity. In defiance of the imperial custom in cinemas of standing for the British anthem 'God Save the King', they made a point of leaving before it was played. They were also incensed when young Afrikaans girls fraternised with members of the armed forces, particularly with members of the RAF. Hot-headed and aggressive,

*The* Zoutpansberg Review and Mining Journal, *a Pietersburg-based bi-weekly newpaper edited by Bosman from April to November 1943*

they provoked fist fights with the soldiers. In a sense they, too, were in a state of war, over unresolved issues between Boer and Briton.

To encourage the war effort, the *Review* ran posters featuring Sergeant Quentin Smythe VC, 'an inspiration to every young South African' with slogans: 'We have the guns, the tanks, the equipment, the courage and the determination. We want the men.'

The manufacturers of Springbok cigarettes adapted their advertising to show dual images – the first of an athlete vaulting a hurdle, the second of a soldier in uniform, rifle in hand, vaulting an equivalent combat obstacle. The slogan labelled them 'Springboks then and Springboks now', with the injunction in smaller type, like a stage whisper: 'Don't Talk about Ships or Shipping.' Further advertising campaigns pitched at civilians advised: 'Lend your money to provide the tools. Send your money on active service. Help to finance the fight.'

In 1943 most Transvaal dorps subsisted on either mining or farming, but with Pietersburg's rich corundum deposits and fine agricultural land it was fast becoming the hub of the Northern Transvaal. Because the town was considered to be of strategic importance, there was also a military camp as well as an air base.

The subjects the new editor chose were not what readers had come to expect. They ranged from visions of the post-war world to poetry, academism to the development of Afrikaans, the war, bilingualism and art. In Bosman's first leading article in the *Zoutpansberg Review and Mining Journal* on 20 April 1943 he stated of Afrikaans:

> *It was a language that lived in the mouth of the people that made it: and this means all the people, and it does not exclude the slaves ... but Afrikaans has been forced into an artificial mould which has made of it a bookish language.*

Ever faithful to his muse, later in the same article Bosman took issue with his colleague Ehrhardt, who had helped get him his job:

> *Mr Planjé recently made a change in a poem that probably remains the greatest of Afrikaans lyrics. The poet had written 'kultuurs', which Mr Planjé altered to 'kulture' on that most sterile of all grounds, grammar. He also justified the change on the score that it eliminated a sibilant. Now, if a poet were to know that there is such a thing as a sibilant, he would never again write poetry. When a poet's sense of sound appears to an ordinary person to be defective, it is only because the poet is concerned with other, secret, harmonies.*

Bosman often returned to his favourite subject, poetry. On 1 May 1943 he wrote a piece titled 'War and Poetry'. At that current stage of the war, he said, it was as well to devote some space to poetry. The piece is worth quoting in full:

141

*In this period of war that is wedged between two great events – between the closing of the campaign in Africa and the opening of the operations in Europe (and all indications are that these will be on a gigantic scale) – it is as well to devote a brief space to a consideration of a subject that is vital to the soul of man – the subject of poetry, whose scope is vaster than that of all history and wars and battles, whose dark mysterious murmurings are more momentous than any stroke of statesmanship, whose wild glories mock with their timeless certitudes the man of reason and the man of action; for their concern is not with the man of destiny but the destiny of man.*

*Poetry, the greatest of the arts, inasmuch it embraces all of the arts, employing all the arts and all its servants, shackling them with the eternal magic of words – chaining them with the eternal power of words – poetry is concerned with man and the earth, with the relationship existing between the earth and man. This is a marvellously inconsequential relationship, bitter and blindingly colourful and incredibly fantastic. It is a dream within an illusion, a yearning that is all the more insistent because its origin must remain forgotten forever.*

*For this reason poesy is illogical, as all truth is illogical, as all reality and truth lie beyond the comprehension of cold and unromantic reason. This is the secret of all the spectacular victories that art has always gained in her age-old conflict with science, art with her swift metamorphoses, constructing her fascinating edifices out of substance much more immaterial than air. (This is what Shakespeare meant with his magnificent question, 'What chisel can cut breath?')*

*And it is a realisation of this profound truth that recently compelled Einstein, that man of science who propounded the theory of relativity, to declare that 'Life is an art'.*

*He did not say 'Life is a science.' He has seen deeply enough to know.*

*English literature boasts two great periods of efflorescence – the Elizabethan era and that period during and immediately following the Napoleonic Wars, at the beginning of the nineteenth century, that has come to be known as the Romantic Revival. The age of Eizabeth produced Shakespeare and his contemporaries; the Romantic Revival brought forth Keats and Shelley and Coleridge. Coleridge died rather more than a hundred years ago. Since then there has not been an English poet.*

*A popular misconception regarding poetry is that it is something abstruse, that one has to be 'brainy' to understand it, or 'intellectual' or 'educated'. The reverse, of course, is the case. While a massive ignorance of the world of affairs might not be an essential requirement for a true appreciation of poetry, it nevertheless helps.*

*The aforegoing statement does not require proof, but if proof were needed, absolutely irrefutable testimony could be supplied by the poets themselves – by the fact that none of our great poets has displayed any capacity for acquiring orthodox learning, and that in the field of straight intelligence there is no positive means of distinguishing between a poet and a moron.*

*What is necessary for the sublimest achievements of the human intellect is nothing more than a simplicity of mind, a childlike and unsuspecting nature, and, if possible, a belief in fairies. The application of this test will show that there are quite a lot of people who are gifted with a genuine aptitude for understanding poetry – and also a lot more who aren't. It will be seen that it is actually against what is known as 'intellectual' people that the portals are barred.*

*If historical precedent provides any reliable guide in respect of a subject to which no rules at all are applicable it would appear that the great epoch of poetry and art come in the wake of great cataclysms. It would appear that a war-weary world, disillusioned with a materialistic interpretation of existence, rushes out desperately for the immortal verities. Thus, a great outburst of creative-artistic energy followed the Napoleonic Wars.*

*One would like to believe that our view is correct, and that the present war will have as aftermath a great artistic revival also: but it would not matter if this should not be the case. Poetry is eternal and can look after itself.*

*The tragedy of England is not associated with any of the events of this war. England's real tragedy is that she has not produced a decent poet since Shelley.*

By May 1943 the African campaign had drawn to a close, shifting the war arena to Europe and raising the question whether Rome should be bombed or not. If Pietersburg readers, considering Rome synonymous with culture, thought that for once Bosman would advocate something more or less predictable, they were wrong.

*The historical argument of Rome being the ancient cradle of Western civilization and the present spiritual home of European culture and civilization is equally valueless.*

*The cultural grandeur of the Ancient World emanated not from Rome but from Athens. The spirit of Western civilization originated in Greece.*

*The Romans were military organizers and imperialists who remained despised barbarians by the Greeks whom they conquered. Rome contributed a great deal to science and state organization, to art nothing. There is every sound reason connected with Western culture for not destroying Athens. There is no reason whatsoever for not reducing Rome to dust.*

On 30 July, still concerned with Mussolini, he wrote:

*The forces that created Mussolini must be stopped ... It is not enough that Mussolini, with his theatrical props pulled out from under him, has been revealed as a sham ...*

*What is necessary is a recognition of the dangers to the world that reside in those forces which made possible the attainment to power of a man like Mussolini.*

By August a new subject had begun to creep into his writing: school teaching and dual-medium education.

*The early Dutch administration at the Cape insisted on this simplification (one language medium) as part of their colonial policy, with the result that French, the language of the Huguenots, who constituted an important part of the population of the colony, died within a couple of generations, leaving Afrikaans only such traces of its influence as are of primary interest to the etymologist and the writer.*

*Which is a pity. In having lost French as the natural medium of expression of a substantial part of its inhabitants, the colony at the Cape lost also a great heritage of cultural treasures. From a restricted point of view it was of definite practical value both to the East India Company and in the interests of the community itself that only one language medium should exist. From the wider aspects of culture of true nationhood, the extinction of French constitutes an irreparable loss to South Africa.*

*We believe it will come to be accepted in time that the individual conception of nationality in the narrowest sense of the term must be expanded to embrace a wider cosmopolitanism. It will not be good enough to be a good citizen of one's own country: there will be those wider duties and responsibilities connected with being a citizen of the world.*

In the same month the £250 000 National Art Centre was nearing completion in Pretoria. Pietersburg readers would no doubt have welcomed an art centre in Pietersburg had such a venture been mooted. Bosman differed utterly, and they must have read his comments with confusion and growing alarm:

*... the real contributions to culture are made not by lavishly financed institutions or by university dons or by pompous Academies, but by individual poets and painters, who get precious little recognition from the world, and less from National Art Centres, during their creative periods in which they shed undying lustre on the countries in which they happen to find themselves at work ...*

*... It is the very essence and soul and life-blood of art, and an essential part of its eternal spirit, that it should be rebellious, and that it accepts orthodoxy of any description as its natural foe ...*

*We believe that worthwhile poetry and art will yet be produced in South Africa. But it will be produced by individual writers and artists who will receive no recognition at all from any National Art Centre or from any other cultural institution.*

*This thought saddens us.*

A little later he compared art and science:

*... Science is based on reason. Art has no basis for existence at all. It is an essential part of the true splendour of art that it should have no foundations. Art is concerned with the human heart and with mortality, with earth and dreams ...*

Bosman didn't approve of IQ tests for the following reasons:

*... if a child obtained good marks in an examination it merely meant that he was good at answering examination questions. And if he got a high IQ all it conveyed is that he was good at answering an intelligence test questions. There was no more to it than that ...*

*There were questions such as what to do if one arrived at the station and found that the train had left. Or how to locate a tennis ball dropped into a grass-grown circular tennis-court with only one entrance. The child with average brain-power would solve this to the satisfaction of the examiner by saying he would walk around the inner side of the court in a spiral fashion, working towards the centre. The half-wit would start wondering what sort of grass it was. So would the genius ...*

*Intelligence tests have only established something which we have already known and which is not worth knowing, viz., that the average intellect will conform in an average way to average tests. But IQs break down when it comes to dealing with the extremes of genius and*

145

*lunacy, which are the only attributes of the mind that are of ultimate value to the world.*

*Intelligence Tests do not measure creative power. No tests can.*

He wrote of Afrikaans theatre:

*There is about the Afrikaans theatre a good deal of that spirit of human warmth that makes every visit to the Old Vic in London an unforgettable experience. That feeling that one gets at the Old Vic, of a strong bond existing between players and audience, of art that becomes exalted through the common touch ...*

*The Afrikaans theatre today has a lot of that atmosphere of simple naturalness – which is really art in its highest form. We think of Pierre de Wet counting over the takings behind the scenes in the Pietersburg Town Hall after the show ...*

*We feel that great things may yet be expected of a theatre that is so close to the soil. An actor who gives a hand in the box office before the play starts has got serious responsibilities towards the audience. He has to give the public not only his best in the way of histrionics, but also the right change.*

One evening in 1943 he'd attended the performance in the Pietersburg Town Hall, and called on Pierre backstage after the show. He told him that he'd been so overcome by one scene in particular that he longed for a telephone booth where he could isolate himself from the rest of the audience and weep unashamedly. In its own context Pierre's response was equally moving: 'Yes, and you know we took nearly £100 tonight.'

Although neither Bosman nor his readers realised it, October was to be his last month in Pietersburg, and he wrote fittingly of poetry.

*Poetry is more than the threading together of magnificently ill-assorted words in an order creating a splendour of rhythm.*

*Words are the most powerful instruments that life holds, and since poetry expresses itself through the medium of these most terrible of all tools it is inevitable that the poet must exercise a stronger influence on the realities of existence than the general and the statesman. How empty are the strategies of reason ...*

Observant readers may have noticed the editor had become fascinated with teaching. And one teacher in particular. There was now a light-hearted banter in his column – a private dialogue for those Bosman-watchers who could read between the lines.

Pietersburg was a watershed in Bosman's career. It was there that the frustrating impotence of the years away was exorcised. Almost without knowing, he found himself researching. The material was there. At 38, he encountered in Pietersburg's dorp life a fresh field of exploration comparable in scope to the Marico 17 years earlier.

In his Oom Schalk Lourens stories he'd portrayed a segment of society to which he never really belonged: now he saw himself as an integral part of the dorp life he would depict. When he was in the Marico he was in his early 20s and separated from the Schalk Lourens community by at least one generation. The adult Pietersburg generation, on the other hand, was his own. Bosman no longer seemed to be peering into a microscope, but at his own mirrored reflection.

In 'Dorps of South Africa' he would write:

> *Dotted over the countryside in no semblance of order, and linked to the outside world, apparently at haphazard, by railway-line and/or road, are a profusion of South African dorps, each with its own strangeness and vagaries, and yet all conforming to the underlying features of a single pattern.*
>
> *They are all fundamentally alike, these country dorps. Small town or village, when you know one you know them all ...*
>
> *The dorps of the Transvaal were founded in a similar enough fashion. They were the places where the wagon-wheels of a party of Voortrekkers had come to rest. The dorp was the business centre of the surrounding farms.*
>
> *And even today the people who live in a town or village are not far removed from the soil. If the changes that take place in the seasons – the spring succeeding the winter and the summer thickening into heavy ripeness – do not lay overt demands on the inhabitants of a dorp in terms of seed-time and harvest, at the same time there is a sullen conforming on the part of these people to those dark tides at whose flow the jacarandas purple overhead and at whose ebb the yellowed fields fall silent ...*

Herman Bosman saw beyond the outer physical features of Pietersburg to the undercurrents he believed gave each South African dorp its unique character. He was captivated by the people of Pietersburg, their foibles and, to him, their strange convictions, which he would later describe as follows in his novel *Willemsdorp*:

> *They were strongly attached to the Bible and to their church. They were potential schizophrenics through generations of trying to adapt the*

*rigid tenets of their Calvinistic creed to the spacious demands made by*
*life on the African veld ...*

And, again from 'Dorps of South Africa':

*There was the veld and there was John Calvin. And the Voortrekkers*
*assumed, without enquiry, that the truths that the veld taught them of*
*life were one with the rigidities of sectarian doctrine, as embodied in the*
*more starless conceptions of predestination and original sin. The spirit*
*of the veld was large. Calvin's, not quite so large ...*

*Anyway, the dorps are an important and significant feature of the*
*African sub-continent. And they are a source of great and abiding*
*interest to the writer and to the person who is a student of life because*
*he is in love with life.*

*The main street with its stores and hotels and bank and the*
*administrative buildings. The houses placed far apart and facing*
*unmade roads. Churches and schools and the golf course and the*
*football field. And the mayor and the bioscope and the co-operative*
*warehouse and the village drunkard.*

The material was there in Pietersburg, but not the spark of inspiration. The
Ella years had become creatively and physically barren.

And then, suddenly, in Pietersburg, the catalyst materialised. Her name was
Helena Stegmann.

# 14

## Helena

For nine years Bosman and Ella had alternately savaged and healed each other, until there were fewer and fewer balms for their wounds. Their behaviour had become increasingly eccentric. Their furniture was painted in neon colours and their piano silver. Neighbours gossiped about their rows and late night parties, where Ella danced in the nude and thunderous Chopin disturbed the peace.

Their life together that had started so optimistically with meteoric flights among the stars now left them marooned in a lunar landscape yawning with craters. Ella was frantic in her search for confirmation she still was his inspiration and a desirable woman, and frenzied in her search for fresh stimulants to revive Bosman's selfhood as a writer and a man.

But it was not until he met Helena Stegmann, a local primary-school teacher, that he found sanctuary. Helena was a fresh experience for Bosman. She was eight years younger than him and Ella, and full of contradictions. At first glance she may have appeared an ordinary-looking schoolteacher, but she had an athletic figure and a graceful way of moving. She also had a gentle way of speaking and an interesting way of expressing her even more interesting thoughts. And suddenly Bosman was entranced.

Helena first saw Bosman one evening in a café, after a film show. Looking up, she was transfixed by the most hauntingly sad blue eyes she had ever encountered.

One winter's day shortly afterwards, the wind bit deep and whipped up the dust, laying it on one's skin like the frost that coated the ground. Helena was in the school hostel when a child came to tell her that there was an 'oom' outside making enquiries about the next-door neighbour. Helena offered to go and see if she could be of assistance.

Outside she found the editor of the *Zoutpansberg Review and Mining Journal*, his hat set jauntily over one eye. The other eye was dripping with the continuous tear of conjunctivitis. Through the standard initial verbal exchange it seemed as though his true personality was laid bare before her. The hat at a rakish angle over the jaunty eye that repelled her was negated by the eye that wept.

*Helena Stegmann (extreme left, back row), as a primary school teacher
in Pietersburg, 1937*

Bosman was enquiring after the whereabouts of the person living next to the school hostel, who was reputed to be an authority on lions. Helena told him that he would be away for the next few days. He then asked whether she could perhaps tell him any stories about schoolteachers, suggesting slyly that there must be a great deal of backbiting among them. It was probably simply a clumsy attempt to detain her a little longer, but she found his approach unseemly, and her reply was scathing.

In a gentler vein, he asked why she had chosen schoolteaching as a profession, and why especially in Pietersburg. Now it was Helena's turn to tease. 'I can't fill out a transfer form. I'm stuck here,' she told him.

Helena told him she believed in belonging to an organisation where promotion depended on service and merit rather than influence. Besides, there would be a pension to make her old age secure.

Encoded in Bosman's DNA was probably the gene that loves adventure, for Bosman was genuinely amazed that she made decisions based on such motives. 'Don't you know,' he asked, 'that every time you close a door another one opens? All you need is the courage to close the first door.'

At dinner Helena recounted their conversation to the other teachers in the hostel. But when the principal remarked that he knew of Bosman and that he was a married man, her heart sank. Helena seldom dreamed, but that night she dreamed of the man whose jaunty eye and hat, and impertinent insinuations she detested, while his weeping eye and gentle admonitions captured her sympathy.

She dreamed he said he had come to take her away from her sadness. For a long time after she had woken the dream was invested with a super-reality surpassing the ordinary reality of every day. She was troubled that the only man who, she believed, might open the closed door for her, was already married. And she was troubled that this man, whose hurtful humour she hated, seemed able to heal hurts far deeper than the superficial ones he inflicted with such unconcern.

Helena made an equally profound impression on Bosman, as he would confess in the novel *Willemsdorp* he would write on dorp life some years later. Lena Cordier (Helena) is invited by Charlie Hendricks (Bosman) to have tea with him at the Café Royal.

*Now, seated in a grass chair beside her he started wondering what it was about her that appealed to him – strongly too, he admitted to himself. Perhaps it was her eyes, he thought. Violet-coloured eyes set in a very white face surrounded with dark hair. Her hair was, however, not really dark enough to afford a really striking contrast to her eyes and face. Also, there were not masses of it; her hair seemed even thin and stringy. Added to this, there was her height, that was above the average, and a slenderness that lent a natural grace to her walk.*

*But Charlie Hendricks felt that it must have been her voice that first made an impression on him. Her voice was low-pitched, and it had a smooth quality to it. Charlie Hendricks felt that her voice was in some way a reflection of her demeanour. It was as though her voice and her gestures, her movements when she walked or when she poured the tea – had been subdued by life.*

*Her voice grew low again – as though hung with dark tapestries, he thought. And yet it was not a joyless voice. It was just that in its tones there was an acceptance of life itself, of its nature and its circumstances, in a measure that Charlie Hendricks found disturbing. And in that moment he realised that, while Lena Cordier's hair was not dark enough to provide a perfect contrast to the violet of her eyes, her voice was. Her voice was darker than her hair, and softer. Her voice furnished a perfect setting for her eyes.*

When Bosman met Helena he was confronted with an identity he had never quite known what to do with. Here, for the first time, was someone who compelled him to reassess himself as an Afrikaner whose family had sided with the British in the Anglo-Boer War.

Helena was the daughter of missionary parents. Like Bosman, she had come from a bilingual Cape Afrikaner environment, except that in her case Afrikaans was the home language. Her mother spoke English, but with a strong Afrikaans accent. Her father, George, after whom the Saulspoort Hospital was named, spoke with such distinguished English diction he was taken for English. He passed on his love of English literature to his children, encouraging them to read Shakespeare when they were still very young.

Helena was an outgoing child who enjoyed group activities such as the Girl Guides and was interested in first aid, veld lore and camp life. She never gave much thought to the solemn pledge proclaiming her allegiance to King and Country.

Once she had left home, she felt that her allegiance to the church demanded monetary donations rather than regular devotion or attendance on Sundays, when the golf course was so alluring. As a teacher in an Afrikaans-medium school she considered it her duty to become a member of the 'kultuurvereniging', but privately she rejected its periodic meetings as superficial. For Helena, culture was ingrained in the texture of everyday life, not something requiring a conscious effort at prescribed intervals. Once, when she had accompanied her mother on a shopping expedition in Cape Town and had encountered a certain hostility when she tried to negotiate her purchases in Afrikaans, Helena retaliated by joining the Ossewa-Brandwag.

Herman Bosman's reaffirmation of his Afrikanerdom was more the result of an overwhelming rediscovery after years spent in a nationality vacuum. Helena's lay in a sense of identity so woven into the fabric of her life it had never been an issue.

In 1926 Bosman had taken for granted his ability to speak the language well enough to teach in an Afrikaans-medium school in the Marico, and during his term of imprisonment his knowledge of Afrikaans stood him in good stead. But with those years in Europe, like a tourist on a permanent in-transit visa, his Afrikaans had fallen into disuse – indeed, disintegrating, even as the names on the forgotten gravestones of his stories were slowly becoming effaced.

By conversing with him in Afrikaans, Helena gradually restored his colloquial use and understanding of the language. This was indispensable, for Afrikaans poets have spoken of their tongue as difficult to translate, an earthy one in which the sounds of the words are often as important as their literal meanings. When he and Helena spoke of the development of Afrikaans as a literary medium during his absence in Europe, Bosman was willing to accept the flowering of the language, but asked for proof of the quality of Afrikaans poetry. Helena gave him the poetry of N P van Wyk Louw to read, in which Bosman found the conflicts too torturous. Bosman gave Helena the poetry of Herman Malan, which she found too esoteric to relate to.

Bosman badly wanted her to understand him as a writer, so he gave her some of his veld stories from the magazines of the 1930s. When Helena read 'Ox-wagons on Trek' she found the writer whose poetry she had condemned as 'too blue' was, in fact, in the manner of the Impressionists, using all the colours of the spectrum. She was so entranced with his talent that she ran all the way from the hostel to the offices of the *Zoutpansberg Review and Mining Journal* to tell him so.

Sooner or later Helena was bound to meet Ella, whose attitude to Herman at that time swung like a pendulum. But the day she met Helena, she seemed so remote that afterwards Helena wondered: 'What have I met? Is this woman wood? Is she grass? Is she flesh?'

Gordon Vorster would later say it so gently in a letter to Helena:

*You met Ella, the violent protector of his dreaminess, and she was veiled from you, her impenetrable blanketed eyes hidden from your yearnings to know more about the man you were beginning to know, after you had sworn to yourself that you never again wanted to know a man.*

*And there they were lost in Pietersburg, eyeless in Gaza, dreaming on the ramparts of Elsinore. He a product of incest and of violent sodomy, murderer, convict, poet, dreamer, ex pimp and abortionist, victim and instrument of death, man of pale and livid wounds, polisher of London doorsteps and tender bleeding lines; and Ella, interpreter of Beethoven and Bosman's needs, shrew, child dancing in the meadows, old, wise woman, lesbian, dreaming dreams while she lit strange fires along an awesome Hellespont.*

*Sheetless, dirty blanketed, stained pillowed they lived with their fearful hysterical laughter. They'd been in the stars too long and yet too bound to earth. And although they were married, both of them wanted a bride.*

*The orderly Helena, loving, over tender, a heart inclined to break too soon, to pity too quickly, a love without reason, trying to break the chains that were once freedoms, the impotence that was no longer proud; trying to heal the braggart wounds that were beginning to hurt.*

*So you rejected Ella as a lover but loved Herman, although you were not in love at all.*

Once Bosman was drawn to Helena, it was inevitable that he should seek through her the way back to his words and his manhood. Helena loved him deeply, but it was a love that did not hinge on physical expression. The course Helena's life had taken before Herman entered it had left her so disillusioned with physical love that she would have preferred to renounce it altogether.

Bosman, on the other hand, perceived a close connection between sexual and poetic fulfilment. He could not once more be a poet without also being a man. Helena knew that to love Herman in her own way would have been simply an extension of her own ego: the only real way to love someone was in his way. And loving Herman Bosman would mean repudiating her own rejection of physical love.

Even so, in their initial lovemaking Helena did not anticipate that total commitment would mean physical capitulation. She was terrified, because she had no means of protection against pregnancy, but she knew that Herman was plagued by even greater terrors and that allowing her own fears to intrude on his would be to reach a crisis point from which he might never find his way back.

The next day Herman wrote Helena a letter telling her what the reinstatement of his manhood meant to him. But even more moving to her was the prose of his letter confirming his words had been restored.

After this Bosman knew that he could never bear to contemplate life without Helena. One day, outside a butcher's shop, Herman said to her: 'You will leave me one day, just as Ella has caused everyone to leave me.' It was an unseasonably hot afternoon for spring and the flies on the carcasses remained quite still when she promised Herman she would never leave him.

By October, Helena was aware of the price of loving Herman Bosman in *his* way. She had missed first one period and then another. Three alternatives were open to her. Her first impulse was to do away with herself, and she would even have welcomed this solution had she not promised never to leave him. The next was to give birth to his child out of wedlock, but Herman was not prepared to consider this possibility. The third was abortion.

Bosman assured Helena he knew the necessary procedure. It was simply a matter of purchasing a syringe and glycerine and applying his knowledge. In due course the foetus came away. Helena was left weak, but not weak enough to alarm her. In fact, she continued to teach for the few remaining days of the third term.

About ten days later – on a Saturday night, towards the end of the Michaelmas holidays – a twin foetus and the afterbirth came away, and after that a flood of blood issued, systematically emptying her body with every pulse beat.

Bosman was taking notes at a political meeting that night. Suddenly he had an uncanny feeling that Helena needed him. He left his pencil and shorthand notes with the nearest man, who could write only longhand, and asking him to record what he could, he hurried to the hostel. It was clear that Helena had to be rushed to hospital, but it was unwise for Herman to accompany her. Herman Bosman, editor of the *Zoutpansberg Review*, the United Party organ, had been seen in Helena's company often enough to be the chief suspect; or, at the very least, a leading witness.

The district surgeon was determined to identify Bosman. A short while before he had been insulted on his wife's behalf when Bosman refused to publish a few lines of poetry in every issue of the *Review* as a 'thought for the day'. This was payback time.

It was wartime and all the blood bank supplies had gone to the armed forces in North Africa. Having satisfied himself that there were no measures he could take to replace the blood Helena was losing, he considered his next priority was unmasking the abortionist. He warned Helena that she could not live through the night and insisted that she reveal the name of the man responsible. Helena was silent. She was determined to live, so that Herman would not be involved in the repercussions of a fatal abortion. She was afraid to sleep. If her concentration lapsed, the determination that was keeping her alive might fail. So she remained propped up throughout the night, aware of the rhythmic ebbing of her blood.

The next morning the district surgeon found that Helena's will had prevailed. She advised him to take the matter calmly – she had no intention of being an abortion fatality. Establishment pressures swept her in diverse directions. There was a detective trying to force a confession from her by telling her that the police had taken possession of the syringe and were ready to identify the culprit. There was the public prosecutor advising her of her rights and reminding her that there was no need for her to make a statement under duress. There was the matron, who appeared genuinely sympathetic when Helena asked whether possession of the syringe was sufficient for conviction and, if so, whether she would make more or less trouble for the owner by revealing his name.

Helena, whose judgement never wavered the night her death had seemed imminent, was trapped in the crossfire. Finally, the matron won Helena's confidence. Convinced that she was acting in Bosman's best interests, she revealed his name.

On the Monday following, the district surgeon's wife brought her flowers and the triumphant message: 'Now he will feel the manacles on his wrists.' Then Helena realised that she had been tricked into incriminating him. For

Helena the seconds, minutes and hours that made up the next few days were measured in terms of her own conscious priorities rather than Greenwich Mean Time.

Herman Bosman was arrested on that Monday, as prophesied. After the manacles had been placed on his wrists, he was marched through the offices of the *Zoutpansberg Review* and detained in prison until a friend put up the bail. The rest of that Monday night Helena was tormented by having inadvertently betrayed Herman. It was during those hours that she made up her mind to find out for herself.

Helena did not possess a dressing-gown, only a coat. Before the night staff went off duty on Tuesday morning she asked for her coat on the pretext she needed a handkerchief from the pocket. Taking advantage of the confusion when the staff changed shift, she threw her coat over her blood-stained night-gown and ran all the way to the Bosmans' home.

She had to hear that it wasn't true. But when she got there, she had no need for words. The condemnation in their eyes was sufficient. But his words did come. They were: 'Haven't you made enough trouble for me?'

Dazed, Helena turned to leave. Halfway up the path Ella came up to her. 'There is something you can do for us. Write a sworn statement denying the truth of the first one.'

Helena did that. She walked to the nearest house with a telephone, that of Solly Marcus, and called for a taxi to take her back to hospital. The matron, aware of the reason for Helena's disappearance, was aghast when she saw her in a state of collapse. Her condition was far more critical even than on the night she had been admitted. On that occasion her priority had been a simple one – to stay alive to keep Herman out of trouble. Now there was no further need to live.

The sleep that Helena slept after her brother Johan had fetched her from Pietersburg Hospital to convalesce was far more of a journey into oblivion than a normal sleep. On the way to the school of Lemana, where her brother was principal, Helena heard from him for the first time of Herman Bosman's imprisonment in 1926, and the reason for it.

A charge of abortion was brought against Herman Bosman and the case was heard in camera. Even though there were no reports on the case itself, the Afrikaans paper *Noordelike Stem* carried a story with a veiled reference to 'a snake among us'. In a small town such as Pietersburg in 1943 local gossip was indistinguishable from local news, and it required little imagination to recognise the 'snake'.

During the course of proceedings the charges against Herman were dropped because, despite what the police had told Helena, the syringe was never found.

For Helena, a sense of waste and desolation was the only conscious feeling to penetrate her numbness. Yet had she known, there might have been a flicker of hope. Herman Bosman had written a poem, only to be published in the middle of the following year in *The South African Opinion*, but there is no doubt it was written for the jacaranda-ed month of Helena's series of deaths that failed to kill her. It carried a message of shame and betrayal, yet was a tender tribute to the generosity of Helena's spirit. Titled 'Leda's Swans', it read:

> *The brown earth of your body*
> *Is cloven in the hoof*
> *Of a daemon, of a satyr.*
> *Amid the village pavements strown*
> *With the purple ash of jacaranda flowers.*

*Helena Lake (neé Stegmann), formerly Bosman, left, with author Valerie Rosenberg, 1973*

Years later Gordon Vorster would write to Helena:

*When Valerie and I left you yesterday, we came away white-faced and afraid and a little ashamed. Not that we were pushing for the facts of your eight years with Herman, but because you saw fit, for the first time, to reveal those years.*

*You ask her to publish. But how to do it? Valerie is a biographer who loves her subject, and loves you. She is most distressed at the possibility of causing you anguish. And yet she has done so by gaining your confidence. I am Herman's friend and, I hope, yours, and the two of us must have formed a team strong enough to con you into opening up those long-rusted locks on the cupboard of your spirit. What you've told us is sacred, a trust, and you gave it to us because you knew that we would use it as objectively, as kindly, as lovingly as we could.*

*In the hours since, we have discussed everything from total suppression to using the tape you recorded, transcribed, as it is. But I think your tape must go on file for the far future when only the researcher of that distant time will feel anguish at his discovery. I know his molecules exist now. I know also that he will love his subject, and you as much as we do, and that he will also attempt a gentleness.*

*And so we have come to the point where research has stopped being scientific and touches the heart.*

*Gently you won him to the world of men until he was able to take a woman. Quietly you shrouded his fears, never allowing one of them to establish an ascendancy, soothing him to the world he was searching for.*

*It was seed-time, but the twin crops could not be harvested. This gleaning was not for him, the reaping was out of bounds. While he ploughed this land, it was to be forcibly barren.*

*Dearest Helena, earth girl, denied her sproutlings, but willingly sacrificing to his glycerine and syringe the fruits he feared were monstrous. Then he deserted you, but he would come back to you, in another chapter.*

# 15

## Come back he did

Come back he did, but a great deal of water would flow beneath the bridge before Helena and Herman met again.

After the court case, Herman's position both as citizen of Pietersburg and editor of the *Zoutpansberg Review and Mining Journal* became quite untenable. He was asked to resign as editor and a Scotsman named Hugh Hayes arrived from Johannesburg to take over.

During the few weeks it took to hand over the reins, Hayes arranged to board with the Bosmans. In the end he invaded both Bosman's home and his moribund marriage.

*A copy of Bosman's certificate of marriage to Helena Stegmann, 18 March 1944*

*Bosman flanked by his ex-wife, Ella (left) and third wife, Helena (right)*

Hayes and Ella were immediately attracted to each other and had consummated the relationship within days. Their rapport extended beyond the physical.

Ella was also Scottish. However, she came with a great deal of baggage. She was extraordinarily superstitious, believed in witchcraft and also accused Helena of being a witch. She maintained that both she and Herman were the products of immaculate conceptions. These eccentric convictions were no deterrent to Hayes. As a Scotsman, he said, he could handle her.

Just as Herman had not forgotten Helena, so she had not forgotten him. When she finally returned from that journey into oblivion at her brother's home at Lemana, she was reminded of her promise to Herman never to leave him. Finally, the reminder became an obsession and she wrote to tell him how sorry she was for what he had suffered on her account. For her part she had been asked to resign at the school and was leaving Pietersburg to stay with her parents in Pretoria.

A reply came from Ella – accusing her of seducing Herman and suggesting her breakdown was unrelated to her abortion. Helena responded with a lawyer's letter. This bitter slanging match was concluded by a conciliatory letter from Herman himself.

By the end of November Ella and Herman were back in Johannesburg. But soon the lure of her new-found fulfilment with Hayes proved too strong, and she decided to return to Pietersburg. Before doing so, she called on Helena in Pretoria and took her to tea.

Much to Helena's surprise, Ella apologised and did a complete *volte-face*. Now, having finally found fulfilment in a satisfactory physical love, she empathised with the relationship that had developed between Helena and Herman. She was on her way to Pietersburg; Herman was alone in Johannesburg and, according to Ella, wanted to see Helena.

When Helena and Herman met a few days later, they seemed to take up where they had left off in Pietersburg a few months before. Poor as they both were, they managed to spend two nights together in a hotel in Johannesburg. Herman accompanied Helena on her return to Pretoria.

Unable to leave each other, they spent the rest of that day roaming around Pretoria together. When night finally came, there was nowhere to go and no money to pay for accommodation, so they wandered back to the railway station, and lingered among the crowds on the platforms while train after train left for Johannesburg without Herman. Finally, an official who had been watching their suspicious behaviour asked them to leave the station.

They were ready to spend the night in an abandoned kiosk – except that it seemed to have squatters' rights as the night urinal for vagrants at Pretoria station. By morning, dirty and exhausted they stumbled into the nearest café, and bought coffee with their last change. Herman – the worse for wear – began to weep, the tears coursing through the grime and soot on his haggard face. His hair was tousled and matted and for a long moment one teardrop clung to the end of a strand of hair. Helena watched fascinated, wondering whether it would fall to the table.

Before he and Helena left the café that morning they had decided that they would be married as soon as possible.

Almost immediately Herman instituted arrangements for a divorce from Ella. He approached his friend George Howard with the request that he testify in court that the marriage between himself (Bosman) and Ella had always been unhappy. But Howard refused him. He dismissed the request as unseemly and ungentlemanly. After all, he said, he was a friend of both Herman and Ella.

On 19 February 1944 – with the help of Bosman's university friend, Fred Zwarenstein – Ella sued Bosman for divorce in a Supreme Court hearing. On 3 March they repeated the process in the Magistrate's Court, although a third document in the Magistrate's Court is dated 6 March with Fred Zwarenstein acting as Ella's counsel. Ella had sued Herman for divorce on the grounds of his adultery with 'a certain woman to the plaintiff unknown', both in Pietersburg and at the Rissik Hotel, Johannesburg. Ella's address was given as 29 Hans van Rensburg Street, their last place of residence in Pietersburg.

On 18 March – about two weeks after the resuscitation of *The South African Opinion* – Herman married Helena Stegmann in Johannesburg.

In Lionel Abrahams's memoir, *Mr Bosman: A Protégé's Memoir*, he draws attention to the well-known street photographer's snapshot of Bosman and his two wives, Ella and Helena. While Ella's forearms and her legs are bare,

> *... Helena's dress and coiffeur are distinctly formal, her expression and attitude quiet, almost held back. But it is her hand Herman is holding. (The way he and she are dressed suggests that this could have been the very day or hour of their wedding. Is it possible?)*

Something about this photograph had disturbed me for years. I compared it with one I have of Helena in *Herman Charles Bosman – A Pictorial Biography* as a smiling schoolteacher with her pupils in Pietersburg. Helena about nine months later on her wedding day – and I'm convinced Lionel Abrahams is right about this – is thin, careworn with suffering, and fragile. A casualty of the price she had to pay – snapped by a street photographer for all to see.

After they married, Bosman's professional and domestic life converged on a single goal – to justify his potential as a writer.

The evening just after Herman and Ella returned from Pietersburg, Benny Sachs introduced them to Leon Feldberg, founder and – at the time – editor of the South African *Jewish Times*. Feldberg and Sachs had decided to try to revive *The South African Opinion* and Sachs believed Bosman should be involved in this venture.

Bosman's run-down appearance and Ella's coarsened, almost depraved look, shocked and embarrassed the Feldbergs. During the course of conversation, however, Bosman began to weave his spell, and Feldberg instantly recognised his talent. He was attracted by Bosman's sense of humanity, his original thinking and humour that reduced them all to convulsions of hilarity. In the end, the Bosmans remained for drinks and dinner. By the end of the evening, Feldberg had decided that, should he and Sachs succeed in resuscitating *The South African Opinion*, Bosman would play a part in it.

Newspaper production during the war was a hazardous undertaking. Feldberg knew that while the revival of *The South African Opinion* would be a literary milestone, it would probably also be a financial failure. He could ill afford another member on his staff, but he offered Bosman the job of literary editor of the *Opinion*. In addition, Bosman was to help where he could on the *Jewish Times*, handling cables and helping Feldberg to produce succinct and telling headlines. Bosman appreciated this opportunity, did all that and even sold advertising space.

If Herman's and Helena's problems were mainly financial at this time, Ella's were spiritual, and therefore far more devastating. The divorce from Herman affected her like an amputation, but what had been mutilated could not be replaced, and there is no way to rehabilitate a damaged soul. The resumption of her association with Hugh Hayes in Pietersburg lasted at most two months. Then she too returned to Johannesburg. Soon Herman began to hear reports about Ella's desperate physical and mental plight. Willie Chalmers, a mutual friend, told him that she was believed to be pregnant, and was wandering around Joubert Park reading the Bible aloud like a demented creature.

She had found employment as a model for the 'life class' at the art school of the Technical College, and her friends George Howard and Gwen Davies were giving her what support they could. Ella accompanied Gwen to parties where she played the piano. Meanwhile she was pouring out her grief in poetry that would not have been easily comprehensible to anyone but Herman.

Bosman had always felt responsible for never having provided the lessons that might have made her a concert pianist. Now he felt compelled to assume responsibility for Ella once again. He began to make regular enquiries about her circumstances and state of health and was often seen hanging about the art school.

On 3 January 1945, Ella married a 25-year-old art student by the name of Donald Harris. In her fortieth year, she gave her age as ten years younger. Despite this marriage, and despite the fact that her pregnancy had turned out to be a phantom one, Herman's sense of responsibility for Ella continued to haunt him. So in the end it was decided that the newly weds would set up home with himself and Helena.

Herman and Helena were then living in End Street, in an old house that had once belonged to the Randlord Sir George Farrar, not far from the End Street Convent oak tree that had sometimes served as the country seat of the shade of Baudelaire. It was here that the Harrises came to live – in adjoining rooms, to be exact.

Helena, who had gone back to teaching to help Herman make ends meet, was suddenly presented with a grown family, for whom she was expected to cook and provide. Worse, the door between the interleading rooms was left open day and night. For Helena it was a malevolent sentry – a spectral reminder of the Pietersburg triangle. In a little volume of Ella's poems it reads:

*Nay, forgive me*
*Who am listening for your quick step*
*Upon the stair.*
*I wandered in an alien throng*
*I thought I should not stay*
*But know not what is wrong.*
*The very strangers knew that there was something*
*Strange in me.*
*They missed the gossamer of your bright presence*
*At my side.*
*Alone, I was a heavier*
*Saddened me*
*Without your star*
*In you that*
*Gladdened me.*

Bernard Sachs says of Ella:
*... The meeting with Herman detonated from her deepest recesses a demonism I would never have associated with her ... The bond between them was not sexual. My appreciation of Ella was that she was lesbian and that her lesbian love in her union with Herman could find full expression in spite of his maleness ...*

*... It was the marriage of two kindred minds. Ella was not only a piano player of concert standards, but she had a brain that could match*

*Herman's. And I don't say this lightly. I cannot conceive of a love more deep and intense than that bound two people together. The lesbian bond is indicated in one of her poems published in a collection after her death.*

*Sorrow drest*
*In pleasantest*
*Green*
*Sits at my right*
*Hand and lies like*
*A forgotten glove next*
*My heart.*
*And I am allowed*
*To hope*
*That the cool and terrible*
*Lesbian thrill*
*Of your violet eyes*
*Shall be the haunted*
*And perpetual palace*
*Of these our dreams.*

Helena shrank from the abhorrent situation and, without realising it, from Herman as well. This was the beginning of a sexual frigidity that, to a degree, would engulf her for the rest of their married years.

Suddenly, three months after her marriage to Donald Harris, Ella was dead. She died on 19 April 1945 as the result of a ruptured ectopic pregnancy. It was reported that an abortion had been performed by a midwife who had been called in to attend to Ella, but Donald's parents suspected otherwise, and reported it to the police.

The next day, for the second time in his life, the police were questioning Bosman about an abortion. Had there been sufficient evidence to convict him, he would have faced not only a charge of abortion but – for the second time in his life – one of manslaughter.

It seems that something like the reasoning in *The Blue Princess* prevailed here, for in letting Herman go, Ella accepted that he would remain hers forever. I think Bosman's poem 'Memory', which I believe mourns Ella's death, must have been written about this time, April being the month of Ella's death.

*An April leaping from a poet's brain,*
*An orange glow across a sinking sky; –*
*Will slow dreams lie upon the grass again,*
*Where now only the dumb-mouthed memories lie?*

*Do memories turn to marble or to dreams?*
*To breathy paint – a sky fly-blown with stars?*
*Or stand they forms entranced by frozen streams,*
*Lulled to the notes of lutes and dulcimers?*

*Yet were my memory made a mummy, still*
*Would I return to greet her in her case;*
*I'd touch with flame her wounden cloth and thrill*
*To view her linen sleep and living face.*

Night after night, Helena lay awake while Herman spoke to Donald Harris of Ella. The bereaved husband had need of comfort, but as urgent as Harris's need, was Bosman's to soothe his own wounds with words.

In the May issue of *The South African Opinion* the 'Talk of the Town' column took the form of an obituary – not exactly a standard subject for this column, but Bosman was not concerned with standard procedure. He wrote:

*On the 19th of last month, under circumstances as heavily fraught with the stuff of high drama as had been her life, Ellaline Sinclair Harris, born Manson, died in Johannesburg.*

*Viewed in a single piece, Ella Manson's life was a complete work of art. She was extraordinarily gifted. There was probably no branch of art in which, had she chosen, she could not have expressed herself with that same degree of outstanding brilliance which she brought to the playing of the piano. And yet she threw it all away. Her first concern was with life, and in the living of it she was the finished artist ...*

*Ella Manson lived her life in terms of an inward certitude, created out of the material of poetry and a dark and brooding romance and drama, in which there could be no compromise with the physical realities, with the concrete laws of existence. Ella Manson could not compromise with the world. No, not ever ...*

*In London she was with a man who aspired to write poetry ... Eventually, through dint of hard persuasion she succeeded in getting this man to throw up his work, and they left on a holiday to the Continent. When this man's employer invited him to come back, Ella had him turned out of the flat. The result was that some months later Ella and this man were wandering, homeless and penniless, in Chelsea. It was winter. In front of the Fulham Road Post Office, eventually the man, leaning his elbows on the window-sill, began to squeal.*

*'It's your fault,' he said, 'look what you've done with your talk. You've landed us in the gutter.'*

*'Yes,' Ella Manson retorted, 'that's exactly what I've done. You told me you were a poet, didn't you? And that's why I've landed you in the gutter. I have always thought that that's where a poet's place is. How can you expect to write at all, if you haven't been in the gutter? Or do you want to be just one of those respectable poets?'*

*Naturally, Ella Manson had hell knocked out of her by life. She did not write about life or make pictures about it. She lived it ... And, of course, she hit back at life. There were occasions when she struck back savagely. A caged spirit seeking to rend asunder the restrictions of mortality. A lion snapping at the bars ...*

*She wrote only for her intimates. She would write a poem in a cafe, on a cigarette packet, on the back of an envelope, in a library book – anywhere, but in a place where the poem would be likely to be preserved. And as she wrote directly from her feelings, in the nakedness of new pain, with the dreadful intensity of an individuality that could never grow tame, the result was that every line she wrote was lava.*

Bernard Sachs considered the obituary too emotional for *The South African Opinion*. But I believe Bosman felt there were no words emotional enough to express his grief. For me it is a searing piece of prose, where he simply opened a vein and bled.

After the Harrises had disappeared from their lives, Herman and Helena needed to heal each other. Bosman appealed to Helena to help exorcise Ella's spectral presence that seemed to reach out from beyond the grave.

He bought her an easel, an artist's palette, some canvases and oil paints, and they both began to paint. He also invited Helena's brother, André Stegmann, to live with them, and slowly they began to heal.

**SHORT STORY**

## In the Withaak's Shade

LEOPARDS?
— Oom Schalk
Lourens said—Oh,
yes, there are two
varieties in this side of the Limpopo. The chief difference between them is that the one kind of leopard has got a few more spots on it than the other kind. But when you meet a leopard in the veld, unexpectedly, you seldom trouble to count his spots to find out what kind he belongs to. That is unnecessary. Because, whatever kind of leopard it is that you come across in this way, you only do one kind of running. And that is the fastest kind.

I remember the occasion that I came across a leopard unexpectedly, and to this day I couldn't tell you how many spots he had, even though I had all the time I needed for studying him. It happened about midday, when I was out on the far end of my farm, behind a koppie, looking for some strayed cattle. I thought the cattle might be there because it is shady under those withaak trees, and there is soft grass that is very pleasant to sit on. After I had looked for the cattle for about an hour in this manner, sitting up against a tree-trunk, it occurred to me that I could look for them just as well, or perhaps even better, if I lay down flat. For even a child knows that cattle aren't so small that you have got to get on to stilts and things to see them properly.

So I lay on my back, with my hat tilted over my face, and my legs crossed, and when I closed my eyes slightly the tip of my boot, sticking up into the air, looked just like the peak of Abjaterskop.

Overhead a lonely aasvoel wheeled, circling slowly round and round without flapping his wings, and I knew that not even a calf could pass in any part of the sky between the tip of my toe and that aasvoel without my observing it immediately. What was more, I could go on lying there under the withaak and looking for the cattle like that all day, if necessary. As you know, I am not the sort of farmer to loaf about the house when there is man's work to be done.

The more I screwed up my eyes and gazed at the toe of my boot, the more it looked like Abjaterskop. By and by it seemed that it actually was Abjaterskop, and I could see the stones on top of it, and the bush trying to grow up its sides, and in my ears there was a far-off, humming sound, like bees in an orchard on a still day. As I have said, it was very pleasant.

Then a strange thing happened. It was as though a huge cloud, shaped like an animal's head and with spots on it, had settled on top of Abjaterskop. It seemed so funny that I wanted to laugh. But I didn't. Instead, I opened my eyes a little more and I felt glad to think that I was only dreaming. Because I would have to believe that the spotted cloud on Abjaterskop was actually a leopard, and that he was gazing at my boot. Again I wanted to laugh. But then, suddenly, I knew.

And I didn't feel so glad. For it was a leopard, all right—a large-sized, hungry-looking leopard, and he was sniffing suspiciously at my feet. I was uncomfortable. I knew that nothing I could do would ever convince that leopard that my toe was Abjaterskop. He was not that sort of leopard. I knew that without even counting the number of his spots. Instead, having finished with my feet, he started sniffing higher up. It was the most terrifying moment of my life. I wanted to get up and run for it. But I couldn't. My legs wouldn't work.

Every big-game hunter I have come across has told me the same story about how, at one time or another, he has owed his escape from lions and other wild animals to his cunning in lying down and pretending to be dead, so that the beast of prey loses interest in him and walks off. Now, as I lay there on the grass, with the leopard trying to make up his mind about me, I understood why, in such a situation, the hunter doesn't move. It's simply that he can't move. That's all. It's not his cunning that keeps him down. It's his legs.

In the meantime, the leopard had got up as far as my knees. He was studying my trousers very carefully, and I started getting embarrassed. My trousers were old and rather unfashionable. Also, at the knee, there was a torn place, from where I had climbed through a barbed-wire fence, into the thick bush, the time I saw the Government tax-collector coming over bult before he saw me. The leopard stared at that rent in my trousers for quite a while, and my embarrassment grew. I felt I wanted to explain about the Government tax-collector and the barbed wire. I didn't want the leopard to get the impression that Schalk Lourens was the sort of man who didn't care about his personal appearance.

When the leopard got as far as my shirt, however, I felt better. It was a good blue flannel shirt that I had bought only a few weeks ago from the Indian store at Ramoutsa, and I didn't care how many strange leopards saw it. Nevertheless, I made up my mind that next time I went to lie on the grass under the withaak, looking for strayed cattle, I would first polish up my veldskoens with sheep's fat, and I would put on my black hat that I only wear to Nagmaal. I could permit the wild animals of the neighbourhood to sneer at me.

But when the leopard reached my face I got frightened again. I know he couldn't take exception to my shirt. But I wasn't so sure about my face. Those were terrible moments. I lay very still, afraid to open my eyes and afraid to breathe. Sniff-sniff, the huge creature went, and his breath swept over my face in hot gasps. You hear of many frightening experiences that a man has in a lifetime. I have also been in quite a few perilous situations. But if you want something to make you suddenly old and to turn your hair white in a few moments, there is nothing to beat a leopard—especially when he is standing over, with his jaws at your throat, trying to find a good place to bite.

The leopard gave a deep growl, stepped right over my body, knocking off my hat, and growled again. I opened my eyes and saw the animal moving away clumsily. But my relief didn't last long. The leopard didn't move far. Instead, he turned over and lay down next to me.

Yes, there on the grass, in the shade of the withaak, the leopard and I lay down together. The leopard lay half-curled up, on his side, with his forelegs crossed, like a dog, and whenever I tried to move away he grunted. I am sure that in the whole history of the Groot Marico there have never been two stranger companions engaged in the thankless task of looking for strayed cattle.

Next day, in Fanie Snyman's voorkamer, which was used as a post office, I told my story to the farmers of the neighbourhood, while they were drinking coffee and waiting for the motor-lorry from Zeerust.

By

**H. C. BOSMAN**

*A page from the 22 March 1935 issue of* The South African Opinion *with one of Bosman's Oom Schalk Lourens short stories, 'In the Withaak's Shade'*

# 16

## Editor once more

Bosman's first issue as literary editor of the new *The South African Opinion* instantly established it as a worthy successor to *The Touleier* of the 1930s, and would be a watershed in the development of South African art and literature, theatre and poetry. A fresh, energised, indigenous culture was unfolding in South Africa, and he saw the *Opinion* as the standard-bearer and mouthpiece of the new revolution in all the arts.

Simultaneously, there was the soaring renewal in Afrikaans literature – the poetry of the 'Dertigers' (the generation of the '30s), notably N P van Wyk Louw, W E G Louw, Uys Krige and others.

Bosman discovered a new-found delight in Afrikaans. He and Helena spoke it in their home to reacquaint him with the vernacular, and to equip him to assess and report on its development during his absence in Europe.

Very early on he dismissed the body of South African English writing of the time as 'colonial literature in the cultural sense of the term' and warned South African writers against seeking overseas acceptance.

*The essential soul of a culture is that it must be indigenous ... Afterwards it can be enriched with the opulent splendours of other cultures ...*

*The place for South African literature to take root is here. Here in Johannesburg. Here in South Africa. It must grow up from the granite of our pavements. From the sun-stricken soul of our veld. From either or from both: it doesn't matter which. It must be created here. It must be born here out of the minds and the blood of our writers. And it must here be transformed into the magic of the printed word. And it is here that our writers must find appreciation and understanding. Here must be our audience, our market and our temple ...*

*We have got the life. The living soul of a culture in its first primitive vigour, naked in its fragrance. Strong in the very fragility of its loveliness. The era of the synthetic quasi-European culture has ended.*

Bosman believed that a culture rooted deep in its own soil was safeguarded against the invasion of foreign ideologies. He urged other English-speaking South Africans to acquaint themselves with the Afrikaans literary development of the time, promising them: 'There is nothing more exotic than what is lying just at hand.'

He insisted that all forms of art should be judged by international standards only, and urged critics not to be too lenient or chauvinistic.

A lecturer in Afrikaans at the time at the University of the Witwatersrand advised students against overlooking anything of merit. The body of Afrikaans literature was small, and anything of distinction was worthy of preservation. Bosman disagreed.

*With so abject an approach on the part of the critic it is amazing that Afrikaans literature has not completely degenerated.*

*Afrikaans as a language and a literature must stand on its own feet. It has still a very long way to go. It must fall or survive on its own merits. It must not be bolstered up with blandishments. It must learn that true strength which comes from self-knowledge, from the humility acquired through self-analysis and self-criticism. It must not be allowed to decay before it has blossomed.*

Bosman condemned fatuous admiration and the absence of constructive criticism. He deplored the acceptance of a piece of Afrikaans as good simply because it was Afrikaans. He cautioned the inclination 'to accept verse as poetry and prose as literature'.

*Before we call a verse-writer a poet at all we must try and remember what it is to be a poet. A poet is no small thing. He is bard and prophet and destiny and doom. Before embarking on what sounds like the start of a fanfare, I should like to point out that a poet is also a fool.*

*For these reasons we must hesitate a long time before we call a good verse-writer a poet. Off-hand, I should say that we must hesitate about two centuries. In the case of a supremely great poet like Isaiah I feel it would be a right and lovely and fitting and venerable thing that the world should hesitate a thousand years. Isaiah would not have it otherwise.*

In Pietersburg Helena had introduced him to the work of N P van Wyk Louw and others and he discovered that, during his absence in Europe, Afrikaans had achieved a remarkable maturity.

*It is almost as though Afrikaans as a literary language crystallised overnight.*

*The Afrikaans writers of today have a kind of volcanic power that the last generation of Afrikaans writers didn't have. Those older writers ... knew where they had to get their material from, out of the life that was*

# Marico Scandal

## A Short Story

### By
### H. C. Bosman

WHEN I passed young Gawie Erasmus by the wall of the new dam (Oom Schalk Lourens said) I could see clearly that he had had another disagreement with his employer, Koos Deventer. Because, as Gawie walked away from me, I saw, on the seat of his trousers, the still damp imprint of a muddy boot. The dried mud of another foot-print, higher up on his trousers, told of a similar disagreement that Gawie had had with his employer on the previous day. I thought that Gawie must be a high-spirited young man to disagree so frequently with his employer.

Nevertheless, I felt it my duty to speak to Koos Deventer about this matter when I sat with him in his voorkamer, drinking coffee.

"I see that Gawie Erasmus still lays the stones unevenly on the wall of the new dam you are building," I said to Koos Deventer.

"Indeed," Koos answered, "have you been looking at the front part of the wall?"

"No," I said. "I have been looking at Gawie's trousers. The back part of his trousers."

I told Koos that if he went on like this much longer people would start talking about his thoughtlessness, and there would be another Marico scandal. Koos admitted that this was so, but asked what was he to do.

"It is a mistake to reason with Gawie right there by the dam, where you are standing in the wet," I said to Koos, "walk with him some distance on to the grass, so that you can wipe your feet first, before you reason with him. And you are not so liable to slip, on the grass."

Koos thanked me for my advice. But I said it was quite all right. I explained to him that I only mentioned the matter in Gawie's interest. I said that I liked to see a young man get on.

Koos Deventer smiled then, in a funny sort of way.

"The trouble with Gawie Erasmus," Koos said, "is that he is not really a white man. It doesn't show in his hair or his finger-nails, of course. He is not as coloured as all that. But you can tell it easily in other ways. Yes, that is what's wrong with Gawie. His Hottentot forebears."

At that moment Koos Deventer's eldest daughter, Francina, brought us in more coffee.

"It is not true, father, what you said about Gawie Erasmus," Francina said, "Gawie is white. He is as white as I am."

Francina was eighteen. She was tall and slender. She had a neat figure. And she looked very pretty in that voorkamer, with the yellow hair falling on to her cheeks from underneath a blue ribbon. Another thing I noticed about Francina, as she moved daintily towards me with the tray, was the scent that she had bought in Zeerust at the last Nagmaal. The perfume lay on her strangely, like the night.

Koos Deventer made no reply to Francina. And only after she had gone back into the kitchen, and the door was closed, did he return to the subject of Gawie Erasmus.

"He is so coloured," Koos said, "that he even sleeps with a blanket over his head, like a kafir does."

It struck me that Koos Deventer's statements were rather peculiar. For, according to Koos, you couldn't tell that Gawie Erasmus was coloured, just by looking at his hair and finger-nails. You had to wait until Gawie lay underneath a blanket, so that you saw nothing of him at all.

But I remembered the way that Francina had walked out of the voorkamer, with her head very high and her red lips closed. And it seemed to me, then, that Gawie's disagreements with his employer were not all due to the unevenness of the wall of the new dam.

I did not see Gawie Erasmus again until the meeting of the Drogevlei Debating Society.

But in the meantime the story that Gawie was coloured gained much ground. Paulus Welman said that he knew a man once, in Vryburg, who had known Gawie's grandfather. And this man said that Gawie's grandfather had a big belly and wore a copper ring through his nose. At other times, again, Paulus Welman said that it was Gawie's father whom this man in Vryburg had known, and that Gawie's father did not wear the copper ring in his nose, but in his one ear. It was hard to know which story to believe. So most of the farmers in the Marico believed both.

The meeting of the Drogevlei Debating Society was

---

*Another of Bosman's short stories featured in one of the earlier issues of*
The South African Opinion *before it was resuscitated in 1944*

*in themselves and that was around them, and in their writings they were animated by the deep sincerities – in their souls' searchings for sublime truths ... But they did not have the creative power to transform this knowing into literary productivity of the highest sort. They didn't have the genius.*

Bosman's views on the work of Afrikaans poet N P van Wyk Louw, though controversial, were understandable. When he first read some of his poems in Pietersburg, Herman virtually dismissed them as decadent. In an early number of the revived *The South African Opinion* he said:

*N P Van Wyk Louw has found substantially all that there is to one side of poetry. And it is significant that what he has found has turned out ashes ...*

*And in respect of expressing this one half of poetry, this half that is heavy with the sombre brutality of the soil – where the emotions are hacked out of the body, and the body is plaited like grass, and the soul is starkly furnished as a bedroom – here Van Wyk Louw is a master. And this is the place also of his defeat ...*

*Realism weaves around itself nets that are never broken. Romance weaves around itself spells that were broken long ago.*

He recognised the strength, sincerity and individualism in Van Wyk Louw's poetry. His negative comments were directed specifically at Van Wyk Louw's disciples. He believed there was room in Afrikaans literature for only one Van Wyk Louw. For those bent on imitating him, Bosman offered two alternatives:

*... to discover for themselves from the wealth of experience of life itself a different way of writing, or to stop writing altogether.*

*Not only is it an unsatisfactory thing to do, to sit down and write in the shadow of N P van Wyk Louw is sterile. The direction which his work has taken, powerful though that direction is, cannot reach to that region of mist and enchantment and torn fantasy and bloody word-blossoming, which is, after all, the ultimate aspiration of all poetry creation. It is a worthy accomplishment when a word of common clay reads like an incantation.*

At a later stage Bosman told the Van Wyk Louw school of writers:

*I have compared the spirit animating Afrikaans writers of today, with the feelings the Elizabethans had. A new language; a live thing of the morning, fresh and with dew on it; young and infinitely flexible and full of dawn-secrets waiting to be discovered. But Marlowe didn't go and write like Fletcher, Rowley like Dekker, Lyly like Bacon. Each was dazzled in his own way; each found a different leafy avenue of his own to wander in; each in terms of his own individuality, his own soul and tastes and temperament ...*

*The Elizabethans were, first of all, extrovert. They created organically. That is how a new literature has got to start. The whole magnificent and monstrous world of outside reality has got to be your material. And this is the real direction that Afrikaans culture is at this very moment pursuing.*

*True poetry embraces the whole universe: the N P van Wyk Louw school are confined within the labyrinths of each writer's ego.*

Bosman maintained that some Afrikaners – writers and readers alike – tended to hamper their literature with too much academic pettifogging about grammar and syntax. The Afrikaner had too much reverential awe for his own creative art, and not enough laughter. 'The poets take themselves too seriously.' He quoted his colleague Ehrhardt Planjé as saying that after mining and agriculture the most important industry in South Africa was Culture, and then riposted:

*You don't have to worry about culture. You haven't got to try and build it up or preserve it. If it is any good at all, God will look after it.*

Bosman charged the Akademie vir Wetenskap en Kuns with having made the writing of Afrikaans verse a highly respectable occupation.

*The writing of Afrikaans prose is today beset by so many artificially created difficulties of idiom and grammar and syntax that the language is losing one of its greatest assets, flexibility. A Malay fisherman at the Cape recently told me a story of a shipwreck. I was thrilled with his Afrikaans, which was curved with the waves and the salt of the sea-spume. A professor would have given him one out of ten for his Afrikaans, because it did not conform to the rules laid down by the Akademie. This thought saddened me. The fisherman's forbears and mine, his on the water and mine on the land, had contributed jointly to the creation of a new language, and the voice of Culture had bidden us part.*

*But I know that the Malay has got the last laugh, for in the end the cultured Afrikaner will have to go back to the Malay to hear the language in its vitality and freshness, strong in being, a thing of continuous organic growth. The Akademie says there is only one correct way of employing a 'voorsetsel'. The Elizabethans spelt Shakespeare's name in six different ways.*

Bosman considered intellectual criteria too sterile to intrude in his jungle of words. Joy was vital to creation.

*I am talking of that divine joy in creation that is also fun. I have come across that spirit here and there among the very youngest of our present-day writers. And I know they are going to produce something worthwhile, some day.*

*Joy is a quality fraught with a gaudy peril. It is so near to love, for one thing. And when you come into the presence of beauty in a gaiety of spirit, let the foolish stars beware. The universe is dangerously poised on the brink of a precipice ...*

*In the work of some of the very youngest of our Afrikaans writers I have begun to detect something of the spirit of high mirth. Look out for them.*

Bosman believed much Afrikaans literature of the time was too parochial, and too remote from the realities of Africa. In this he anticipated contemporary writers by a full three decades.

As Bosman had written in Pietersburg the previous year, he not only rejected academism, but all synthetic devices to promote art like competitions, festivals and sponsorships.

*If a genius has produced a work of genius, there is no board of judges drawn from the ranks of his contemporaries that is competent to assess the value of the contribution which he has made to world thought. That is only something which the future ages can determine – and the future ages never go wrong ...*

*If a new national culture has struck legitimate roots, if it has got the authentic ring, if it has got a genuine spark, no matter how dim, you will be quite safe in leaving it alone. There is nothing in this world that can destroy it. You don't need to try to stimulate it with cheap artifices.*

*If it is a genuine spark, you can't kill it even with a 'kunswedstryd'.*

He blamed the indifferent quality of Johannesburg art during the early '40s on official support.

*We feel that to allow the South African artist to go on, year after year, turning out things that would be looked at askance if they were produced by a student at any third-rate Chelsea art school, is not to protect him at all, but to connive at his becoming, not only a hopelessly bad artist, but also, and this is a lot worse, a most unpleasant character.*

At the same time he was convinced that great painting would be produced in South Africa – despite and not because of well-meaning official patronage.

*It's got nothing to do with our artists and writers. It's got everything to do with Africa. You can't go wrong here. The soil is thick with life, ancient with learning, heavy with inspiration.*

Enthusiastic as he was, he advised aspiring artists to forget everything they'd admired in other artists and learn from life itself, for to Bosman life and art were one.

Naturally, Bosman would most often return to the subject that was closest to his heart throughout his life: poetry and the word. For him the word was a religion – probably the only one he ever recognised. Contained in the molecule of the word were the ultimates with which he was concerned. It was not only that he had chosen the word; it also seemed to have chosen him. And there was nothing he could do about it. In January 1946 he wrote:

*In the beginning there was the Word. A word is the most powerful thing that there is. It is also the most alive thing that there is. A word has got swallowed up inside it the whole of creation.*

*A language and poetry are one. Words are themselves poems. A language is not simply the medium, the vehicle, through which to give body to an idea – something for clothing poetry with. The word itself, the sound and the look of it, its life and shape altogether apart from its meaning, has got its own magic and its own poetry.*

What he had written on poetry in the 1930s and the year before in the *Zoutpansberg Review* made it clear that his views on this topic could never be anything but subjective. If the word was his only religion, poetry was his only god.

*Poetry is anything that a poet does. And a poet is nothing more or less than a divinely inspired madman.*

*A poet gets his gift direct from God. And it's a hell of a gift. And whether the poet wants his gift or not, he can't get rid of it. It is a curse from which he can't escape ... You can tell if a man is a poet by the things he writes. But you can tell far better if a man is a poet by the things he lives ...*

*In whatever words a poet strings phrases together he creates poetry, no matter what his intentions are, or whether he has got his tongue in his cheek. In spite of himself he wreathes enchantments ... A poet cannot be insincere with his genius, no matter what length he goes to, hoax or no hoax. And a man who hasn't got the spark of poetry inside him can turn out only tripe, no matter what length he goes to, hoax or no hoax.*

Bosman insisted that all aspiring poets should, initially at least, subject themselves to the discipline of orthodox rhyme and metre. For one thing, they owed it as a tribute to the poets of the past. These basic techniques could only be discarded once they had been absorbed in the poet's very breath and bloodstream.

*That man is not a poet who can't lose himself for hours in a discussion as to whether there really is such a thing as a spondee in the English language ... The first couple of words will tell you if the person who has written it knows anything about the structural foundation of poetry and about words ... or whether he is simply writing like that because he doesn't know any better.*

Before Bosman had ever gone to Pietersburg, the previous year when he was down on his luck, he had written a controversial 32-page pamphlet on the Jewish question, which he had then tried to sell to prominent members of the Jewish community. The matter was eventually raised in Parliament.

In April 1944 (approximately a year later) his essay, 'The Boer and the Jew', traced the similarities between the Afrikaner and the Jew and suggested that after a year in the employ of, first Solly Marcus and then Leon Feldberg, his thinking had changed.

Afrikaners and Jews were both oppressed peoples who had come to the Transvaal under pressures of various kinds, he said. The mode of travel differed slightly.

*The Boer packed his belongings on to an ox-wagon; the Jew's baggage was booked through to Johannesburg and came up in the guard's van.*

He said that the Afrikaner and the Jew had not yet found each other, but they would.

*So much is inevitable. Life did not just dump them down here together for nothing.*

In his comparison he says:

*... when writers in the past have characterised the Boer War as having been the last of the 'gentleman's wars', there is no need to enlarge on the fact that what made it a gentleman's war was because the Boers were in it ...*

Leon Feldberg, owner/proprietor of both *The South African Opinion* as well as the *Jewish Times*, was a cultured man of great charm, and was constantly enchanted by Bosman's original mind and humanity. Their mutual admiration society which had started the night Benny Sachs had introduced them, soon flowered into a rather special friendship.

Aware of the fragility of Bosman's sensitive spirit – rather like Oom Jim Flattery had been years ago in the Marico – he was concerned at the price it could still exact. He felt an anxious almost paternal responsibility for him, and was always ready to get him out of trouble.

As far back as the 1930s George Howard had said that among all the young men of Johannesburg's early '30s, looking on, looking back, looking forward and expressing themselves in anger, Herman was unique. 'He threaded his personal rages with a splendid kind of laughter that was always spiritual medicine to the heavily burdened. He was a life-line to the despairing.'

The end of the war was to spawn a breed of 'protest writers' who would be called either 'angry young men' or the 'beat generation', depending on which side of the Atlantic they were located. As early as June 1944 Leon Feldberg was as aware of Bosman's compassion and impotent anger as George Howard had always been. One Sunday morning in June Bosman, Leon Feldberg and Helena went together to research 'Shanty Town'. What he subsequently wrote is as valid today as it was then.

> *What was most interesting about Shanty Town was the human side. One felt in the place the warmth of a strong and raw life. Deplorable though their economic circumstances were, there was about these men and women and children a sense of life that had no frustration in it ... Was there anything about us, about this party of white visitors, that the residents of Shanty Town could genuinely envy? In our hearts the answer was, no ... And when we left, a native woman asked us if we were going to send blankets. It was a perfect snub, whose imputation could not be lost even on the most obtuse. A duchess could not have administered it better ...*
>
> *If life is spirit, what the natives of Shanty Town bear about them is not poverty but destiny.*

Towards the end of 1946 Bosman welcomed the first edition of a rival paper, *Vandag*, produced by Ehrhardt Planjé and the poet-playwright Uys Krige, just returned from the war. Bosman wrote:

> **Vandag** *in its new form is a South African journal for letters and art. The standard is high. Uys Krige's 'Ballade van die Boorde' is a particularly fine piece of work. As a publication devoted to the furtherance of the interests of South African culture,* **Vandag** *is very welcome in our midst. Editorially it is in competent hands.*

During the following years Bosman and Krige developed a high regard for each other. When Krige's *Sol y Sombra* appeared, Bosman wrote a most favourable review in the *Opinion*.

Although they were both born at the Cape, Herman grew up in the Transvaal. Uys Krige thought that he and Bosman each reflected his own particular regional brand of humour. Uys Krige considered himself an exponent of the humour of the Mediterranean wine-growing countries: a brand of humour that was extrovert, eloquent and expansive to the point of overstatement. He believed Bosman identified with the humour of the Transvaal Afrikaner, which resided in subtleties like ambiguities, understatement and the throw-away line.

Krige once came out of Broadcast House in Johannesburg to find Bosman berating an African for the merciless way he had been flogging the donkey pulling his cart. Uys called across to him: 'That's right, Herman – your good deed for the day. Tell him that after his mother a man's best friend is his horse.'

Bosman was derisive. 'Uys, you were always master of the cliché.'

Uys was delighted. 'Ah, but do you know what a cliché is? It is that which is worn threadbare next to the hearts of men. An indifferent poet – *much* more indifferent than I – said it. His name was Sir William Watson.'

As early as the end of the first year of the new *Opinion*, public opinion on the literary editor ranged from 'eccentric' to 'downright dangerous'. Still, Bosman's reputation as a literary icon was beginning to flower. Johannesburg academics and Professor J Y T Greig, head of the Department of English at Wits, who had published three books on English usage, always held up Bosman to his students as a fine English stylist.

Also, a group of students used to gather each month to wait for *The South African Opinion* to appear. They would then repair to the Devonshire Hotel in Braamfontein, near the university, and read Bosman's articles together over a glass of wine and talk of the doctrines he spread.

As he had just written: leave it to the future ages. They never go wrong.

# 17

## Disciples and disasters

The office of *The South African Opinion* was wedged into the premises of the *Jewish Times* on the sixth floor of His Majesty's Buildings. It was in the strong-room, to be exact, with a window knocked through an outer wall. So, in a certain sense at least, Bosman was surrounded by an aura of top security.

Although he was writing well on the *Opinion* and establishing himself as an essayist and an arbiter of literary and artistic standards in South Africa, Bosman had a burning desire to resuscitate *The Touleier*. But Blignaut, the other half of *The Touleier* team, had left for London in 1939 and was unlikely to return.

Bosman once suggested to Uys Krige that they should start a *Touleier*-type of magazine together. Uys's reaction was to question him jokingly about one or two of the other Bosman-Blignaut enterprises, and Bosman withdrew into his shell. Years later, he told Uys that his need to publish a literary magazine had been an extremely urgent one, and his response – though jocularly intended – was a deciding factor in Bosman's eventual decision to leave the *Opinion*.

So, there was no-one with either the enthusiasm or the money. Or so it seemed, until into that strongroom walked someone whose enthusiasm for reviving *The Touleier* almost matched his own. His name was Reinhardt (Rip) Oberholster. Many years previously he had read those first few issues of *The Touleier* in Lichtenburg and, without ever having met Herman Malan, had assessed him as the finest writer of short stories in South Africa.

Towards the end of the '30s, he had discovered some of Herman Malan's material reprinted in *The Ringhals* and had gone to the publishers, Brill Brothers, in search of the author. They had referred him to Jean Blignaut, who explained that Herman Malan had died in Europe but that he, Blignaut, still had works of his that he would continue to publish in *The Ringhals* from time to time.

That seemed to be that. The 'finest short-story writer' would produce no more. Until one day Rip found himself in the Johannesburg Public Library, idly paging through copies of the *Opinion*, when he read a piece of prose that bore the unmistakable stamp of 'the late' Herman Malan. He went straight to the offices of the *Opinion* to establish the identity of Herman Malan/Bosman.

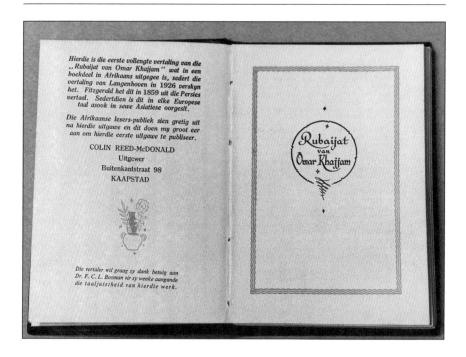

*Preliminary pages from Bosman's translation of the* Rubaiyat of Omar Khayam, *1947*

His knock was answered by Helena, who most days after school helped out with clerical work to take some of the pressure off Herman. She vaguely thought she recognised the caller. They jogged each other's memories, and it transpired that once when Rip had passed through Pietersburg, he had spoken to Helena about Herman Malan, the remarkable short-story writer.

After Helena told Rip that the man he had been searching for since 1931 was her husband, they also discovered that Rip's wife was the daughter of Dominee Ziervogel, who had lived on a farm adjoining that of the Flatterys when Bosman taught at Zwingli in the Marico.

Rip Oberholster could quote Bosman's short story 'The Man-eater' almost by heart, a fact that persuaded Bosman of the excellence of his taste in literature and almost allowed him to overlook Rip's regard for Rudyard Kipling.

Oberholster's enthusiasm for resuscitating *The Touleier* was quite disarming. But there were problems. There was still a war on and newsprint was strictly rationed. The two rebel magazines, *The Ringhals* and *The New Sjambok*, had long since ceased to exist, and Bosman and Rip tried to acquire their previous weekly 100 lb paper quota. Rip arranged an interview in Pretoria with Colonel Kruger, controller of paper allocations at the time.

Colonel Kruger listened to their case and agreed, on condition that they clearly stated in the name that the new paper incorporated *The Ringhals* and *The New Sjambok*. This was totally unacceptable to Herman and Rip. *The Ringhals* and *The New Sjambok*, they explained, were primarily remembered as scandal sheets and if their names appeared in the masthead of the new paper, it would damage its image. They tried to persuade the Colonel that in their efforts to resuscitate *The Touleier* they were giving him an opportunity to participate in a major South African literary event.

Whether he was persuaded of any distinction between *The Touleier* and the other papers is not clear, but Colonel Kruger would have none of it, and refused to accommodate them any further.

Having failed to revive *The Touleier*, Rip Oberholster decided to settle for second best – the publication of an anthology of the Schalk Lourens stories that had appeared in *The Touleier*. Together he and Bosman went to see Sarel Marais, then head of the publishing department of Afrikaanse Pers-Boekhandel. Marais had little faith in the short story as a selling line, however. He said that Mr O J Bekker, the general manager of the company, was the only other man he knew who shared Oberholster's enthusiasm for the short story. Marais agreed to publish and distribute such an anthology at Bosman's and Rip's expense. But they were unable to put up the money required, and this scheme also foundered, and so one disciple disappeared from Bosman's life.

The Bosmans' income was never quite sufficient for a comfortable life, so to augment their meagre finances, Helena joined the staff of Damelin College as an Afrikaans teacher. By this time ex-servicemen were flocking home to complete interrupted studies. Mr Damelin needed someone to take the English poetry class, and the obvious choice was Herman Bosman. He gamely did his best – for the few lessons that he lasted.

Helena recalled the rowdy students were difficult to control – a just retribution for the way Herman had once plagued a schoolmaster at Houghton College. Bosman's self-confidence ebbed visibly before this mass attack on his psyche. His lessons were abysmally ineffective: he never succeeded in communicating with the students, who called him 'old poi-etry' in parody of his own pronunciation.

Bosman told Helena before class he would walk to school along the tramlines as slowly as he could, hoping that disaster might intervene and relieve him of the responsibility of that day's lesson. It never did.

Lionel Abrahams, a member of that class – gives his own impressions:

> *Close up and hatless he seemed rather loose-jointedly thrown together*
> *and was evidently very nervous, anything but debonair and at ease.*
> *Today he was trapped between the intensity of his passion for the subject*

*he was trying to tell us about and his strangulated embarrassment at facing a roomful of unstudious adolescents who were impatient with his deep vision of poetry which was not going to supply them with a few swottable exam answers ... [He presented] us with his words and intentions as though with conjured visible entities; the silvery-soft voice and strangely paced hesitant speech with its rapid brief phrases punctuated by pauses, slow weighty emphases and sharp, appealing exclamations testing agreement. ('Hey? Hey!')*

After a few weeks Bosman was prepared to concede that the experiment was a failure and to seek a less soul-destroying means of augmenting their income.

Early in 1946 Mr Damelin suggested to Herman Bosman that he teach the art of short-story writing to Lionel Abrahams, a young boy who had come to the college from the Hope Training Home for the Handicapped. Mr Damelin showed Bosman some samples of Lionel's writing and a meeting was arranged in Mr Damelin's office.

Mr Damelin was not there at the appointed time, but Bosman and Lionel had no difficulty in identifying each other. Lionel remembered Bosman from the poetry classes he had given at the college. Bosman suggested that they talk things over in his office at *The South African Opinion*, but after they had gone a few yards it was clear that the walk to His Majesty's Buildings would be rather far for Lionel. Instead, they went into a nearby café. Donald Harris was there with a friend, and Bosman introduced Lionel, saying: 'He is going to be the best writer in South Africa.' Even allowing for a touch of playful humour, Lionel was quite overcome by this extravagant compliment.

Twice a week for the next 18 months, Bosman tutored Lionel, for the sum of £5 a month, passing on to him not only some of the craft of writing short stories, but a feeling for the force of great literature, an excited sense of vocation, and – most important of all – an insight into his own artistic credo. During this time, Lionel became aware of the privilege of communicating with an author as unique in his art as in his personality. Lionel and Gordon Vorster would recall his Grecian pronunciation of 'poi-etry', which became his nickname, 'old poi-etry'.

Lionel's vivid and personal impressions of his interaction with Bosman are quoted from his *Mr Bosman: A Protégé's Memoir.*

*... his enunciation unmarked by any trace of an Afrikaans accent. He always sat restlessly, his shoulders angled as if he had fallen into the armchair, his legs not only crossed but screwed together, his hands expressively at play, sometimes toying with his hat, sometimes shaping or, mime-like, 'presenting' what he was saying. He seemed electric with*

*excitement, and the energy affected not only his posture and gestures but even his clothes. His twisted hat, textured tie, jacket, velskoen boots seemed to have been chosen for freedom and then loosened, rumpled, blown awry by a psychic wind of some kind. He grew a light narrow fringe of moustache along the rim of his upper lip, which had for me the curious effect of deepening his privacy, his air of guarded secrecy. His sharpish nose symbolised the intensity of his interest in whatever surrounded him. His mouth and penetrating eyes, when not commanded by excitement, awe, embarrassed discomfiture or wild, applausive laughter, characteristically bespoke kindly amusement.*

*As I grew familiar with him over the following months, it was Mr Bosman's laughter that came to seem perhaps the most extraordinary thing about him. Though hearty and free, it sometimes carried all sorts of implications. Like a bolt of lightning or a ceremony, it illuminated and altered what it touched. But even without laughter he produced an aura which had a way of intensifying the moment. His eyes had something to do with it, the eyes often hidden along with the breadth of his brow under the wild tilt of his hat. They were vividly blue, and tangled sandy brows contributed to their expressiveness. When they weren't flashing excitement, awe, apprehensiveness or moments of secretly explicable terror, they were beaming tenderly shrewd amusement that could take off wildly into hilarity or deepen to a look that cherished whatever or whomever it was resting on. And his hands also played their part, dancing with the meaning, shaping and reshaping it, as he spoke.*

Lionel reports Bosman's advice:

*You have to write and write ten years – for the wastepaper basket ...*

*Don't be precious about what you produce. I once abandoned a whole heap of manuscripts on top of a cupboard in London. You must know there is more where that came from ...*

*... he recognised Poe's greatness, [but] made no pretense of understanding him ...*

*Study the traditional poetic forms, discover the power in them, try your hand at them. Only when you've mastered that discipline can you set yourself free to write without rhyme and metre if you need to.*

When at one of Bosman's last parties a guest asked Lionel whether he had entered a certain short-story competition, he replied in the negative and was asked why not. Before he could respond, Bosman, who was standing nearby, intervened: 'Tell him, Lionel, it's because the rules said the entries would be judged on merit. We don't want to be judged on merit. We want to be judged on genius.' Bosman's genius did not include such academic notions as merit.

There was a practical side to Bosman's humility as a writer. It encompassed not merely an author's willingness to take a humble job to earn a living, as once he had done, but also his willingness to take a humble attitude towards the tools of his art. He impressed on Lionel the need to place before his ego as a writer the disciplines of grammar and technique and his material. For Bosman, these things, like the elements of poetry, were imbued with almost magical properties.

He once cited Mark Twain, who during his period as a printer's apprentice had learned the true value of a comma by handling the comma in its metal form. Bosman also believed that Twain's best works were written when he thought of himself as a journalist. Once he began thinking of himself as a writer, he lost his humility, thereby losing something as an artist.

Bosman emphasised to Lionel the necessity of writing only what he knew of life. If the writer's material is life, he should open himself up to his experience of life. It was never enough for Bosman to observe clinically. He had to commit himself to a deep involvement with humanity. Abrahams observed:

> *... his more precious gift was to awaken me to the importance of humour, as a source of delight in reading, a powerful resource in writing with an aesthetic dimension close to that of poetry, and a heroically significant, appropriate and realistic attitude to life.*

Bosman's faith in his pupil was vindicated. Besides being a major contributor to a South African poetry anthology titled *Thresholds of Tolerance* in 1975, Lionel in 1977 won recognition for his novel, *The Celibacy of Felix Greenspan*. Prior to this, he and Nadine Gordimer were commissioned to compile an anthology of South African literature titled *South African New Writing*; and he was represented in several other collections. Herman Bosman remained his major literary influence. After Bosman's death, Lionel became his first unofficial literary executor and first posthumous editor, publishing six books culled mainly from his literary relics.

One of the soldiers who came home from the war was a young poet-artist called Gordon Vorster, who wished to publish some of his own work in *The South African Opinion*. He vividly recalls his first interview with the literary editor, whose work he had read in Italy and North Africa during the war. It was with a feeling of awe that he entered the strongroom with its iron walls and safe door on the sixth floor. Afterwards he concluded that this was, after all, the obvious place for a man with such prodigious talent to work – 'enshrined like a jewel in the tomb of Tutankhamun'.

They were ideal drinking-mates, because Gordon Vorster brought a certain poetry to his drinking experiences that Herman appreciated. One way and another, Vorster and Bosman did a fair amount of drinking together. Before lunch Bosman's preference was for tea and scones or anchovy toast, taken in sombre tea lounges with leather-padded seats, mostly Fanny Farmer's or Madeleine's. Both the fare and the surroundings were probably chosen to satisfy the mood of nostalgia for London that beset Bosman at times.

On some of these occasions Bosman's first wife Vera, with whom he maintained a light-hearted and teasing relationship throughout his life, was invited to join the party. She would often be seen with them lunching on curry at the East African restaurant or sipping Turkish coffee at Lucullus.

In the afternoons Herman and Gordon were usually thirstier. They drank a great deal of beer, and Gordon wrote a short story about drinking at the Commissioner Bar which appeared in the *Opinion* of October 1946.

*You have to go down some steps to get to this little lounge, and one day, while I was having a drink there with a friend who was telling me all about madness and how sane it was, I saw a very inspiring sight. I was facing the door and I was the first one to see it. A woman of about thirty, very pale and haggard looking, like a worn-out old skull, was walking slowly down the stairs. As she came into the lounge she smiled at my friend and my friend winked at her, and it was very wonderful and friendly and dignified, so I asked my friend if he knew her, and he said no, and so I thought it was very much more wonderful and precious a happening than I had imagined previously. I felt fortunate that I had seen something so lovely happen right before my eyes, in Commissioner Street of all places, right before my eyes, in this sad little lounge where they sold beer that tasted like wood.*

*The woman sat down and started drawing a wonderful picture in the dust on the table ... Her actions had been so possessive and determined, as well as full of purpose, as are the actions of a painter who takes the first energetic strokes upon a new canvas. It was while I was drawing this comparison that I thought of the possibility of her being an artist, so I explained my theory to my friend, so he told me that, though she was admittedly an attic dweller and an artist, she was not one of paint but of life. I thought his words very beautiful because my friend is a lunatic.*

*My friend spoke to her.*

*'What,' he said, 'do you fancy for the dogs tonight?'*

*'Yes,' I asked, 'what? It is Wednesday.'*

*She answered, 'Try three and five ...'*

185

*'Do you,' I asked, 'believe in leprechauns?'*

*'To hell with you,' she said.*

*'Yes,' said my friend, 'To hell with you. Of course she does. Everybody does, everybody must. What is a leprechaun?'*

*'It is an Irish kind of a fairy,' I answered.*

*'Yes,' he said, 'I know now. She believes in them.'*

*'You go to hell too,' she said to my friend.*

*'No,' said my friend. 'I won't. I like you ....'*

*'I,' she said, 'will not go soft for any man. Men are bunk.'*

*'Yes,' I said. 'Men are all bunk. Women too.'*

*'Yes,' said my friend, who like us was very drunk, 'yes, yes, yes. Everybody is bunk.'*

*'The world,' said the woman, 'is bunk, and we are all rubbish. Bunk to the communists. Bunk to the communists and capitalists and conservatives and the O.B. (Ossewa-Brandwag) and you and me and all these other fools who are drunk today ... and the ones who are sober.'*

*'To hell with everybody,' said my friend.*

*'To hell,' said the woman. 'I used to play basketball at school and I wrote compositions.'*

*'Yes,' said my friend, 'it is all very fine.'*

*'Wonderful,' I said.*

*'You go to hell,' they said.*

Bosman had a fondness for a light red claret, preferably from a bottle with a red triangular label. They frequented places such as the Glossop and Heath's Hotel in President Street that had a Palm Court. Gordon recalls:

> *We drank, laughed and were bloody superior, criticising everybody who dared put pen to paper. But we hated each other as well, because I was brash and he had the wisdom of many disillusionments. I believed in people and with some reservations, had stars in my eyes about them; he accepted people unreservedly, with all the muck.*
>
> *At that time I was starting life, at twenty-two, while Herman was summarising, ending, tying up the loose ends so that he could die five years later.*

Often a few days or even weeks would pass during which they did not see each other. Then Vorster would call on Bosman at his office 'in the safe' at the *Opinion*. The exchange would go something like this:

Bosman: 'Where have you been?'

Vorster: 'Working.'

Bosman (kindly and gently): 'It would please you to know that I have also been working. You have not been alone. While you've been working in your studio I have been in my office working.'

In these apparently inane words that others might have mistaken for non-communication, there lurked a world of communication that through their few years together became their special property.

Once Gordon brought Bosman a particularly long poem to be considered for publication. It was very carefully set out without capital letters or punctuation, in the manner of E E Cummings. All the words were spaced on the page in the form of representational symbols, like the early Dylan Thomas poems. Bosman leafed through it hurriedly and said: 'Ag, yes. I haven't had time to read it all, but I can see just from the way it looks that it must be good. And I see you have used a number of the's and a's. First class words, those.'

Bosman would discuss Gordon Vorster's short stories in strange terms that would possibly baffle most others. 'I can see you are a great writer just by the way you type. You seem to hit the S-key just a shade harder than the others. It gives it a particular distinction.'

Meanwhile, towards the end of 1946, Helena and Herman moved from their house in End Street to another at 16 Sovereign Street, Kensington, which they rented from the well-known Afrikaans singer Chris Lessing at what Bosman thought was an exorbitant rental. There was a perfectly plausible rationalisation for the high rental, though. The house had a large garden and Chris Lessing had been cultivating flowers, which were sold on the street by a team of vendors. He persuaded Helena and Herman that they could augment their income by following the same practice. They could even use the same vendors.

Somehow the venture did not flourish as well with the new tenants. The vendors would vanish for the day and return in the evening with their flowers bedraggled and unsold. It was only later that the Bosmans learned that while they were paying Chris Lessing's men to sell flowers, he had retained them on his own payroll to assist with renovating jobs on the side. What with diminishing profits from the flower-selling business and an excessively high rental, the Bosman economy was far from buoyant.

Herman once told Uys Krige rather gloomily that when he switched on his radio of an evening and heard Chris Lessing sing songs like 'Die wapad is my woning', he just did not seem to enjoy that kind of song any more.

Meanwhile things were not going so well at the *Opinion* either.

Even at the best of times the magazine's finances had not been robust, but by the end of 1946 they had reached a precarious state. The *Opinion*, like all unsponsored papers then and now, were dependent on advertising revenue to survive. Thus the literary editor found himself producing a monthly paper – and pounding the pavements selling advertising space in the company of his friend Gordon Vorster. Bosman sold space on behalf of the *Opinion* only, while Vorster represented a whole stable of magazines. They went anywhere and everywhere and turned out to be highly successful salesmen.

It was thirsty work, though, and much of their commission went to finance the great quantities of beer they had to consume to keep them going. Shoes were another occupational casualty: soles were worn through within a single instalment of the magazine they were trying to keep afloat. Gordon patched his with stout pieces of his C to C cigarette boxes, which always made them good for another few kilometres. Herman's feet were more tender, though, and he had to fit the thinner bits of cardboard in which the reams of office stationery were packed.

For Bosman the financial problems of the *Opinion* were compounded by other difficulties. He found himself increasingly at loggerheads with Benny Sachs in their old love-hate relationship. Helena recalls at least one occasion when they actually came to blows in the strongroom. She intervened when it seemed as if Herman was bent on hurling his opponent through the window.

At the same time Leon Feldberg, owner of the publishing company, had decided to accept an offer from Lily Rabkin that her magazine *Trek* should amalgamate with the *Opinion*.

Meanwhile a man called Colin Reed-McDonald had conceived the idea of translating some of the classics into Afrikaans and founded the Afrikaanse Kulturele Leserskring to promote the marketing of these translations throughout the country. He approached Bosman and invited him to become general secretary of the Leserskring at a salary of £60 a month. He was to be based in Cape Town and his home would be a Cape Dutch house provided at the company's expense.

The whole scheme seemed infinitely more attractive than staying on as literary editor of the *Opinion*, where things seemed to be going from bad to worse. Simultaneously, their farcical sideline of selling cut flowers was about to plunge them into bankruptcy. In the end an Act of God decided the whole thing for them. A devastating late-summer storm one day left the garden two feet deep in hail, with every flower decapitated. Confronted with this, the Bosmans gratefully accepted Reed-McDonald's offer. Gordon Vorster accepted a similar offer from the same company to represent its interests in the Free State and parts of the Cape.

The February issue of 1947 was Herman Bosman's last as literary editor of the *Opinion*. In his last contribution in the 'Talk of the Town' column he wrote of cathedrals.

*I can't sense in it the romance of human habitation. Throughout the centuries the people who entered the cathedral came there as visitors, and they wore their Sunday clothes and they were on their best behaviour, and they were quite unnatural. They came there in a spirit of religious awe, and they felt good, somehow, and solemn, somehow, under the vault through which they could see the sky; and they thought that God was there – forgetting that He was in their homes, where they lived, and in the taverns, and in the market place where the money changed hands.*

In March he started work for Reed-McDonald. His first job was the translation into Afrikaans of *Omar Khayyam*. He completed it by mid-April and was paid £50. He owed much of this achievement to Helena, who had given back to him a vernacular he had mislaid and in which he could now create more poetry.

By May of 1947 the Bosmans had moved to 98 Buitenkant Street, Cape Town. The third member of the family was Helena's brother André.

Even in those days one could not expect very much for the £7 10s a month Reed-McDonald budgeted for rental; so it was hardly surprising that the Cape Dutch house turned out to be a semidetached cottage in a slum area, where Helena's 'bourgeois Kensington furniture' seemed almost ostentatious.

They arrived at the beginning of a damp, chilly Cape winter to find both water and electricity disconnected. They had their first meal in an old fly-blown café called 'The Original Joe'. The *plat du jour* was tripe – probably the 'original tripe' that came out with Van Riebeeck, Bosman estimated. The idea must have appealed to him, for he was the only member of the trio who could finish his meal.

The Bosmans started unpacking their furniture directly after dinner. About two hours later, just when the straw had accumulated to a depth of about two feet, two gentlemen callers arrived. They introduced themselves as the sales staff of the Cape Town branch of Colin Reed-McDonald's organisation and explained that they had been instructed to board with the Bosmans whilst taking orders for the entire set of books, only two of which had been translated by then. Helena graciously offered them the only spare bedding at her disposal – the straw in the passage. One caller hastily withdrew and went in search of a hotel. The other hung around hopefully for a while.

It took at least a week to have the electricity and water reconnected, but by that time their visions of Herman happily translating the classics while Helena and André did the clerical work had evaporated. A letter arrived from Reed-McDonald, modifying the arrangements and instructing Herman to commence selling the translations from door to door. Even a born salesman

*Bosman's sketch of Helena correcting schoolwork (Collection of Humanities Research Center, Austin, Texas)*

like Bosman found selling an entire series of translated classics a little difficult when only two volumes of the series existed, and Helena and André wondered vaguely where all the clerical work would come from which they were expected to do.

Soon after Herman's brother Pierre added his own touch of unreality to this mad hatter's tea party. At that time he was studying medicine at Cape Town University – having spent his way through his inheritance with great thoroughness in a remarkably short time. He was pretty well destitute when he arrived on their doorstep with the intention of remaining on as a house-guest. Herman and Helena allowed him to stay simply because there was nothing else they could do. Pierre was drinking heavily at this time. One evening he arrived very much the worse for wear. Herman was not at home and Helena tried to be as tactful as she could. Suddenly Pierre said to her: 'You don't know what it is like to have a murderer for a brother.'

Helena lost her composure and ordered Pierre from the house. When Herman arrived home shortly afterwards, she told him about the incident. Herman left the house to look for his brother in the rain-drenched streets of Cape Town. Eventually he found him in a public bar. Neither of them ever discussed the matter, but Pierre never returned to the house, and thereafter they were permanently estranged. Nor did Helena speak to Pierre again – until, that is, the day of Herman's funeral five years later.

Funds were running out and debts accumulating. The £50 Bosman had received for the translation of *Omar Khayyam* had been used to transport their furniture from Johannesburg and there were no other resources other than what Herman could earn selling the non-existent series of translations. Simple book-keeping showed there was no way they could stay solvent. Far more ominous than the debts, though, were the first signs of Herman's failing health. During this black period in Cape Town he suffered the first of a series of heart attacks. His colour drained to a ghastly greenish-grey and Helena watched him fighting for breath. She had only a half-crown, but it was enough for a tiny bottle of brandy from the nearest bottle store. She mixed it with water and gave it to him. It was quite unorthodox treatment, but somehow it seemed to revive him.

This misfortune was enough to make them abandon their ill-starred Cape Town venture and return to Johannesburg. Helena wrote to her mother explaining their predicament, while Bosman wrote to Leon Feldberg asking whether it was possible for him to be re-employed. Mrs Stegmann advanced them the money to finance their journey back to Johannesburg and Feldberg assured Bosman of a job, even if it had to be selling advertising space once more.

Herman returned to Johannesburg as soon as possible. Helena stayed behind in Cape Town, where she worked as a teacher for just long enough to clear up the accumulation of debts.

Meanwhile *The South African Opinion* had amalgamated with *Trek*, under the latter name, and true to his undertaking to Feldberg, Bosman found himself selling space as well as writing articles for *Trek*. In fact, he had started contributing to *Trek* while still in Cape Town: several of his impression pieces appeared in the 'Talk of the Town' column. At least three of these dealt with his experiences in Cape Town and were later republished in *A Cask of Jerepigo*.

Where others might have crumbled, he never lost his talent for turning anything into an adventure. He thrived on the rainbows he created from it, and wove them into literature.

*Helena and Herman Bosman photographed towards the end of his life*

# 18

## Seed time and harvest

It was still winter when the Bosmans were reunited in Johannesburg and found accommodation in a house at 19 First Avenue East, Parktown North, the home of Mrs Pope, a widow with four children. The house had lovely, rambling grounds with wild parts where the children played, a rose garden that would be a sea of blooms in summer, and an orchard whose blossoms were still tight little nodules on skeletal branches when the Bosmans moved in. But by the time their fruiting season came, the Bosmans would be long gone.

The Bosmans had a large room with their own entrance, but their privacy was not inviolate. There was a fire blazing in the living room, but the warmth it spread did not reach the regions where they lived.

Shadows were infiltrating, for Bosman's public person was still haunted by spectral reminders of his imprisonment long ago and not so long ago, to be dredged up for discussion over library counters and telephones. A reputation has that kind of habit.

Bosman's first novel, *Jacaranda in the Night*, was published in January 1947 when he was still literary editor of *The South African Opinion*. In fact, parts of it had appeared in essay form in that magazine in 1945. *Jacaranda* originated in Pietersburg, in the sense that both the material and the inspiration were there. The material was the South African dorp in the veld and its people with their idiosyncrasies, which always appealed to his fascination with human beings. The inspiration was Helena, who finally gave him back his words and restored his manhood.

The setting is Pietersburg, called Kalwyn in *Jacaranda*, in a deliberate allusion to Calvin, whose teachings governed the lives of the people. The theme is the undercurrents of dorp life in general, and in particular the pettiness contained within the walls of a primary school in a dorp like Pietersburg.

The story of the publication of *Jacaranda* is a saga on its own. In their efforts to resuscitate *The Touleier*, Bosman and Oberholster made the acquaintance of Sarel Marais of Afrikaanse Pers-Boekhandel, a post-war publishing house dedicated to stimulating local English publishing. Prior to that, most writers in English were compelled to publish overseas. Towards the end of 1945 APB ran an English novel competition and asked Bosman to adjudicate.

Early in 1946, while Vera Sawyer, Bosman's first wife, was on sick-leave, Herman, in his usual unaccountable way, asked her whether he could use her address to receive a letter. Despite his marriages to Ella and Helena, Vera, who could never deny him anything, agreed.

The letter Bosman eventually received was dated 24 January 1946 and in it APB informed Bosman that the manuscript *Frustration* had been received as an entry in their English novel competition. The letter and manuscript bore Vera Sawyer's name and address.

In the literary column of *The South African Opinion* of July 1946 *Frustration* was listed among the novels accepted for publication. The name of the author was given as Vincent van Dam. The September issue carried a short paragraph to the effect that *Jacaranda in the Night* by H C Bosman had been accepted for publication by APB.

It turned out that *Frustration* by Vera Sawyer (Vincent van Dam) and *Jacaranda* by Bosman were one and the same novel. Somewhere between July and September adjudicator Bosman revealed his identity as author.

*Jacaranda* was not awarded any prize in the novel competition. The first prize was shared by Elizabeth Charlotte Webster for *The Expiring Frog* and Daphne Rooke for *The Sea Hath Bounds*.

The reviews of *Jacaranda* were only lukewarm. *The Rand Daily Mail* paid mild tribute to Bosman's ability to capture the pettiness in an Afrikaans-medium dorp school. The 'villain village rake' was described as 'well drawn', but Bosman's treatment of the heroine was considered 'sentimental, even lachrymose'. *The Sunday Times* said: 'It exhibits the same qualities of wild and wayward imagination as do the short stories on which, hitherto, he has built his reputation.'

C W Hudson reviewed it sympathetically for the March issue of *Noord en Suid*. It was an unusual novel, he said. The small town of its setting was complete with its love of scandal, its narrow outlook on life, its boring sameness, its dearth of culture. 'This stifling environment is the background of undercurrents of human emotions and passions which are concealed to the public eye, but nevertheless present.'

Prof. E Davis, writing in the April issue of *The South African Opinion*, penetrated to the heart of the author's intention:

> *It was almost as though there had been some reason for that queer mischance whereby the settlement of Kalwyn had not been spelt in accordance with orthography, almost as though it had come about through some inner understanding of the fact that the lore of the veld was not quite the same thing as Calvin's teachings.*

194

Of the heroine he said:

> *You realise that her being a bitch (meant here in the sexual sense) is only the outcome of her spiritual magnanimity. She scorns to set a price on herself. And so in the end, in the dusty Dostoevskian end, she becomes more precious than rubies.*

The publication of Bosman's first novel should ordinarily have been cause for rejoicing, but its controversial reception was like a stone thrown into the pool of city and suburban libraries. The widening circles spread to Parktown North. One day, out of natural curiosity, Mrs Pope borrowed *Jacaranda* from the local library. A widow living alone with her four children, she was understandably alarmed to find that she was harbouring not only the author of a book that in certain quarters had been labelled sordid, but also a man whose person was surrounded by whispers of a scandal in Pietersburg involving charges of abortion, and who had a prison record for the crime of murder.

At first Mrs Pope was nervous of confronting the Bosmans, but eventually she summoned up sufficient courage to repeat what she had heard. Bosman was stunned, but he gave her a couple of names to telephone for references as to his character. Helena, concerned for Herman's feelings, came to Mrs Pope and kept repeating: 'But my husband is a good man.' It was almost as if she felt that repeating this might exorcise this obstinate spectre from the past.

Of course, both Helena and Herman knew that once their landlady had spoken, there was no longer any question of remaining. Bosman simply told Mrs Pope: 'You have made me feel like a randy dog. We will leave in the morning.'

Years later, Mrs Pope was to write to me:

> *I was not proud of the episode. I felt that here was a man just out of prison and in a highly neurotic state, and I could perhaps have helped him. When I said this to a friend, she said that he was beyond my ken and that I could not have done anything for him. I think this is true, but I need not have given him an extra kick, which is why I feel bad about the whole thing even to this day. I was given the opportunity of behaving like a responsible adult and I did not.*

Arthur and Kate Kohn, friends of the Bosmans, were living on a plot in the Muldersdrift area, a few miles to the northwest of Johannesburg. They insisted that the Bosmans come and live with them immediately.

It was towards the end of winter and it was still quite dark at six o'clock in the morning when Bosman had to catch the early bus to Johannesburg. His observations inspired an untitled essay that appeared in the September issue of *Trek*. What colours were to the Impressionists, words were to Bosman, who painted his picture as surely as he wrote it:

*I have several times wondered why our South African artists don't paint the early morning landscape more often. When the koppies and valleys are swimming in mists. And the plantations are dark masses with a soft grey light behind them and the blurred horizons are wrapped in theology.*

*Perhaps they leave that part of the day alone – that part of the day before the sky is red – because it is so much more difficult to catch those griseous tones, leaden and ashen-silver tints and neutral greens, and patches that are the colours of dove wings: it is not just anybody that can cover a canvas with different kinds of slaty greys and still not make the thing look like a night scene. It takes a real artist to paint a landscape in dun shades – and yet to reveal it as a world filled with the morning's clean light.*

The Bosmans remained with the Kohns in Muldersdrift for about a month. The time-consuming and tiresome travelling to and from Johannesburg and the lack of electricity made it difficult for Bosman to work on a project of his own when his regular day's work was done. At the beginning of summer they moved to the Sydney Hotel in the centre of Johannesburg. But now Herman's claustrophobia and nightmares about incarceration in prison gave Helena great cause for concern. So she suggested that as a therapeutic catharsis he write an autobiographical novel chronicling his experiences in prison.

Ever since Bosman had – to a greater or lesser degree – contributed to Lago Clifford's description of his prison experiences in Stephen Black's *Sjambok* in 1929, he had been mentally and emotionally preparing himself for this task. Now he set up his typewriter and began to work on his prison memoir, *Cold Stone Jug.*

In the October issue of *Trek*, Bosman had written a profile of his publisher, Sarel Marais of APB, acknowledging his contribution to English South African literature, 'fundamentally and intrinsically our own'.

*We have nothing in the way of a living school of contemporary English South African writing, such as creates the mould of a people's thinking and acts as the strongest simple inspiration in the unfolding of people's spiritual consciousness. In other words, we have a handful of individual literary figures, mostly novelists, writing in and about this country in English; we haven't got an English South African literature in terms of South African culture.*

*South Africa, her cities and her dorps and her veld, her polyglot and her polychromatic population, her hard beauty and her sullen contrasts, offers the writer a literary raw material rifted with dazzling ore. And I believe that English South African literature needs only a small measure of encouragement to enable it to enter upon a period of great creative efflorescence.*

By November 1946 he had attracted another publisher: the Central News Agency advised him they had accepted a series of short stories for publication titled *Starlight on the Veld*. On the day he received this news Bosman in his exuberance split the back seam of his only reputable pair of trousers. Patiently, Helena mended them as she had done many times before.

On 4 January 1947 Bosman wrote to William Wolpert of the CNA asking for *Starlight* to be dedicated to Leon Feldberg. It was finally published late in 1947 as *Mafeking Road*. In the documentary film of Bosman's life, *The Storyteller*, Gordon Vorster called it a major literary event in South Africa.

*It is the finest collection of short stories that has ever been published in South Africa.*

*I say that very definitely – I ask you to forgive my prejudice – I am enormously prejudiced. It was a fine thing to happen to South African letters.*

The evening of its appearance the Vorsters and Bosmans celebrated with a slap-up dinner. The food in neither the Sydney Hotel, where the Bosmans were staying, nor the East London Hotel, where the Vorsters had their rooms, qualified for such an occasion, so they laid in supplies from the nearby delicatessen: ham and beef rolls, salad and lots of rough claret.

At that time Mary Morrison Webster of *The Sunday Times* was one of the most highly regarded reviewers in the country. When the review copies of *Mafeking Road* came out, Bosman took her to dinner. Miss Webster later recalled the incident:

*When he handed me the review copy after a meal in a dingy Johannesburg hotel, I had felt apprehensive both on his account and mine. I knew nothing of his work and had no clue to his history. But after reading a few of the stories in bed that night, I felt a strange elation. Here, I realised, was no amateur author but a writer of genius.*

Miss Webster's review appeared on 14 December under the headline: 'South African author Herman Bosman makes a valuable addition to our literature.' Early that morning Herman and Helena had walked across from the Sydney

Hotel to *The Sunday Times* offices to wait for the newspapers. With mounting excitement they read:

> *One of the best things to have happened in South Africa for many a day is the publication of* Mafeking Road *by Herman Charles Bosman (Central News Agency). Last year, it may be remembered, Mr Bosman published his first novel,* Jacaranda in the Night, *a book in which, in spite of certain crudities, it was impossible not to detect an element of genius.*
>
> *In* Mafeking Road *the suspicion that Mr Bosman has, as a writer, what it takes, and that his contribution to South African literature may be significant, is simply confirmed.*
>
> *For nearly twenty years, whenever the South African short story has been under discussion, the name of Pauline Smith has immediately been mentioned with 'The Pain' and other of the tales in her collection cited as classic pieces in this genre. But whereas Miss Smith's handling of her themes is essentially feminine, Mr Bosman's, though equally delicate, has a male perceptivity.*
>
> *All the stories, as a matter of fact, are recounted by an imaginary character, Oom Schalk Lourens of the Marico Bushveld, whose memory takes him back to incidents of the days of the Vierkleur, of the troubled interlude under Sir Theophilus Shepstone, and of the First and Second South African Wars ...*
>
> *Here is a collection of short stories of the first water – a collection so rich in human interest, historical matter and poetic fancy that it compares more than favourably with any other national collection of our time.*

The next day, in his letter of thanks to Mary Morrison Webster, Bosman wrote: 'You have put me on Olympus among the immortal.'

A week later *The Rand Daily Mail* said:

> *Here are twenty-one short stories, eighteen of which are perfect of their kind, flowering effortlessly from a root of genius that cannot be gainsaid.*
>
> *Here are stories which spring from the author as naturally as a stream bubbles out of the ground. They resemble the stories of Pauline Smith. They also resemble the stories of Chekhov. Sometimes they are about nothing very much at all, since what appears to be nothing very much can be as mysterious and significant as what is commonly regarded as important. But on whatever theme he is writing, Mr Bosman enters into the very spirit of his landscape and his characters.*

*Mafeking Road* not only established Bosman's reputation as a writer in South Africa, but also elicited an enthusiastic reaction from overseas. About September 1948, the Anglo-African Shipping Company of New York wrote to Mr Wolpert of the CNA saying that an agent who had read *Mafeking Road* had suggested that some of these stories be submitted to *Harper's Magazine*. At the same time, the London office of the CNA offered to publish a Schalk Lourens story, 'In the Withaak's Shade', in an anthology of international short stories. For this Bosman would receive five guineas.

Bosman did take a number of his stories to Lindsay Smith, the Johannesburg representative of the Anglo-African Shipping Company, who told Bosman he would be able to place them. He was so delighted on Bosman's behalf that he offered to reduce the company's commission. Bosman never turned up for his cheque, and Lindsay Smith had no idea where to find him, for by that time he had moved from the Sydney Hotel.

Shortly afterwards Bosman was invited to a private audition at the South African Broadcasting Corporation with a view to reading his own short stories over the air in a programme. Bosman was enchanted with the prospect of a new career that would widen his horizons. He saw himself as a Quentin Reynolds, J B Priestley, a man who spread his gospel not only with a dipping-pen and Quink ink, but through microphones and on short wave. Perhaps even the stage ... His eyes were bright with expectancy and soft with Walter Mitty dreams when he emerged from the studio. The sound engineer approaching him was no mere man, but a messenger of the gods bearing tidings. 'Yeah, well,' said the emissary from Olympus, 'that's the way it is. We just can't use a junk voice like that.'

Those were the days when a stylised delivery had become fashionable and the gravel-textured voice of Carey Wilson in *The Passing Parade* was all the rage. Herman's was a light voice, beautifully used, but unsuitable for narrating a series. He was, however, eventually invited to do one broadcast in the *From My Bookshelf* series.

In March 1949, the CNA advised Bosman that in the 'Africa Reporting' section of the *New York Times* book review of 20 February Alan Paton had said:

> **Special mention should be given to Bosman's Mafeking Road, *a collection of short stories thought by many to be of international stature.***

Bosman must have written to thank Alan Paton and in his letter he must have used the word 'kind', for in his reply of 29 March 1949 Paton said:

> *My reference to your book was not kind. It was a judgement uncorrupted by kindness or by any relationship with you whatever. I hope you will treasure it as a jewel, flawless and unique.*

About this time Roy Campbell in London began to write to Bosman, care of the *Trek* editorial offices in Johannesburg, to ask permission for the BBC to read some of the *Mafeking Road* stories on the air. Something very strange appears to have happened in those offices, because the first few letters were returned to Campbell with an inscription indicating that Bosman was unknown at that address. Eventually Campbell reached Bosman, however, and by the end of July at least two stories had been broadcast from London.

The Bosmans' accommodation in the Sydney Hotel was a single room with a washbasin. It was in these cramped quarters that he started writing *Cold Stone Jug* on his battered Corona typewriter. The typewriter had originally belonged to Helena's brother André, who brought it with him when he moved in with the Bosmans in their house in End Street.

*Cold Stone Jug*, 'A Chronicle: being the unimpassioned record of a somewhat lengthy sojourn in prison', was published by APB in January 1949. An advance notice appeared in *Die Vaderland*, probably as much in tribute to the publishers as to the book itself.

> *With his* Jacaranda in the Night *and* Mafeking Road *Herman Charles Bosman has won for himself a considerable reputation, both in South Africa and overseas. In the near future Afrikaanse Pers-Boekhandel will publish another novel from his pen,* Cold Stone Jug, *a strange, compelling story of life in a South African jail. It is no attempt at a reasoned sociological treatment of prison life – merely a statement of brute reality.*
>
> *The main features of the novel are the tight story line and the rapid but penetrating characterisations. A large number of warders and prisoners are fully drawn in their several dimensions so that each emerges as a live individual.*
>
> *The novel is neither bitter nor pessimistic; nor is there any trace of false sentimentality. It is a novel well worth reading.*

Mary Morrison Webster had seen the manuscript and had suggested that Bosman in some places delete the word 'gaudy', which he had used over-frequently. It was one of his favourite words. Besides, although he may have invited her opinion on the assumption that it had to be at least as lyrical as her assessment of *Mafeking Road*, he never tolerated criticism of his work. Ever. In the end Mary Morrison Webster did not review his book for *The Sunday Times*.

In *The Star* of 20 February 1949 the reviewer got close to the heart of the matter when he said:

> *This is a rather difficult book to classify ... It is a story of a prison sentence and has the twin advantages of being true to life and well*

*written. On the other hand, I cannot help wondering about the intention of a book like this.*

*A good deal of it is valuable for its revelation of life in prison, as long as we are members of a community where crime and convictions have their place, we must share a communal responsibility of their consequences. At the same time it is certain that a number of people less socially minded will enjoy this book for its coarseness and sensationalism.*

*The characters are well drawn and living and if they seem all to be touched with some primitive rawness, it is probably not to be wondered at, when the very walls and bars of a prison carry their own inevitable and characteristic prison smell in spite of all the scrubbing.*

*The book is vital and very interesting, but tough like its subject.*

It was tough all right, especially for a reviewer so sheltered from the harsh realities of life that he could find in it nothing but coarseness and sensationalism for 'people less socially minded'.

On 19 February, Charles Eglington's review in *The Rand Daily Mail* said:

*Anecdotes emphasising the more sordid side of prison life are time and time again dragged in, not only gratuitously but with apparent relish.*

*These blemishes are regrettable because Mr Bosman has an extraordinarily interesting story to tell at times; when his mood of wry detachment and the casual way in which he writes are suited to his subject matter, he tells it vividly and with insight. Some of his descriptions, stark and very sharply done, make one shudder and fill one with a terrible sense of desolation. The characters are cleverly and accurately drawn and the prison argot in which they all talk is very well handled.*

*As a writer Mr Bosman has fine qualities which are not absent from* Cold Stone Jug; *he has trueness of ear, trueness of eye and insight into human experience.*

Of Bosman's humour he said:

*It is so often, if not cruel, then callous.*

Bosman telephoned Charles Eglington to tell him that he had liked the review and would like to meet him. That afternoon they took tea together in a cafe. During the course of conversation, Charles Eglington, himself a poet, soon found that he was in the presence of an extraordinary human being. Later he recalled his first impression of Bosman:

*Very tense. Very calm in a tensed way ... A fairly highly strung person, enormously intelligent. He had a sharp penetrating sort of intelligence and often made comments on life and on literature which, on first hearing them, struck one as being eccentric, but later on, when one could get him to amplify his remarks, one found that he looked at life and literature in a most unusual way. In fact, I don't think I have met anyone who quite had his idiosyncratic way of looking at life and literature.*

Perhaps it was necessary for a decade to pass before *Cold Stone Jug* would find its place in South African literature. *Jacaranda* had been well received and *Mafeking Road* eulogised.

*Cold Stone Jug* was a commercial success and sold out within about seven months of its appearance, but critics, even poetical ones, agreed that it was difficult to classify. It was not a novel, nor was it quite an autobiography. It was neither a memoir nor an essay, nor even poetry, although it contains all these elements. Apart from admitting cautiously that it exposed a sociological disgrace in that the very system that prevailed among warders and prisoners bred further corruption, critics seemed baffled by Bosman's consistent refusal to appeal to the reader's compassion.

If a sensitive critic like Charles Eglington found the humour callous, the reason had to lie in the fact that the only humour possible within prison walls is callous humour. Had Charles Eglington met Bosman before he had written his review, he would have understood that no humour could have been callous enough to insulate the naked nerve that was Bosman in that 'cold stone jug' where he lived nearly four years of his young manhood.

Perhaps *Cold Stone Jug* appeared just a fraction too early. Black humour was just gaining acceptance in another hemisphere where the more sophisticated were delighting in Evelyn Waugh's *The Loved One* and in Christopher Fry's *A Phoenix Too Frequent*, in the cartoons of Charles Adams of *The New Yorker*, and maybe in Thurber. It was 20 years before people would be able to appreciate Saul Steinberg's cartoons in *The New Yorker*.

If *Cold Stone Jug* was black humour before black humour became fashionable, then the main criticism must have been that it was ahead of its time. Gordon Vorster believed *Cold Stone Jug* ought to have been left to mature like wine in a cask until the taste improved. 'And I am not talking about the taste of the wine either,' he said, 'but rather the taste of the drinker.'

In 1960, nine years after Bosman's death, Edgar Bernstein would sum up contemporary South African literature for the South African Pen Club, and draw a perceptive comparison between *Mafeking Road* and *Cold Stone Jug*.

*In a class of his own is Herman Charles Bosman, that sensitive poet, too cruelly buffeted by life, who died too young. Bosman, in the short stories of* Mafeking Road, *puts the rural Afrikaner into English fiction in a way no other writer has done. These are masterly stories, in which the art is in the telling more than in the incidents; the picture is lit with benevolent humour, and the men in the veld come alive as Bosman creates them. Grimmer, starker, more forceful is his* Cold Stone Jug, *an autobiographical novel of prison life. I know of few stories which plumb deeper into emotions of prisoners.*

When Bernstein called *Cold Stone Jug* 'the laughter that was really crying', he paid it the ultimate tribute.

It must have been in the period just after *Cold Stone Jug* was published that Bosman finally turned his attention to the novel on city life that he had promised himself he would one day write. Only it just wouldn't gell. As far as I'm able to date 'Johannesburg Christmas Eve' (the novel fragment now in Texas), it started optimistically enough with a description of that Christmas Eve in the 1920s when he met Vera Sawyer. But he could not have started writing it earlier, for there is about it the maturity of style he was using in the middle '40s. In addition, the novel's Greek nightclub owner and his cabaret sound suspiciously like George Pitusus of the old Criterion Hotel on the corner of Jeppe and Rissik streets in the post-war years. Finally, there is the indisputable evidence that the manuscript was typed on the Corona typewriter which Bosman used from his sojourn in End Street right through until his death.

In many passages Bosman's source material reads almost like a personal diary, for example:

*He meant that his mother was a white woman, and that she had an Afrikaner surname, that was either Hollands Dutch or Huguenot French – a name like Bonthuys or Van der Merwe or Du Plessis or Malan – and that she had grown up in a household in which the father, mother and children had spoken not English but Afrikaans.*

*Though he was an Afrikaner and a white man, and belonged to the numerically larger section of white South Africans, it was strange how deep-seated was the sense of racial inferiority that Gideon van Blerk had in regard to his fellow-citizens, who were white, like he was, but were English-speaking, who were co-heirs with him in the white man's overlordship in the southern part of Africa, but who spoke English while his own language was a form of Dutch.*

The novel remained unfinished to the point of being barely started. In fact, he abandoned it after only thirty-six pages. There seem to be at least two considerations that influenced his decision to leave it aside. This was also to be the story of Vera, and in 1948 there was not much more to say of Vera than the poem of his university days, which recalled only the raindrops in her hair.

There is a delicious passage in 'Johannesburg Christmas Eve' worth quoting for its insight into Bosman's city impressions. It tells the story of Mletswha Kusane, who worked in a bakery. One night when the mixing machine broke down, he was promoted from treading dough for ordinary bread to treading dough for confectionery because, of all the black workers, he sweated least.

> *What the night foreman didn't notice was the effect that this unexpected promotion had on Mletshwa ... Mletshwa suddenly started chanting in the Sechuana tongue a song that he had made up about himself, in the same way that any primitive African makes up a song about himself when he finds that, by chance, he is standing first in a line of pick-and-shovel labourers digging a ditch ...*
>
> *'Who is he, who is he, who is he?' Mletshwa chanted, going left right, left right, in double quick time.*
>
> *'Who is he chosen by the Great White Man*
>
> *'To walk fast in the fine meal with the broken eggs in it?*
>
> *'Who is he but Mletshwa? ...*
>
> *'Who is he but Mletshwa Kusane whose kraal is by the Malopo?'*
>
> *When the night foreman looked again, Mletshwa was leaping up and down in the tub. One hand was raised up to the level of his shoulder, balancing an imaginary assegai. His other arm supported an equally imaginary raw-hide shield. What were not fictitious were the pieces of dough clinging to his working pants and shirt and even to one side of his neck. The night foreman was not a little surprised to see a nigger performing a Zulu war-dance in a kneading trough at that time of night. Especially when white splashes of dough could have passed as war-paint ...*
>
> *It was only a little later that the night foreman noticed what other effect the violent exercise had had on Jim Fish: he was sweating like a dozen niggers; the sweat was pouring off Mletshwa as though from a shower-bath ...*

Also found among Bosman's literary relics that went to Texas was a fragment of a second novel, later referred to as 'Louis Wassenaar'.

It must have been during this period – somewhere in 1949 – that Bosman tried his hand at a number of Johannesburg sketches as well. This was a series which may or may not have been intended for publication. The sketch as literary form was becoming fashionable – that fragment of life that is neither short story nor poetry, yet contains elements of both.

During the same period he also wrote another play. Its title was *Street Woman* and it was set out in the fashion of something intended for publication under the name Herman Charles Bosman, which he used exclusively during the latter years of his life. The theme is mostly the eternal triangle. More importantly, though, he writes of the female vagina as a 'receptacle of filth', the classic image in the male impotence syndrome.

In both *Street Woman* and the sketches he used the names Marta, Veronica, Polly, Bennet. Bosman had a habit of using names derived from those of people he knew. I can spot Mara and Vera, and just can't believe they were names simply chosen at random. To me, in both the sketches and *Street Woman* he seemed less the magical weaver of words he had been at other times in his life.

It was April 1950 when Bosman started writing his 'Voorkamer' series of Bushveld sketches for *The Forum*, at the rate of one a week. Format apart, there are some marked differences between the Oom Schalk Lourens stories and the 'Voorkamer' sketches. Whereas the former encompass the entire Marico landscape, the latter are mostly fragments of conversation in Jurie Steyn's 'voorkamer', where the people of the district gathered to await the arrival of the mail.

This difference in setting is brought out subtly but convincingly. Without any specific descriptive passage in either series, one is immediately aware that with Oom Schalk Lourens one is outside where the horizons are wide, and in the later series one is inside where the walls are for leaning against. Even the dust smells and tastes different.

The 'Voorkamer' series is also set in another age. Progress had come to the Marico since the days of Oom Schalk and his frontiersmen, when the main preoccupation was survival and the preservation of the chosen way of life. Vital issues had become casual reminiscences. The main occupation now seemed to be 'geselskap', something in which Bosman himself must have participated during his stay in the Marico in 1926.

There are further differences in the distinctive characteristics of the humour of each. The runaway switchback sense of exaggeration coupled with the casual throw-away line of the Schalk Lourens stories as opposed to the low-key, mildly funny observations with the occasional 'non-ending' type of ending in the 'Voorkamer' series.

In the early 1930s Bosman might even have considered these hackwork. But by 1949 doing hack-work seemed no longer to be an offence against his integrity as a writer, but a valid part of a writer's lot. He had come to

*Portrait in oils of Herman by his wife, Helena, 1947*

accept his position in South African literature, writing and living his own life in whatever capacity he had to.

Bosman was taken to task for returning to the Bushveld for these impressionistic pieces when, as the critics suggested, there was a perfectly good war in Korea he could write about. His critics misunderstood the whole point, however. Bosman was not merely South African but African.

A war in Korea was for Americans or Koreans to write about. He never wasted time in replying to such criticism. Or any criticism. That was probably one reason why he refused to discuss his work. He knew what it was about – Africa. And he had stated it in print in all those essays in *The South African Opinion*.

Stephen Gray, then Professor of English at the Rand Afrikaans University, rates these conversation pieces highly:

> *There is the perfection of his language, again not to be confused with some oafish prattle, but a meticulously composed prose that catches the most lyrical phrasings of Afrikaans and gives us an invigorated English.*

Gray was right, though, in calling these 'blood-money stories'. In contrast to the 1930s, when Jean Blignaut saw him turn out 'The Gramophone' in three hours, Bosman now laboured over these sketches until the early hours of the morning. Helena would wait up for him, and if on rereading they felt that the work had slipped below standard, he would rewrite it until they were satisfied.

Throughout the period immediately after their return from Cape Town, Bosman continued to work for Leon Feldberg and contributed articles to *Trek*. In particular, extracts from two articles published in 1948 bear quoting, because in them Bosman anticipated by 45 years the thinking of the new generation of Afrikaans writers.

> *You mustn't ask me to approve of the artificial efforts being made by a section of the Afrikaner literati at establishing cultural links with the Hollanders and the Flemings, in order to stimulate interest in the creation of a 'Dietse' (Low-German) literature. Afrikaans is not Low-German. Its name tells you that it is an African language.*
>
> *The resemblance that exists between Afrikaans and the languages of the Low Countries is something fortuitous and meaningless ... the poet must know that Afrikaans is more different in spirit from Nederlands than from Chinese.*

He believed South African English literature was so much poorer than Afrikaans because:

> *The Afrikaner accepts himself as part of Africa. Out of his own traditions and history and background, out of the stones and the soil and the red guts of Africa, he is fashioning a literature that has not reached a very high inspirational level – let us make no mistake about that – but that has struck an authentic note, somehow, and that you can feel has got a power in it that must become an enduring part of the Afrikaner's national heritage.*

Of African literature he went even further. He said Africans had a marvellous world of knowledge and experience right in Johannesburg to fashion into great literature. The white man should keep away from this material: only the black artist could do justice to it.

*We have stolen enough from the kaffir. Don't let us have the cheek to go and try to poach on the preserves of his life's bitternesses as well, without having shared them. In any case, how can a white man get into a black man's skin and vice versa? That sort of thing is presumption, and can produce only falseness in art. No, they must write their literature. We must write ours. Only thus will we be able to meet each other in honesty, as fellow-artists, on a footing of equality.*

His words were prophetic.

# 19

## A fragile biochemistry

Bosman returned from Cape Town, his status changed from literary editor to contributor to *Trek*, and headline composer and advertising salesman for the *Jewish Times*. He now shared an office just behind His Majesty's Buildings with the cartoonist Abe Berry (whose initials matched his own) in High Court Buildings.

After the Bosmans had left Muldersdrift, they moved into a room in the Sydney Hotel in Fraser Street, which Bosman found frighteningly claustrophobic. While he was working in High Court Buildings he was stuck in one of those open lifts with trellis doors. Bosman afterwards told Helena that he had been stuck midway between two floors. Whilst the people on the upper floor could see only his head and torso, those below could see only his lower half. What initially were merely passers-by offering assistance were transformed by his imagination into a circus audience fascinated by the spectacle of two mismatched halves of a freak displayed in a cage. Only – this was free.

In sheer animal terror Bosman was trying to rip the lift to pieces, while the expression on the faces of the spectators changed from concern to horror. For him they were transformed into a howling mob enthralled by the ritual of blood and doom that invests the bullrings of Spain or the cockfights of Malaya.

A year later when Bosman was stuck in the same lift and took the incident calmly, the caretaker didn't recognise him when she recounted the story to him. He 'tsk-tsked' sympathetically, and 'wondered how people could act so mad'.

Bosman's genius came at a high price. He very probably suffered from a bi-polar disorder, and lived his life at the mercy of his fragile body chemistry. Perhaps his condition would have been more treatable today. Benny Sachs would write much later, 'the voltage he carried was too high'.

On the night of 27 May 1948 the whole of South Africa was sleepless, listening to the radio as bulletin after bulletin announced the progression of the first National Party victory since 1929. Some thunderstruck United Party supporters broke bottles of whisky and swore never to drink again. Ex-servicemen even shot holes through their radios, especially when the news came from Standerton that General Smuts had lost his seat.

*Bosman's sketches of Helena asleep (above) and at her toilet (right) (Collection of Humanities Research Center, Austin, Texas)*

Herman Bosman was one of the crowd in front of *The Rand Daily Mail* offices, where results were being posted on a board facing on to the street. When Gordon Vorster asked him later how he reacted when the Nationalist victory was finally proclaimed, he said: 'I didn't do anything ridiculous at all. I behaved with perfect decorum. I merely took off my hat, placed it on the pavement, jumped on it three times and replaced it on my head.'

In post-war Johannesburg the housing shortage was extremely critical. Bosman, flushed with victory after the election, lost no time in contacting his local Member of Parliament. 'Today you are answering the phone,' he said, 'but tomorrow your butler will be doing it. I am a writer living in a

*Top: A Bosman watercolour, lodged at the Humanities Research Center, Austin, Texas*
*Bottom: Herman and Helena Bosman on holiday*

hotel. I can't eat their food and I can't work in these conditions. Will you please get a flat for me in Johannesburg.'

Besides Bosman's contributions to *Trek*, by early 1948 he had begun publishing Afrikaans versions of his Schalk Lourens stories in the magazines *Brandwag* and *Ruiter*; but his output was slender and his creative energy channelled in order of priority.

While they were waiting for the Member of Parliament to provide them with a flat, the need for more elbow room became so desperate that Herman and Helena decided to take over for a month or so an art studio vacated by Gordon Vorster and Cecil Skotnes in the Roma Hotel. The two artists had given up the studio because at this time Vorster was studying art and he and Cecil Skotnes found the rental of £5 a month high.

Besides needing more space to live, Helena wanted to paint a portrait of Herman with the oil paints and easel he had bought her after Ella's death. She chose to paint Herman looking down, because his penetrating blue eyes had such a hypnotic effect on anyone looking into them.

Bosman also painted and sketched. Over the years he made over a hundred impressionistic water colours or pencil sketches. These included studies of the veld, graveyards, rural scenes, but often his subject was Helena, bent over her school books correcting homework or engaged in some cosmetic rite. There is one of her asleep, different from the others in that it seems to be quite Japanese in its simplicity. It appears almost analytical, but also shows great insight and tenderness. The line of her nose is firm, without hesitance or nuance. It is a leaden line, like that of a stained-glass window, where the light around it is of much more importance than the actual line itself.

In using these harsh lines to create an ethereal effect, Bosman probed deeply, ruthlessly; and through this harshness he showed enormous sympathy for his subject.

One night Helena was asking Gordon some questions concerning impasto, glaze and varnish. The questions were nonsensical to Bosman. 'Ag, if you are a painter you can paint,' he said, and got up and left. He meant it, for had he not been pointing out for eight years in his writing that the Bushmen had never needed art lessons?

Once, when Gordon Vorster asked him where he had learnt French, he replied in the same vein: 'You are a poet, aren't you? You don't need to learn French, you simply speak it.'

A short while after they had taken over the studio, the Bosmans found a flat in Saratoga Court, Bellevue, and Helena's brother André joined them once more. André was tall and cadaver-thin, shy until he warmed up, and then you glimpsed a delightful sense of humour, and one of the most remarkable memories I have ever encountered. Whenever I needed to correct dates and places they had stayed in my research, André could reel them off. He also had Helena's gentleness and warmth, and he did most of the family driving.

He had been a Divinity student at Stellenbosch when he had nervous breakdown. He was a patient in a sanatorium until Helena and Herman took him to stay with them. He became Herman's copy-holder wherever he was working. They looked after him, and he looked after them.

By the end of 1948 Bosman's health was failing. He complained of fatigue and felt in desperate need of a holiday. They consulted their budget and Herman was doubtful, but Helena calculated that they had enough money for two return train tickets to Port Elizabeth and – as an ex-girl guide – suggested they hike most of the way to Plettenberg Bay. Helena packed into Herman's haversack a few cooking and eating utensils and into her own some blankets. They took a train to Port Elizabeth and from there a bus to Jeffrey's Bay. On the way they enquired as to the best route to Plettenberg Bay. They were advised that the inland route was safer and easier, but much longer than the coastal road. It was not recommended to hikers, because in parts the only way was over the beach itself, and there was a scarcity of fresh water. Besides, nobody had ever heard of anyone ever walking it before. That settled the matter. This was a challenge Herman Bosman could not ignore.

Their source of information proved correct. Towards sunset Bosman was so thirsty that, in spite of Helena's warning, he consumed the entire contents of a can of condensed milk, which only made him thirstier. Helena's girl-guide knowledge to the rescue, she remembered that in this part of the country the houses were not to be found on the escarpment where they had been making their way, but at the base. Helena was right. They found an almost abandoned farmhouse where the servant directed them to a freshwater stream and a grove of trees where they could spend the night.

Morning found Herman again deathly pale and they had only gone a little way when he was obliged to lie down in a donga. Chilled, Helena recognised the same greenish-grey pallor she had come to fear in Cape Town. When he recovered sufficiently to walk again, they were still debating whether Bosman was well enough to continue, when a gust of wind plucked at Helena's head-scarf. Her sudden reaching for it was mistaken for a signal, and a passing lorry driver ground to a halt. Helena ignored their original ground rules about 'no hitchhiking allowed'. She simply thanked him and accepted.

They rode in the back of the open lorry with sacks of mealie-meal and arrived in Plettenberg Bay looking like two badly made-up ghosts in a high-school play. Even so, Helena was chilled by Herman's pallor. By the time he collapsed in the first available tent, she knew. This was a second heart attack.

For the first few days he did nothing but sleep, while Helena nursed him. As his condition gradually improved, she bought a primus stove and a flatiron from the nearest general dealer and washed and ironed their clothes and cooked for them. Her will that had kept her alive in Pietersburg Hospital now bargained with God for Herman's recovery. And He listened. For a while.

Once Herman had recovered, it was as though he had found a new world to explore. There was the timber shed built by the Dutch East India Company, its roof open to the sky and its walls spilling geraniums. There were the old whaling pots from the one-time whaling station on Beacon Isle, and the original sailors' beacon around which the courtyard of the old Beacon Isle Hotel had been built. Along the creamy stretch of beach towards Robberg were the remains of a monolith commemorating a shipwreck centuries ago. And right at the end was the tiny footpath that could take one over the saddle of Robberg to Bird Island, where the waters were Caribbean-clear, deserted except for the occasional angler and his gillie.

Refreshed at the end of their holiday, Herman was reluctant to return home via Port Elizabeth, the terminal point of their return ticket. The scenic and historical regions of Knysna and George appealed to him, so he proposed that they hike as far as Knysna, take the branch-line train from Knysna to George and spend a day there before making the connection to Johannesburg. With no excess mileage, all cost free. The ticket examiner thought otherwise. He was suspicious enough of Herman's alleged misunderstanding, but when he saw the Bosmans spending their last money on a meal with two glasses of wine, he felt it his duty to warn them that in Johannesburg the train would be met by Railway Police.

It was. For the umpteenth time in Herman Bosman's life he was flanked by police and frogmarched to the charge office. For Helena this was quite a new experience, and she felt foolishly ignorant of the form. She was undecided whether to lag behind and perhaps be taken for one of the spectators, or to catch up and identify herself once and for all with the little procession. Before she could make up her mind, they had reached the office, where Herman telephoned Leon Feldberg.

Feldberg agreed to pay the difference on their tickets against Bosman's wages, and they ended their holiday in laughter all the way to Saratoga Court.

It was a happy ending to the last holiday they would ever have.

# 20

## Excursions and trips

Early in 1949, after *Cold Stone Jug* had joined *Jacaranda in the Night* and *Mafeking Road* in the bookshops, the Bosmans decided that the time had come for them to own a motorcar. Since Herman's income was still modest, he chose a modestly priced car – a somewhat dilapidated Opel, of which the radiator seemed to be permanently brokendown.

Helena had begun to take driving lessons and was progressing well, but neither she nor Herman was a confident driver, so André did most of the family driving. After they had acquired the undreamed-of-luxury of their own car, the Bosmans took frequent weekend jaunts into the countryside with the Vorsters; to get really close to nature – as in the time at Rustenburg Kloof.

Gordon took over the wheel of the Opel. On the way they stopped once to take on board a couple of demijohns of rough claret with a red triangular label, and very many more times to top up the leaking radiator. When they arrived at the camping site, Herman was offended that on their way to the remotest spot they could find, they passed many other campers who had also brought along rough claret in bottles with a red triangular label. He decided these were low-class people who should be discouraged from getting close to nature. So he proceeded to discourage as many as he could.

He mounted guard in front of the site they had chosen and cast an evil eye at all approaching cars in search of a spot to camp. He had the most extraordinary penetrating blue eyes, and he knew that if he concentrated really hard, he could hypnotise them into leaving. It worked. Car after car ground to a halt, but never decanted any campers. Magically, after a hushed conversation among the passengers, they would leave again.

One enormous man and his wife had already pitched their tent by the time the Bosman-Vorster quartet arrived. Early in the evening the Bosmans and Vorsters prepared little hollows in the ground in which to sleep, filling them with dried grass and leaves for warmth. After they had settled in for the night, their neighbours became quite drunk and rowdy.

The enormous man stood outside his tent, yelling to his wife: 'Marie! Come outside here, you bloody woman, before I come in there and knock your block off!'

Marie continued to ignore him, and only when a full-scale war seemed imminent, she appeared. 'Well? Wha-cha want?' she enquired gracefully.

'Just look at that goddam moon, willya!' he replied, his face radiant with tenderness.

The journey back was uphill. It had taken them about three hours to get from Johannesburg to Rustenburg. Now, with the radiator giving distress signals, it took nearly seven hours to get home.

But there was another excursion to the Hartbeespoort Dam near Brits. Vorster recalls that one moment all four of them were standing together, transfixed by the thunderous waters eddying far below; the next moment, glancing back towards the bank, he saw Herman on hands and knees, trying not to look as he felt his way back along the endless yards that separated him from safety. This was no ordinary attack of vertigo. Herman told Gordon that far below he had seen a flight of birds that looked like mossies, but which he knew to be vultures.

Bosman's imagination, pierced with 'the mad glories of the poet' that endowed us with memorable lines and graceful images, exacted its price in the form of his delicate psyche.

There were other trips, too, memorably described in 'The Recognising Blues' – posthumously published in Lionel Abraham's literary magazine *The Purple Renoster*, and later in a hardcover collection of Bosman's *Almost Forgotten Stories*. David Butler has fittingly included it as part of his repertoire in his one-man show *A Touch of Madness*. Dagga-rooker Charlie is passing a men's outfitters when he has a really bad attack of the 'recognising blues'.

*I would first make up a name in my brain, a name that sounded good to me, and that I thought had the right sort of a rhythm. And then the first person I would see, I would think that he was the man whose name I had just thought out. And I would go up and address him by this name and shake hands with him, and tell him how glad I was to see him. And a name I thought up that sounded very fine to me was Sir Lionel Ostrich de Frontignac. It was a very magnificent name.*

*And so I went up, bare-footed and in my shirtsleeves, to the first man I saw in the street, after I had coined this name, and I took him by the hand, and I said, 'Well met, Sir Lionel. It is many years since last we met, Sir Lionel Ostrich de Frontignac.'*

*And the remarkable coincidence was that the man whom I addressed in this way actually was Sir Lionel Ostrich de Frontignac. But on account of his taking me for a bum – through my being bare-footed and in my shirt sleeves – he wouldn't acknowledge that he really was Sir Lionel and that I had recognised him dead to rights.*

*'You are mistaken,' Sir Lionel Ostrich de Frontignac said, moving away from me. 'You have got the recognising blues.'*

Bosman still went night-wandering with George Howard from time to time, just as they had done in the '30s. It was on nights when Bosman was unable to write that George was aware of a different, more fearful quality that distinguished day from night far more distinctly than the setting sun.

George recalls one evening when they had bought a bottle of wine on Louis Botha Avenue to take home for dinner with Helena. They passed an African, a middle-aged man dressed in domestic servants' clothes and looking very tired. 'If you are going up Sylvia Pass you will need this,' Herman said, handing over the bottle of wine.

After he had been thanked many times, they parted. Herman told George seriously: 'There are ghosts among the rocks on Sylvia Pass. I know, I have encountered them. This man will need all the wine in that bottle for courage before he gets over Sylvia Pass.'

In 1950 Rudolph van Ryneveld opened an artists' cellar opposite Johannesburg's Marshall Square in Ferreirastown. People spoke excitedly of the Bohemian night life that had come to dull Johannesburg. There were great clouds of incense imported from Italian monasteries and French cathedrals. Evidently, anyone who came down from pavement level was invited to paint or draw or write poetry on the walls of the cellar. On display on one of the walls was a portrait of Ella painted by Donald Harris.

When George Howard took Bosman there and he saw it for the first time, he became very agitated and cried, 'Police! This mob of Philistines must be locked up at once.' He left muttering, 'It's an insult to art.'

During the night Herman and George trod the paths of Poe and Baudelaire, and during the day he and Gordon Vorster stimulated each other to laughter. The humour was not black, but the colour of gathering shadows. They would bandy about phrases such as 'When one door closes another one shuts', or 'What you miss on the swings you lose on the roundabouts'. On that trip to Rustenburg, wherever they saw a notice reading 'Storting van Vuilgoed Verbode', they would make up stories about Dutchmen, who could be so undesirable that their presence was forbidden everywhere.

Bosman loved hoboes and would frequently sit down with them on a pavement corner on the sunny side of the street and enquire how the season had gone in Durban that winter. Once, when approached by a tramp near the Glossop Hotel, he confided to him that he was working that block himself. On another occasion a hobo charmed him when he appealed for some small change, assuring him: 'And I am not going to waste it on food either.'

There was a story often told among delighted friends as proof of his eccentricity. When he went to watch Laurence Olivier in the film of *Henry V*, he brought the house down by jumping up and shouting: 'Vive la France!' This was probably no mere colourful gesture. Bosman never did anything to impress. His enthusiasm and identifications were always very real – real enough to convert him in that moment into a violently patriotic Frenchman.

But he was aware that his wild reactions might one day be interpreted in a bad light. Bosman felt it necessary to warn Vorster that their exuberance could easily be mistaken for certifiable lunacy, and that they ran the risk of being locked up forever. The shades of his *Cold Stone Jug* memoir lurked in his memory.

It was also during this period, while they were living in the Sydney Hotel and Saratoga Court, that Herman finally stepped down from his pedestal and accepted the 'mob' as part of humanity among whom the artist had to work. In the heady days of the 1930s he identified his profession as 'poi-et' and despised the mob from the windows of his ivory tower. Perhaps he had begun to find his pedestal sterile.

Jane Eliza Hasted, a fellow writer of the time, recalls that once, while the Bosmans were still living in the hotel, she called on Herman to say goodbye. She had been compelled by circumstances to take regular employment in Cape Town.

She remembers them sitting in the tiny deserted lounge while an African, dressed in one of those short canvas suits that were then standard uniform for cleaners, cleaned from dark corners cigarette ash and 'stompies', crumpled tissues and tram tickets – standard litter of the Saturday night bar trade. Bosman discussed with her his 'writer's credo', that the writer's true environment was in the world amongst people, in whatever capacity he or she had to work. This, rather than the ivory tower, was the treasure house of experience from which a writer should draw.

Bosman was as convinced as ever of his genius, but his arrogance of the 1930s seemed to have been replaced by a maturity where he considered communication with all humanity vital. The writer had to relate to life and humanity. His development in life was his development as a writer. The gift of the writer was a trust, and he owed it to that gift to endure whatever hardship came with it. In the end, his fundamental gift as a writer was his self.

More and more, Bosman came to practise what he had preached to Jane Hasted that day. Gordon Vorster remembers how needlessly embarrassed he was about introducing a deity like Bosman to the odd relative who might be a tradesman or postmaster. Bosman would practically monopolise the new acquaintance. He would enter into an entrancing conversation with the journeyman on tonguing and grooving, or he would question the postmaster about current stamps and ask him whether he really put the mortise key in that lock every day? And he would slap his thigh with enthusiasm. And this would not be a conscious effort at collecting material for some future book, but a genuine attempt to communicate with warmth and friendliness.

It was after the winter of 1949 that Bosman decided to give up his position with Leon Feldberg and deliberately take a non-creative job as proofreader for *The Sunday Express*. With three books published, and his Johannesburg sketches temporarily shelved, he felt it time to attempt a major work he would write only at night. Gordon Vorster's wife, Yvonne, was then secretary to Kenneth Sampson, general manager of *The Sunday Express*, and used to eat her lunch sandwiches at Herman's desk every day.

Bosman never told a joke, but everything he lived or said was cause for laughter. Conversely, he seldom took part in serious discussion in the weighty pontifical sense. His most serious statements were humorous or eccentric. Charles Eglington observed that it was only on further reflection that one discovered the truth in jester's trappings.

At the beginning of 1951 Bosman decided that with his own regular salary at *The Sunday Express*, his royalties, Helena's wages as a teacher and André's as a copy-holder, he could finally afford to become something he would have scorned to be in the 1930s: a man of property. Helena's mother lent them the money for the deposit and they left the flat in North View and bought a house in Milton Road, Lombardy East, which they called 'Paradise Regained'.

His more Bohemian friends muttered among themselves about Herman's total aboutface. 'Has he really become all that bourgeois in his mature years?' they asked one another anxiously and winced at 'Paradise Regained'. 'It must be one of Herman's little jokes.'

They were right to wonder. This was a conscious break with Bohemianism. On visiting George Howard's flat in Rissik Street about this time, Bosman reproached him for painting his wardrobe silver-grey. George had no respect for the grain of the wood, he said. George was reminded of the time when Herman and Ella had once shared a flat with him in Wroxhame House and had delighted in their silver-grey piano, but he said nothing.

Bosman's friends had always sponged on him, as he did on them, but now they could do it in a high-class manner. He could even offer them a proper bed with enough sheets, not just a corner on the floor with a couple of sugar sacks.

For Herman, who always thought of Helena in terms of earth and seed and harvest, having his own plot of ground was an inexpressible joy. 'Look,' he told her delightedly, 'I can spit on it and it belongs to me, right down to the centre of the earth.'

Because they were in Lombardy East they planted four Lombardy poplars, and when the tight winter nodules unfolded themselves into tender green leaves, Herman kissed them and did not care a damn whether his Bohemian friends thought him bourgeois. After the Lombardy poplars had taken, he and Helena dug holes for fruit trees. Helena's mother warned them that they should only order trees from the Cape, as the local ones were prone to crown-gall. But Herman was too impatient so they planted local trees. And they all had crown-gall.

One Sunday, while Yvonne Vorster was in hospital, Gordon took his two-year-old daughter Marianne to lunch with the Bosmans. Herman took her out to the vegetable garden and showed her the potato patch, where together they chose those they wanted for lunch. At table, Herman sat next to Marianne and fed her potatoes. Everyone knew that it was a very special moment for them both.

So Herman finally descended from among the stars. He had a secure job with a regular salary and a house in suburbia where he grew his own potatoes. He himself describes the transformation best in 'The Poet', perhaps one of the last poems he ever wrote.

*... Instead of a sky panoplied*
*With flighted images I'd sooner have*
*A mealie-field to gaze on: I would try*
*To keep the growing earth within the sound*
*Of my blood. The Fates were careless when they gave*
*Me banished things in superfluity –*
*Lost facts brooding like temples instead of ground*
*For seed and harvest ...*

One evening Helena was busy in the kitchen when Herman offered to go out and water the plants. 'You might pull out a few weeds while you are about it,' Helena called after him.

But Herman loved all growing things. His weeds were as vital and important to him as his potatoes. He explained: 'These little weeds lift up their heads and they bare their chests and they say: "This lovely water is for *me*!" How can I pull them out?'

Here I am reminded of the poem, 'Seed', which to me signifies Helena and belongs here.

*The farmer ploughs into the ground*
*More than the wheat-seed strewn on the ground*
*The farmer ploughs into the ground*
*The plough and the oxen and his body*

*He ploughs into the ground the farmstead and the cattle*
*And the pigs and the poultry and the kitchen utensils*
*And the afternoon sunlight shining into the windowpanes*
  *of the voorhuis*
*And the light entangled in the eyes of his children*
*He ploughs into the ground his wife's brown body*
*And the windmill above the bore-hole*
*And the bore-hole and the wind driving the windmill.*
*The farmer ploughs the blue clouds into the ground;*
*And as a tribute to the holocaust of the ploughshare*
*The earth renders the farmer in due season*
*Corn.*

Gordon Vorster finishes our little documentary film, *The Storyteller*, by telling us that poem could only have been written in this country by an Afrikaner. And although it is written in English, it is an Afrikaans poem.

That is the wonder of Bosman – he wrote Afrikaans in the English language.

# 21

## Return to Pietersburg, to poetry and Poe

When Herman and Helena moved into their home in Lombardy East, Herman knew very well that his time was running out and that he had to be clear about his priorities. He badly wanted to attempt another major work, so he divided his time into proofreading by day, and saving all his creative writing for the evening in his own study.

A B Hughes, editor of *The Sunday Express*, thought well enough of Bosman to offer him a position as a columnist. Barbara Grace, editor of the women's section of the paper, would have placed a weekly column at his disposal any time he wanted it. He refused both offers.

When Bosman's 'Voorkamer' series in *The Forum* was already nine months old, he published the short story 'The Missionary' in the January 1951 issue of *Spotlight* magazine, followed by 'The Traitor's Wife' in February. The editor, Brian Lello, believed these to be the start of a whole new Schalk Lourens series. He was not to know how little time and energy were left to Bosman. The same applied to the Schalk Lourens stories he was translating and writing for the bilingual magazine *On Parade*.

Bosman's health was failing fast. Earlier, while they were living in Saratoga Court, George Howard once came upon him posting a letter at the Jeppe Street Post Office – ashen pale, sweating and trembling, and wearing a heavy coat though the day was warm.

He gave George Howard the impression of being vaguely melancholy. One evening during a musical gathering at his flat he told George: 'I think I am finished. I know in my heart that no girl will give her love to a poet if there is a rugby player around. I was never any good at rugby. I don't think Keats and Shelley could play rugby either. There is a terrible feeling of impotence if you cannot handle a rugby ball stylishly.'

Paradise Regained meant an enormous improvement in his working conditions. Previously he had had to write wherever he found himself and with whatever means he could muster. Now, for the first time, he had his own study where he could write undisturbed.

It was a simple south-facing room, and the tools of his craft were the Corona typewriter and an ordinary, small wooden desk with a rickety strut between the three drawers on the right and the lefthand side. In moments of

*Bosman's desk and his beloved Corona typewriter*

*Bosman with a copy of one of the three books he published in his lifetime*

meditation Bosman must have propped his foot there, for eventually it gave way and was never replaced.

For poetry, even the poetry that is loosely called prose, he still used his ordinary dipping-pen and a bottle of Quink ink, which he also used when writing letters to his friends.

The atmosphere was one of almost monastic simplicity. There were his dictionaries and his *Roget's Thesaurus*, but there was no room on his desk for such luxuries as a reading lamp: he worked by the light of a single overhead fitting. The only picture on the wall was one that Helena had painted in End Street after the Harrises had left. It was an impression of blacks on their way to work, appearing out of the early morning mists around End Street as though materialising from ectoplasm.

The major work he was now writing was later titled *Willemsdorp*. The setting was Pietersburg once again. His novel on city life had been abandoned unfinished, and he thought that he would do a better job on dorp life. He had treated the same subject in *Jacaranda in the Night*, and although it had about it the feel of roughness and undercurrents of dorp life that satisfied him at the time, he knew it would not stand the test of time. So he decided to attempt the same theme again on a larger canvas. He cast his net wider than the pettiness of school politics and encompassed broader issues, including the people and machinery that brought out the English newspaper.

He wrote 145 pages before deciding that his efforts were unworthy. He found the people still puppet-like and two-dimensional, like those who inhabited *Jacaranda*, and his dorp far too cardboard-like to endure. So he abandoned this first version to do another, for *Willemsdorp* meant a great deal more to Bosman than just another story. In a way he must have known that this was to be his last season of writing.

It was his third try at Pietersburg, but it was more than a story retold; it meant finding better ways to say things. As he wrote his second attempt, Pietersburg seemed to come alive. Just by the film of dust on your skin and the taste of it in your mouth, you know without mistaking that this is Pietersburg 1948. There are no obvious devices such as a description of the landscape, a resurrection of the koppie or the grass. One simply knows one is in Pietersburg, and one knows the way a butcher's shop smells and sounds, even when it is closed and silent. And one knows the way a bar smells in Pietersburg, and that atmosphere of revelry that is almost depressing.

The setting and the characters are the same as those of *Jacaranda*, but in *Willemsdorp* Bosman, having penetrated his environment, recedes from it sufficiently to avoid the risk of subjective involvement that might colour his work with sentiment.

When he wrote *Jacaranda*, he was still very close to his heroine in time and experience. In fact, by the time he wrote *Willemsdorp* Bosman might even have acknowledged the validity of the criticism levelled at *Jacaranda*, that his treatment of his heroine was 'lachrymose'. In *Willemsdorp* the main characters, Lena Cordier and Charlie Hendricks, represent only those aspects of Helena and Herman that are relevant to the story.

In Charlie, the small-town journalist who probably could not get a better job in the city, there is no vestige of the poet. Similarly, his portrait of Lena is an accurate physical description of Helena, but there is virtually no attempt to transpose her psyche onto the heroine. Only because it is crucial to the story does he depict her as one who 'scorns to set a price on herself', which makes her in the Dostoevskian sense 'more precious than rubies'.

Willemsdorp is also an improvement on *Jacaranda* in terms of character development, in the quality of the humour – which is as gentle as Oom Schalk's, but so much quieter – and in the plot.

It has been suggested that even the second version of *Willemsdorp* is incomplete, because the ending seems unsatisfactory. It certainly lacks the subtle thrust so characteristic of all Bosman's endings. However, Gordon Vorster, who had watched Bosman preparing himself for death over his last four years, is sceptical. 'It would be so unlike Bosman to die without finishing the novel,' he said. 'How could he not go to his typewriter and give it even a temporary finish?'

My own reaction to *Willemsdorp* was an uneasy feeling that Bosman had gone too far and said too much. On closer examination of the manuscript it seems that the novel was just about finished and that Bosman was merely experimenting with endings. There are in fact three possible endings, and perhaps he had not yet made a final choice by the time he died.

An alternative ending would have been Hendricks's last visit to the Wondergat, where Sergeant Brits is waiting to remind him that the murderer always returns to the scene of the crime.

Personally, I would have chosen yet another ending, though. In it Sergeant Brits, in his enthusiasm for front-page coverage of the most dramatic murder investigation ever to have taken place in Willemsdorp, appears at Charlie Hendricks's home. He advises him that they are holding a prestigious figure as chief suspect, and says he would like Hendricks to be present when the two final pieces of evidence are turned up that will identify the murderer. This could happen any moment.

Hendricks, knowing that these two pieces of evidence must identify himself as the killer, has no choice but to accompany Brits, who is in fact performing an unconscious arrest of the real murderer.

Had he lived long enough to publish *Willemsdorp*, this is the kind of Bosmanesque ending I think he would have chosen. Also, if Schalk Lourens had been telling the story, this is the point at which I believe he would have knocked out his pipe on his veldskoen. To quote Oom Schalk one more time:

> *... it is not the story that counts. What matters is the way you tell it. The important thing is to know just at what moment you must knock out your pipe on your veldskoen, and at what stage of the story you must start talking about the School Committee at Drogevlei. Another necessary thing is to know what part of the story to leave out.*

Apart from his labours on *Willemsdorp* and his regular job on *The Sunday Express*, Bosman was working on another two projects during those last months of his life. There was the weekly deadline to be met for his 'Voorkamer' series for *The Forum*. Also, Sarel Marais of the APB had requested that he edit an anthology of English South African poetry to be published later in the year.

So, virtually every night he worked in his study, for as long as his declining health allowed. Helena would bring him tea at about nine o'clock. The nights he wrote his 'Voorkamer' sketches, he would drink as many as six Cokes as a stimulant. Sometimes he drank Helena's home-made gingerbeer instead.

On the nights he worked on *Willemsdorp*, there was no deadline other than that imposed by the flow of his prose and his own physical stamina. On these nights he always had a large bottle of that rough claret with him.

When late at night Helena tidied his study after he had finished or could no longer work, she would collect and store away scraps of poetry and fragments of prose, bits of imagery and phrases that were probably meant as notes for either his poetry or *Willemsdorp*, or both.

Having watched anxiously during those long months when he groped for the fugitive words, she knew he was writing well at that stage and treated everything he wrote with great respect. The following is an example of this nocturnal gleaning.

> *A pebble dropped in the water making brass-wire bangles ... Her laughter had an ornamental sound as though it was wearing jade earrings and bracelets ... A grove of black wattles, heads bent forward, was riding on push-bikes into the night ... The evening was like a thinker with his hands in front of his face ... A lonely cloud, rigged with square top and topgallant sails on the foremast, beat across the blue Atlantic of the sky ... Ears and eyes lassoed together with a pair of horn-rimmed spectacles ... Over the shoulders of the trees a lone sunset cloud was trailing to the wind like a scarf ... He would wear his fear jauntily; he would make of his terror a gay thing: something light, frivolous ... a*

*feather in a hat ... A dense tuft of hair standing straight out from his*
*forehead made a verandah for his face ...*

Throughout these last months of Herman's life, he and Helena treated each
other with gentleness and affection. She called him 'Hermantjie', while his
term of endearment for her was 'diertjie' (little animal). On many levels, other
than the physical, their relationship satisfied all Herman's needs in his
dying days.

Throughout his lifetime there persisted traces of *The Blue Princess* syndrome
– 'In losing this princess she remains mine forever'. This theme of lost love,
which also emerged repeatedly in the Schalk Lourens stories, seems to have
been so rooted in his psyche that this 'lostness' often exerted an attraction far
more potent than when the love-object was available.

As a basis for surmising a second such affair one has the tantalising
suggestion by Bosman himself in his poem 'Arrival', with its opening lines:

> *After twenty years*
> *I again had tea with you.*

If Bosman had written this in the last year of his life, this would place the
source in 1931, the year of his *Blue Princess*. And in this case the inspiration
could not have been Vera, with whom he had continued to take tea regularly
ever since his release from prison, but Ellie Beemer. But I suggest this merely
as conjecture.

Quite apart from these two physical loves, there is also the suggestion of a
continued involvement with a fantasy love, for what degree of 'lostness' could
be more enduring than the grave? And among his later undated poems, one
entitled 'Memory' begins: 'An April leaping from a poet's brain ... '

April was the month of Ella Manson's death. The poem seems to have been
written after that. But in the final stanza he expresses a commitment to the
dead, who, possessed of a new dimension by virtue of their very condition,
seem to have tugged at his heart more strongly than those who merely happen
to be living.

> *Yet were thy memory made a mummy, still*
> *Would I return to greet her in her case;*
> *I'd touch with flame her wounden cloth and thrill*
> *To view her linen sleep and living face.*

The latter is reminiscent of Edgar Allan Poe, whose influence persistently
found its way into Bosman's life and writings. As far back as the 1930s Poe
had become for Bosman a guide in his own explorations into themes that had

intrigued the Decadents. In *The Blue Princess* there was a poem titled 'A Princess Sleeping', with the title note: 'A buttonhole broken from the flower-bed of Baudelaire, my brother who forgot'. And even here he says:

> *Maybe your teeth are laughing*
> *At the moist white worms*
> *That still play with you*
> *Whimsically,*
> *And swell your body with a sly jest,*
> *And make believe*
> *That your flesh,*
> *Fragrant with the earth's most ancient*
> *Perfume,*
> *Is big with a pink child.*
> *(Rejoice, my soul; behold my princess sleepeth).*

This poem could have been so easily derived from Poe's 'The Conqueror Worm' below:

> *But see, amid the mimic rout*
> *A crawling shape intrude!*
> *A blood-red thing that writhes from out*
> *The scenic solitude!*
> *It writhes! – it writhes! – with mortal pangs*
> *The mimes become its food,*
> *And seraphs sob at vermin fangs*
> *In human gore imbued.*

According to the Bosman bibliography of the University of the Witwatersrand, Bosman never published another poem after 'Leda's Swans', which appeared in *The South African Opinion* in 1944, seven years before his death and shortly after Helena's abortion in Pietersburg.

But he continued to write poetry during all those years. It would appear that he produced about 25 poems during this period. These are mostly introspective and often difficult to understand. It seems as if Bosman wrote them only for himself, to clarify things for himself or to summarise his life.

Gordon Vorster called Bosman's poetry his 'laboratory'. He also believed it would be a long time before people understood it.

In the literary column of the July 1948 issue of *Trek*, Bosman published an essay on Poe containing some rather matter-of-fact observations on the influence Bosman felt Poe ought to have on other writers, in South Africa and overseas.

*Where I feel that Edgar Allan Poe has more than ordinary significance for us writing in South Africa is in regard to the struggle he put up to get American literature on the map. He was fated to arrive on the scene at the beginning of the creation of an authentically American literature, just as we in this generation find ourselves at the same literary cross-roads in respect of South African literature. Writing in English in this country, are we going to write English or are we going to write South African?*

In the same essay Bosman estimated what he believed to be the scope of Poe's influence on the entire art landscape of the next century. He discussed Poe's influence in relation to Chopin, Baudelaire, D H Lawrence, Coleridge, Mark Twain, Max Adler, Bret Harte, Artemus Ward, O Henry and Stephen Leacock. In fact, in relation to just about everybody except himself. In view of the enormous influence Poe exerted on Bosman, the intellectual type of statement he makes in this essay leaves one with the strange unsatisfied feeling of things left unsaid. How could Bosman, who despised the intellectual approach, confine himself to intellectual observations on Poe and so totally ignore the fantasy?

There had to be a reason for this kind of omission; and perhaps it lies in another essay Bosman wrote on Poe as an introductory passage to an unpublished story. It was undated. Yet we know that the typewriter was the same one Bosman began to use for his private writing after Ella's death in 1945. The longest time that could have separated the two essays was three years, but they could also have been written at almost the same time, one for public consumption and one for himself. The second essay certainly says all the things Bosman omitted to publish in the first, maybe for the same reason that the poetry he was writing at this period of his life was also not intended for others. He writes:

*Edgar Allan Poe, poet and plagiarist, charlatan and genius – whose genius I place next to Shakespeare's – has haunted my mind from my earliest youth, as he has ghostlike frequented the brains of men of letters and music and coloured pictures from Baudelaire down to the present day. How could it be otherwise when men with magical minds so much mightier than my own for a century crowned him in their spirits with the wreaths of the bay-tree – how could it be otherwise than that I, as a youth seeking under an African moon the divine influence abroad under the Thessalian mountain, when I encountered his name and the well-known daguerrotype of his likeness and the story of his life that held more than common interest – and finally his writings themselves – should from that moment of first meeting have recognised his grandeur in the dark gold of doom, and his genius in the estranged lustres of the Pierides?*

*Recognise him I did. Know him – let others assume for themselves that individual advantage. I knew that I could never know him. Schizophrenic, paranoiac, fraud and liar: these were the things that went to bejewel his genius, to rococo his arabesques, to introduce that element of painfully unnecessary baroque ornamentation into the tragic drama of his life, without which he would not have been able to write a single line of poetry. He was at once insanely heroic strutter and white-livered abject coward; at once angel and friend; at once saint and criminal; at once a clear-thinking inductive logician – a master of scientific reasoning – and a steepled, irresponsible dreamer in the hot lair of the poet's fantasy that is so uncomfortably close to – and yet at the polar extreme from – the opium smoker's den of visions.*

*In my early adolescence I encountered and recognised Edgar Allan Poe. I recognised in him those characteristics that I have just enumerated. And if you skim the list again quickly you will see that he had just the ordinary everyday human qualities writ large.*

Long before Gordon Vorster was shown this piece by Bosman on Poe, so strangely like his own on Bosman at the beginning of this book, Gordon speculated in a letter:

*Did he really laugh all those loud uncontrolled laughs or – and the thought gives me cold shivers – was he crying? Is this why his marriages were divorces – and, stranger still, why his divorces were more enduring than his marriages? And did he, in killing, bestow life?*

*If this is Bosman, then the whole accepted character of Bosman built up on a series of authentic but non-sequitur anecdotes falls apart in the face of what was probably the most authentic thing about him – this laughter-that-might-have-been-crying.*

During those years between Vorster's first meeting with Bosman in the strong-room of *The South African Opinion* and their period as contemporaneous guests in the Sydney and East London hotels, only a stone's throw away from each other, there had been a great deal of discussion on Poe. In fact, the only book that Gordon Vorster says he ever stole from the Kimberley Library as a very young boy was an edition of *The Collected Poems of Edgar Allan Poe*, which he later presented to Bosman and which Bosman refused to accept, and which Gordon Vorster insisted that he keep, and which, in the end, he did.

This was a promising basis for collaboration when around 1950 Sarel Marais of APB asked Bosman to compile an anthology of English South African poetry. This was a nationwide project advertised in all parts of the Union of South Africa. The avalanche of responses was quite terrifying and Bosman asked Gordon Vorster to help him make a selection for publication.

A number of distinguished contributors were considered, such as Alan Paton, Anthony Delius, Charles Eglington, Lionel Abrahams and Nadine Gordimer. Gordon Vorster's one effort was almost a hundred pages long.

The criteria for acceptance were quite unusual. Many entries that might have been approved by academics were unceremoniously thrown out. Bosman's aversion to university had not been merely a matter of juvenile rebellion or an excess of high spirits. He genuinely believed that academism was not only harmful but downright dangerous.

So academic criteria were out. Herman and Gordon were looking for poetry with memorable lines. That was in fact the ultimate test – the ease with which the lines could be remembered. Titles also played a part in the selection. Any poem called 'Thou Art Waiting at the Gate, My Lord' was automatically eliminated, while a piece titled 'Poem' would be worth considering. A poem with a title like 'Pissed in Gaza' instantly qualified. It was not even necessary to read it: only a poet could have thought up a title like that.

Naturally, such unusual standards necessitated a great deal of correspondence. Awkward questions had to be answered and some of the budding poets even had to be encouraged. The most perplexing letters to be written were those to entrants whose efforts were considered unacceptable but who might improve if they were given a hint or two. Some replies were downright provocative. They would return the contribution, saying that they had already read the source material from which it was drawn. 'We received our copy by air-mail.' (This was the 1950s.)

Some of the letters had to be written in Afrikaans. After ten years of study in English, Gordon Vorster was unsure of the required form of address for someone who might be a friend but was undoubtedly also a senior. Uys Krige fell into this category. Vorster wanted to tell Krige that his poem was on the right track but did not quite qualify for the anthology they had in mind. He had a shot at it and produced something like '*Geagte Meneer Krige, hiermee stuur ons u gedig terug ...*' He showed it to Herman.

'Hell, you don't write a letter like that to Uys. He will never understand such Afrikaans.' Herman grabbed a sheet of notepaper. Plunging his dipping-pen into a bottle of Quink, he wrote:

> *Liewe Uys, (That's how you start off a letter to Uys. Now let me see. He'll want to know how I am.) Ek het baie siek gewees met die griep.*

*(This is about the most common form of Afrikaans you can write: real low-class stuff, but it's beautiful. Now we have to ask how he is.) Hoe gaan dit met jou? (Now to the point.) Hierdie gedig is sommer 'n klomp kak. Jou vriend, Herman.*

They had been working on the project for the better part of a year when Herman died. After that there was no more fun in it for Gordon. He lost interest, closed the files and sent them back to Helena to advise contributors that the project had been cancelled.

Meanwhile, Sarel Marais was under the happy illusion that after so much time spent on the selection, something quite splendid was about to emerge. He was furious when he heard the outcome.

*Gordon Vorster*

# 22

## Not quite the end

*If thou didst ever hold me in thy heart,*
*Absent thee from felicity awhile,*
*And in this harsh world draw thy breath in pain,*
*To tell my story.*
**HAMLET,** *Act V, Scene II*

The last year of Herman Bosman's life was a preparation for death, and his friends were aware of it.

After having observed Herman pale and in ill health for some years, George Howard believed one can choose the hour of one's death. 'Not quite in the physical sense, but in a spiritual one. It's not a question of sadness. There is no finality in sadness. Only finality in tiredness. When that time comes, one says to oneself: "This is much about the end".'

In that final year Gordon Vorster observed, in Bosman, a similar kind of acceptance.

*To some he may have seemed written out. There were the indicative factors of his bourgeois attitudes, a certain reaction to recognition locally and overseas, his holding only a proof-reading job, and over a year's worth of "Voorkamer" sketches delivered to* The Forum *with the regularity of unpaid accounts. Apart from the odd mention that he was working on a novel, he said nothing about* Willemsdorp.

*What would have happened to him had he lived? To Keats? To Shakespeare? Shakespeare did not live past his middle years either. Even if he had reached fifty, what would it have mattered? Extending oneself in whatever branch of the arts does not always express itself simply in an ascending or descending graph. You can take your work so far and then, before you are even aware of it, you become repetitive – an unproductive caricature of yourself. You can stay in the doldrums for a long time with all those self-doubts. Then suddenly you are hitting it again and hitting it hard. Herman may have been either just about played out, or ready to break out in a new form.*

In those last months before Bosman died, he showed his concern for Helena. One day he put his arm around her waist and said thoughtfully: 'And what's going to happen to you?' Then he answered himself, 'Ag no, you'll be all right.'

For his brother Pierre, on the other hand, he felt no concern whatsoever. Throughout the four years since that night in Cape Town when Helena asked Pierre to leave the house, Herman had refused to respond to his brother's overtures. Seven months before his death he received what was probably the last letter from Pierre, in which he rather pathetically asked after the health of everyone and added that there was no hatred in his heart for either Herman or Helena. 'I would be very pleased to receive a letter from my brother.'

Herman failed to reply. Pierre might just as well have been talking to a wall.

The last communication from Pierre prior to this was towards the end of 1949. In October of that year Bosman received a letter from Pierre informing him that he had 'temporarily' abandoned his course in medicine at the University of Cape Town and had become a proofreader for *The Cape Times*. He had also completed a short novel and asked Herman's advice on possible publishers.

Herman did not respond. Another letter followed in December 1949, in which Pierre wrote how pleased he was with the security his job as proofreader was affording him. The rest was an entreaty directed at Herman asking for whatever shred of brotherly care or love remained in his heart.

Once again there was no response. Herman had finally broken with Pierre, the brother to whom he had framed a message of encouragement in court that day when he was sentenced to death; whose realist school of writing he had once scorned; who bummed off him when he was down and out himself, and who had filched Helena's busfare to buy a drink; who had never paid his debts to Herman even though he was Elisa's sole heir; who had never offered Herman any assistance during the months of affluence before he had consumed his entire inheritance.

One of Bosman's friends, Nancy McDermott, visited the Bosmans one Sunday afternoon in 1951 and asked Herman if there was anywhere he would like to go in her newly acquired 1934 Austin.

'Yes, yes,' he said, speaking in staccato phrases. 'I'd like you please to take me to Hendrieka.'

Hendrieka?

Once he used to walk to work past Brixton cemetery and had started to weave tales around a grave over which a white angel was poised. He was convinced that the angel was watching over a little Afrikaner girl, Hendrieka, who had died long ago.

So Herman, Helena and Nancy set out on that Sunday afternoon for Brixton cemetery, where he bought an immense armful of flowers 'for my Hendrieka'.

236

They threaded their way through the Chinese and Jewish section. As they approached Hendrieka's grave, Helena and Nancy hung back a little, leaving Herman to go on alone. They saw him take off his hat. When they approached he was staring and saying: 'Yes, yes, God knows no difference.'

They looked at the gravestone. It bore the name of a boy. It was a Portuguese name. Even the remotest possibility of Afrikaans parentage was excluded. It was a story Bosman himself might have written.

Although the Bosmans had moved into Paradise Regained at the beginning of the year, quite typically they threw a house-warming party in October. George Howard felt a strange reluctance to attend the party that Friday evening and did not go at all. Ehrhardt Planjé was there briefly. He felt compelled to go for Herman's sake, and felt an equally strong compulsion to leave quickly for his own sake. Fred Zwarenstein was there, as well as Benny Sachs, Lionel Abrahams, Charles Eglington, Barbara Grace, the Vorsters, Mary Morrison Webster, Nancy McDermott, Jumbo Posthumus, Lewis Meskin, Kate and Arthur Kohn and David Goldblatt.

That evening Bosman spent almost 20 minutes on the couch with Benny Sachs, reciting Baudelaire's French translation of Edgar Allan Poe's 'The Masque of the Red Death'. Inspired by the thunderstorm raging outside, Charles Eglington declaimed a speech from King Lear, choosing an appropriate moment to make his exit into the driving rain.

The Vorsters left shortly afterwards and managed to get their car away fairly easily, but when the next guest tried to leave, he found that his car was bogged down in the mud. Herman helped him try to dig it out, but without success. The harder they tried, the deeper it sank into the bog. This car happened to block the way for all the others, which meant that all the remaining revellers were marooned and had to stay the night. So they made themselves as comfortable as they could wherever they could – even on the floor.

The next day was Saturday, and of all those present only Herman and André had to work. Yet, Herman and Helena did not leave their guests and go to bed, but chose to try and sleep on the dining table instead.

George Howard, although absent from the gathering, would ever after refer to it as 'The Last Supper'. And on reflection it seems to have been charged with the same kind of the symbolism of that event.

Someone covered Herman with a blanket and in jest pulled it right over his head. Helena was picking out the notes of the funeral march on the piano. One of the guests, David Goldblatt, whispered to someone else that it looked like a burial rite. The guests were a little rowdy and for the rest of the night Lionel Abrahams watched Herman twisting uncomfortably in a sleep in which there could be no rest for him.

Most of the morning was spent in excavating cars. That afternoon Herman and André worked their usual shift from 2 pm to 2 am to get *The Sunday Express* to bed on time. Herman drank Coke after Coke in an attempt to stave off his fatigue, but when he finally got to bed that night, he was in a state of complete exhaustion.

When he awoke on Sunday morning he was far from well. Towards mid-morning, quite suddenly, he came to Helena and asked her to get André to take him to Edenvale Hospital. 'It's a matter of life and death,' he said.

Helena recalls that when he arrived at the hospital, he volunteered the following particulars: 'Born Kuils River – and you can put down "died Edenvale Hospital".'

The doctors and staff exploded in gales of laughter. Only Helena knew that this was the same brand of humour that had permitted Herman to laugh in the shadow of the gallows noose. Within an hour or so the doctors considered his condition quite satisfactory and he was discharged.

Helena and Herman went to rest after lunch. It was then that he felt a tremendous pain and a tightness round his chest, so vice-like that he could hardly breathe. When this happens, one has a desperate need to break wind or vomit, to emit something from the mouth to relieve the pressure. Herman went to the toilet and tried to do this, locking the door behind him as was his habit. Almost immediately Helena heard a strange groan and the sound of Herman falling against the door. Then total silence.

She cried for help. A next-door neighbour, a policeman, came and helped her open the door and carry Herman to the bed. He was in a coma.

André went to look for a doctor. While they waited Helena massaged Herman's limbs. Neighbours gathered and offered either advice or warnings while Herman lay dying. Helena could see that they could no longer wait for André. For the second time that day, they rushed to Edenvale Hospital. This time, no questions. No jokes. Herman Bosman never regained consciousness. The trolley on which he lay was left at an awkward angle at the top of an incline, with the brake not firmly enough in place. Suddenly the trolley began to move down the slope. A nurse caught it and wrenched it back. When they had straightened Herman again, Helena slipped her hand beneath the blanket. She could feel no heartbeat. He lay quite still.

Helena went and stood quite alone in a dark corner. The only message she could think of to send after that spirit that had left so abruptly was: 'Run, Herman. Run!' The date was 14 October 1951.

The obituaries that appeared over the next few days were his friends' expressions of grief. Their lives would never be the same.

In *The Star* Edgar Bernstein wrote:

*The sudden death this week of Herman Charles Bosman at the early age of 46 has removed a remarkable personality from the local literary scene – a man as kindly as he was jauntily Bohemian and as sensitive as the books he wrote.*

In *Forward* on 19 October Bernstein recalled the shades that had coloured Bosman's laughter all those years:

*There was something about Herman Charles Bosman (whose death last Sunday at the age of 46 has cut a unique talent from South African literature) that put me in mind of a twentieth century version of Hals's 'Laughing Cavalier'. An incurable romantic in an unromantic age, he had a way of shrugging off the crisis of our times as a joke in rather questionable taste. His jaunty shrug was a gesture touched with the arrogance of the caballero, and it irritated those who did not understand his psychological make-up. But the crestfallen laughter that usually tinged it made it bearable to his friends.*

In his personal letter of condolence to Helena, Bernstein wrote:

*I wanted to say some words of homage yesterday, when the minister asked if anyone wished to say anything; but my heart was too full to speak. I grieved for Herman and for you and for all of us who are swept along and shaken and bruised and broken in the waste accident of life. I thought of Herman over all the twenty years I have known him, and was privileged to be his friend; the great soul that was in him and the rich talent that was his; the pain of life that wounded him always, and all of the dislocation and hardship which he had to endure. And I thought of you and the healing role you played in his too quickly ended life. He told me more than once of the great debt of gratitude he owed you for the anchorage he had found with you. He cherished you in his innermost heart as his rock and his comfort no less than his wife and friend.*

*Once in a conversation he said to me: 'Helena saved me ... Yes. It was just like that: I was being destroyed, and she saved me.' We fell silent and did not speak again for some minutes. I always found Herman's silences as eloquent as his words. The thoughts flowed between us, and we knew what each other was thinking. I realised just how deeply he meant what he said, and in the years that followed, those words were always with me, and I could not help noticing again and again how much of his life was built on you, and how much of inner peace you brought him; it was the first time, in all the long years I knew him, that he ever attained to such peace.*

239

Leon Feldberg, the Jewish businessman who had befriended him, looked out for him, got him out of trouble, and to whom Bosman had dedicated *Mafeking Road*, wrote in the *Jewish Times*:

> *The sudden death of Herman Charles Bosman has robbed South Africa of a fine writer, and the Jewish community of a good friend ... He was a close personal friend of mine and I had a deep respect for his unusual nature and talent ...*
>
> *From our very first handshake, I realised that he was a person quite out of the ordinary, imbued with qualities of the spirit that made him sensitive to all kinds of things the average person does not notice ...*

In deference to a staff petition for compassion and consideration of the widow's feelings, A B Hughes wrote a straightforward piece in *The Sunday Express*, omitting any mention of Bosman's gaol record. In the November issue of *Trek* Benny Sachs, recalling 30 years of association with Bosman, said:

> *Bosman just couldn't fit into a uniform or a straight line, and his course through life was on that account jagged and hard.*

Lily Rabkin of *The Forum*, for which he had spent many a Thursday night struggling to meet his Friday morning deadline, said:

> *The unexpected death of Herman Bosman has brought a complex sorrow - sorrow at the sudden loss of a valued friend, sorrow at the sudden loss to South Africa (and the world) of a very rare and real creative talent.*
>
> *It is at times like this that one realises sharply that art is not an abstract entity, that it is the product of the mind and body of man.*

Lionel Abrahams, his pupil and disciple, wrote in the November issue of *Common Sense*:

> *He could write funnier humour, and novels, short stories and poems of greater impact, imaginative power and originality than anyone in South Africa. But his legacy to our literature is contained not alone in his writings, but in his life as well ...*
>
> *Herman Bosman once told me that a scientist can work out for you, if you plant so many bags of seed in a field and use so many tons of fertiliser, how many sacks of mealies you will reap; but that if you asked God how much you would get if you sowed in this field, He would say: 'I don't know. But have a try. You'll get a LOT' ...*
>
> *If anyone asks me (the substitution must be forgiven), how great is Herman Bosman? then I must also reply: 'I don't know. But it's a lot.'*

Jean Blignaut was in England and not too many people there would have cared had he written a tribute then. For him, Herman died twice, and both times he was in the wrong hemisphere. He wept awhile, but in time he did write his tribute to Herman Bosman, *My Friend Herman Charles Bosman*, published in 1980.

A wire was sent to Pierre, who came at once. At the funeral parlour he gazed into the coffin for a long time, his head turned to one side. Ney Blignaut, Jean's brother, thought it looked as if Herman's features had been transmuted into marble.

George Howard felt it looked as if they had been sculpted with great attention to detail by Michelangelo, whose pietas and depositions from the Cross have made him the incontestable master sculptor of the dead.

Gordon Vorster was tearless, in a trance-like state of shock. Helena put an arm round him and comforted him. 'There, Gordon. Think of it as one of Herman's little jokes.'

Among the other mourners were Leon Feldberg; John Cope, editor of *The Forum*; T F Sutherland, J Hopkinson and L Anderson of *The Sunday Express*; G Read of *The Rand Daily Mail*; William Wolpert of the CNA; Lionel Abrahams; George Howard; Lex Malan, son of Herman's uncle Charles; B Bransley; W J Elsmore; Dr Eddie Roux; Helena's brother André, and Nancy McDermott.

At the graveside Vera handed Helena a poem titled 'To Helena – a birthday poem'. Herman had written it before his marriage to Helena and had given it to their mutual friend Gwen Davies to pass on to Helena. Gwen had kept it during all those years and passed it to Vera in error at the funeral. When Vera saw the title she handed the poem to Helena. It was only then that Helena discovered for the first time that Herman had once been married to Vera Sawyer.

Gordon Vorster was in deep shock that day, but at a later stage he wrote to Helena:

*A white-gloved hand held a silver platter of rose petals out to you. With a most gracious movement you raised your right hand, took some petals and held them poised above the coffin of the man who had held you in thrall for eight years. You had, so you say, known him as saint and as monster, lover, friend, enemy, you had loved and bathed him, chided and praised him as if he were your beloved Beethoven for whom you could make beds and scrub floors. And now he was dead and you didn't believe in death.*

*As you took the petals of roses a miracle occurred. Your hand, slowly and with indescribable grace, danced a slow pavane dance across the space above him, your fingers curling and extending, your wrist subtly turning, and your hand was Pavlova-swanlike in the grace, charm and elegance of your benediction – your hands having, to me, been flights of angels singing him to his rest. You relaxed your arm and touched a wind-disturbed lock of hair that was disturbing you gently.*

After the other mourners had left and George Howard was alone, he placed among the flowers on the grave a page torn from a book of poems. Its subject had been a cause for laughter 12 years earlier on the day of that chance meeting outside the British Museum. It was Swinburne's premature requiem for Baudelaire.

*Thou art far too far for wings of words to follow,*
*Far too far off for thought or any prayer.*
*What ails us with thee, who art wind and air?*
*What ails us gazing where all seen is hollow?*
*Yet with some fancy, yet with some desire,*
*Dreams pursue death as winds a flying fire,*
*Our dreams pursue our dead and do not find.*

But I think Bosman had already written the most memorable graveside lines in his magical story, 'Funeral Earth'.

*We had a difficult task, that time, (Oom Schalk Lourens said), teaching Sijefu's tribe of Mtosas to become civilised. But they did not show any appreciation. Even after we had set fire to their huts in a long row round the slopes of Abjaterskop, so that you could see the smoke almost as far as Nietverdiend, the Mtosas remained just about as unenlightened as ever.*

Later:

*When Commandant Joubert stooped down and picked up his handful of earth, a strange thing happened. And I remember that other war, against the Mtosas. And we knew – although we would not say it – what was now that longing in the hearts of each of us. For Commandant Joubert did not straight away drop the soil into Fanie Louw's grave. Instead, he kneaded the damp ground between his fingers. It was as though he had forgotten that it was funeral earth. He seemed to be thinking not of death, then, but of life.*

*We patterned after him, picking up handfuls of soil, and pressing it together. We felt the deep loam in it, and saw how springy it was, and we let it trickle through our fingers. And we could remember only that it was the time for the sowing.*

Gordon Vorster drove his wife Yvonne and the two widows, Helena and Vera, back to the house in Lombardy East. Pierre joined them there. That day at the funeral Helena had spoken to him for the first time since the evening in Cape Town when she had asked him to leave the house.

When much later the Vorsters drove away from the house in Milton Road, Gordon was reminded of the night of the party, when he was the last guest to back his car out of the driveway. The sign with the name 'Paradise Regained' had been painted in poster paints and the rain was washing out the words ... in much the same way as the names on the gravestones of Herman's stories were gradually being obliterated, season after season.

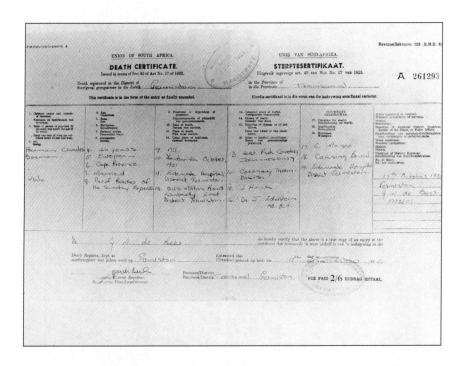

*The death certificate of Herman Charles Bosman*

*Patrick Mynhardt as Oom Schalk Lourens*

# Epilogue: The future ages

Although Bosman died with only three books published, he would become South Africa's best-loved literary cult figure and its most written-about writer.

It started with a trickle.

Several times over the years since Bosman's death Yvonne Vorster was obliged to undergo surgery, and each time she took only Bosman's books with her. When encased in plaster from her neck to her feet, she read in *Cold Stone Jug* the passage where Bosman describes how once during his years of incarceration he was selected to go outside the prison walls to erect a bracket.

How bright the colours seemed and how flower-like the people, and how precious the few steps from the shut-in dun-coloured world to the spectacle of real life that somehow continued to go on beyond the prison walls, and how he tried so hard to make those steps last as long as possible, extending his nerve ends and sensibilities so that he would not lose the super-reality of those few seconds.

One of the nurses noticed Yvonne's collection of Bosman books and became a regular visitor during her spare time. She told Yvonne that she belonged to a Herman Bosman reading circle that met at regular intervals to discuss his work. This was the first time any member of the circle had had the privilege of meeting someone with a personal connection with Bosman; so, visit by visit, the nurse accumulated a series of anecdotes to be passed on to other members.

In the 1940s, students used to gather at the Devonshire Hotel to read Bosman straight from *The South African Opinion* and *Trek*. That original three-book trickle had bubbled into a lively stream, and by the early 1980s, 12 more books had been culled from his literary relics and salvaged from the stacks of reference libraries. Their titles crowd bookshelves all over South Africa and beyond:

Lionel Abrahams, Bosman's disciple and literary executor, interested Human & Rousseau in publishing *A Cask of Jerepigo* (a collection of essays in 1957), *Unto Dust* (a collection of veld stories first published in 1963), *Bosman at his Best* (a selection of his prose writing in 1965), then in 1971 two collections of his 'Voorkamer' sketches, *Jurie Steyn's Post Office* and *A Bekkersdal Marathon*, and a volume of poetry, *The Earth is Waiting* (1974).

I came in like the filling in the sandwich with the first comprehensive biography, *Sunflower to the Sun* (1976) – later renamed *The Life of H C Bosman*; then came Bosman's novel *Willemsdorp* (1977), his second novel on dorp life in South Africa which I brought back from Texas. My *Almost Forgotten Stories* (1979), *Uncollected Essays* (1981) and *Herman Charles Bosman - A Pictorial Biography* (1981) followed.

Stephen Gray had added *Selected Stories* (1980), and in 1981, apart from my two, another three books appeared: Jean Blignaut's collection of Bosman's early verse *Death Hath Eloquence*, his memoir *My Friend Herman Charles Bosman*, and Patrick Mynhardt's prose selection *The Bosman I Like*. In 2001, following many insightful and informative prefaces and introductions to his various collections of Bosman's work, Lionel Abrahams's sparkling memoir, *Mr Bosman: A Protégé's Memoir* appeared in the October issue of the literary journal *English in Africa*. Bosman had become one of South Africa's most written-about writers.

After Lionel Abrahams, Stephen Gray and Craig MacKenzie systematically re-edited and republished all of Bosman's works in their 14-volume Anniversary Edition between 1998 and 2005. This series includes Gray's meticulous collection of Bosman's poetry, *Wild Seed* (2004), which gathers all of Bosman's poetry barring the four poems sent to me in 1972 by a fellow inmate of his in Pretoria Central Prison in 1928/9.

When people ask me – and they often do – how the Bosman papers came to be in Texas, I tell them the following story.

Some time after Bosman's death in 1951, Helena married his old friend from their Young Communist Party capers, Raymond Lake. The babies she had been unable to have during Bosman's lifetime – Jonathan, and then the twins, Rosalind and Marian – arrived in quick succession. Helena was exhausted, and without the facilities to care for Bosman's literary relics.

Professor Joseph Jones, a visiting lecturer from the Humanities Research Center at Austin, Texas, then on a talent hunt, approached Helena with a view to acquiring them for their holdings of Commonwealth literature. And it seemed at the time the best solution to safeguard them.

As it happened, I was a student at the University of the Witwatersrand at the time and attended Professor Jones's lecture on Arthur Miller's *Death of a Salesman*.

However, my own first encounter with Bosman happened when my English lecturer, Phillip Birkenshaw, lent me a copy of *Mafeking Road*, which I read all through that night. I was so entranced that I tried (unsuccessfully at that time) to secure the television rights in conjunction with my film colleague Ashley Lazarus.

*David Butler as Bosman in* A Touch of Madness

When Bernard Sachs's Bosman biography came out I found there was still so much more I wanted to know about Bosman. So I asked Paul Roos of DALRO (then the Bosman agent) to arrange for me to meet Helena Lake.

We met in the library at Fairmount Preparatory School where she worked as a librarian. That Highveld winter's afternoon, to the happy sounds of children playing and the school bell tolling the half hours, I asked her permission to research H C Bosman's life story.

We arranged to meet again at her house in Linbro Park. Helena somehow believed in me, and her supportiveness became my rod and my staff, and changed my life forever.

When I asked her what other writers were doing on Bosman, she reeled off a discouragingly impressive list of projects, mostly focused on a particular aspect of his work. There was stiff opposition – such as half a dozen distinguished academics – and myself with so modest a CV as to be (quite correctly) accused of impudence.

We cut to the chase. I began oh-so-hesitantly to interview the list of friends and relatives Helena had suggested, until I met Bosman's first wife Vera Sawyer. When Vera told me Bosman had spent only six months in the Bushveld, and not a year as was generally supposed, it pointed the way. This was something not even Helena had known. I had a mission.

From then on I took everything back to source: birth certificates, marriage certificates, death certificates. In the newspaper morgue of the Johannesburg Public Library, I found the story of the Bellevue tragedy. In the Johannesburg Reference Library the copies of the gutter-press papers with 'Lago Clifford's' account of prison. And suddenly an exciting story was emerging with a momentum of its own.

Using librarian Shora de Saxe's excellent bibliography, I worked chronologically, matching the events in Bosman's life to what he wrote. I had reached the point in my research where I needed to read the Bosman papers, but the items I requested from Texas were illegible. Phillip Birkenshaw took one look, and then advised me to go myself.

On Lionel Abrahams's advice, I'd applied to the Human Sciences Research Council for a subsidy, and while awaiting the outcome Lionel told me that a doctoral candidate (an expatriate South African living in Texas) was here and had mentioned she had the Bosman papers available to her exclusively for two years. I didn't think this was the function of a research centre, and assumed that if she was here she couldn't be using the papers. I confirmed with Texas and arranged to go, except that I was broke.

Serendipitously, the Alitalia Italian Airline representative at that time had just read one of my magazine articles in *Artlook* and was filling a guest list for an inaugural flight. When I told him how I believed in the 1% chance, and how badly I needed to go to Texas, he believed in it, too. I virtually hitched a ride as far as Rome.

My film-maker friend and colleague, Ashley Lazarus, loaned me the money for the rest of the fare against my Chagall lithograph, advising, 'Go now, work hard and come back soon.' This all affirmed my faith in a philosophy I live by: my faith in the 1% chance. Every time I hit a problem, it was somehow solved for me. Whether it's God, Herman Bosman, or a benign writer's muse who rewards hanging in there for the 1% chance, it translates into optimism at its highest. An act of faith I recommend to all stalled writers. And somehow it works out at a whole lot more than 1%.

En route for home, in London I met Jean Blignaut and we went together to the British Museum newspaper library at Colindale for copies of *The Sunday Critic*. On my return flight to Johannesburg, I happened to be carrying a banned book, so customs took my luggage apart. Once home, I phoned customs to retrieve my book and was referred to a Mr Flattery.

Again serendipitously, he turned out to be a relative of the same Flattery family with whom Bosman had boarded in the Bushveld. He made it possible for me to meet Willie and Joey Flattery, who took me to their old farm 'Middelrand' and then to the school at Heimweeberg where Bosman had taught them.

I finally arrived home to find the Human Sciences Research Council had granted me the research subsidy that repaid my debt. As Hannibal Smith says in the *A Team*, 'I like it when a plan comes together.'

When I returned from Texas with *Willemsdorp*, Gordon Vorster was fascinated with what I had found and suddenly I wasn't alone any more. Together we taped hours of interviews, and much of what he wrote for me at that time became the basis of work quoted here.

Human & Rousseau published *Sunflower to the Sun: The Life of Herman Charles Bosman* in 1976 and *Willemsdorp* in 1977.

Meanwhile, I'd had the fun of 'discovering' Bosman's old magazine stories, fast becoming confetti in the Johannesburg Public Library stacks. When initially I had a hiccough in finding a publisher, with Helena Lake's permission, *The Sunday Express* (where Bosman worked before his death) ran an opinion poll. They published one story a week, inviting readers' comments. The replies see-sawed from 'No thanks, H C Bosman is grossly overrated,' to 'Yes please, they are a real treasury lighting up my otherwise drab Sundays.'

This also attracted both publicity and publishers. We practically had an auction on our hands. Bosman's future ages had spoken. Howard Timmins Publishers, quickest off the mark, sent novelist Pamela Jooste (then their representative) to close the deal. And Gordon Vorster christened them *Almost Forgotten Stories*. These were the foundation for what would later be published by Ad Donker as *Ramoutsa Road*, a volume recently republished by Jonathan Ball.

I followed these stories with a collection of Bosman's journalism (again published by Howard Timmins) as *Uncollected Essays* the following year. Later, Struik must have acquired Timmins, for I have since found among old correspondence two covering letters for cheques to me by Struik.

The Bosman experience changed my life forever. It prompted me to adapt his stories for theatre, television and a documentary film, permitting me to work with exciting talents I'd never otherwise have had access to. Most of all, it enriched my life with Helena's friendship, and *Sunflower to the Sun* is dedicated: *For Helena, who opened up the long-rusted locks on the cupboard of her spirit.*

It also brought me the friendships of actor-raconteur Patrick Mynhardt, and the multitalented artist-poet-film-maker Gordon Vorster. Circa 1972 when I first shared my research with actor Patrick Mynhardt, that original three-book trickle became a current, and then rapids. He brought Bosman's works down from the bookshelves and into people's lives. What he and Victor Mackeson had started as dinner theatre in Pretoria would make theatre history with his six one-man shows that toured South Africa, Europe, Israel and New York. By the time he'd adapted them for audio tape and video tape, he was a legend in his own time.

Actor-broadcaster Cecil Jubber also produced a documentary audio tape with the live voices of Helena, Gordon Vorster, Pierre Bosman, Bernard Sachs, Edgar Bernstein, Fred Zwarenstein, Charles Eglington, Jumbo Posthumus and Nancy McDermott.

My own foray into theatre happened in May 1985 when Nicholas Ellenbogen of the Natal Performing Arts Council commissioned a four-hander workshop piece of Bosman's stories to celebrate the opening of the Playhouse's Loft Theatre. We called it *The Storyteller*. Mike Swinton directed an ensemble cast – Roger Dwyer, Stephen Gurney, Bruce Young and Phillipa Gutridge.

More recently still, actor-playwright Nicky Rebelo and David Butler held a magnifying glass up to Bosman in *A Touch of Madness* – a sobering glimpse of what Bosman called the 'chinks through which there glows the fire of insanity'. Genius exacts such creative energy that it can unbalance both mind and body chemistry.

I have tried to relate the story chronologically, but three things happened simultaneously: Patrick Mynhardt's supper theatre, my Bosman biography (*Sunflower*), and the documentary film of Bosman's life (*The Storyteller*). The title *The Storyteller* was a natural choice. By then, the Bosman stories had taken on a life of their own, and in a sense they named themselves, and no other name would do.

If we're talking about 'the future ages', I need to tell you straight away that the story doesn't end here. For me it is part of a continuum. Anything I don't finish – and I expect there will be much – will be part of the next biography, and I feel privileged to pass the baton.

As I've said, I *have* tried, and still *am* trying to tell the story chronologically, but if we flash forward to talk of David Butler, I must mention Bosmanophile Craig MacKenzie.

Craig became an instant Bosmanophile the night his parents took him as a 14-year-old boy to see Patrick Mynhardt first perform Bosman at the Lyric Theatre in Durban. He didn't know it then, but as in my case, it changed his life forever. He ended up writing a doctorate on the South African short story with Bosman as its centrepiece and was then part of the Anniversary Edition project (together with Stephen Gray) to re-edit all of Bosman's works from scratch.

I'd like to conclude with the rest of the story about the documentary film. I had finished *Sunflower* when the SABC commissioned Independent Films to make a documentary film of Bosman's life.

Patrick Mynhardt did the *Cold Stone Jug* material, Peter Grosset directed, Gordon Vorster did most of the storytelling and shared his own intimate view of Bosman with us. This means that although I was credited for scriptwriting, it was really only the linking bits of commentary that Patrick and Gordon hadn't already told.

In his wonderful speaking voice enriched and burred with that trace of an Afrikaans accent, Gordon Vorster also read that part of 'Veld Maiden' film-makers call the 'set up'.

*Frans Welman was in some respects what people might call a hard man. For instance, it was something of a mild scandal the way he treated his wife and the kaffirs on his farm. But then, on the other hand, he looked very well after his cattle and pigs. And I have always believed that this is more important in a farmer than that he should be kind to his wife and the kaffirs.*

Then Oom Schalk comes upon John de Swardt painting studies of the veld.

*He had a piece of white bucksail on a stand in front of him and he was painting my farm. He seemed to have picked out all the useless bits for his picture – a krantz and a few stones and some clumps of kakiebos. 'Young man,' I said to him, after we had introduced ourselves, 'when*

*people in Johannesburg see that picture they will laugh and say that
Schalk Lourens lives on a barren piece of rock, like a lizard does. Why
don't you rather paint the fertile parts? Look at that vlei there, and the
dam. And put in that new cattle-dip that I have just built up with
reinforced concrete. Then, if Piet Grobler or General Kemp sees this
picture, he will know at once that Schalk Lourens has been making
improvements on the farm.'*

*The young painter shook his head.*

*'No,' he said, 'I want to paint only the veld. I hate the idea of painting
boreholes and cattle-dips and houses and concrete – especially concrete.'*

A little later in the story, the following exchange occurs:

*John de Swardt then took me into his tent and showed me some other
pictures he had painted at different places along the Dwarsberge. They
were all the same sort of picture, barren and stony. I thought it would
be a good idea if the Government put up a lot of pictures like that on
the Kalahari border for the locusts to see. Because that would keep the
locusts out of the Marico.*

*Then John de Swardt showed me another picture he had painted and
when I saw that I got a different opinion about this thing that he said
was Art. I looked from De Swardt to the picture and then back again to
De Swardt.*

*'I'd never have thought it of you,' I said, 'and you look such a quiet
sort, too.'*

*'I call it the "Veld Maiden",' John de Swardt said.*

*'If the predikant saw it he'd call it by other names,' I replied.*

Gordon stops reading and confides to camera: 'Now, you see I'm supposed to
stop there, but I can't. Look what comes next.'

He continues:

*'But I am a broad-minded man. I have been once in the bar at Zeerust
and twice in the bioscope when I should have been attending Nagmaal.'*

Again he suggests to camera: 'Now that's a good place to stop, but I can't. You
just can't do that to Herman.'

He continues:

*'... So I don't hold it against a young man for having ideas like this.
But you mustn't let anyone else see her unless you paint a few more
clothes on her.'*

In sharing the actor's experience with us, Gordon invites us into the screen adaptation with him. It is one of the best documentaries I've seen – and it was a privilege to have had the good fortune of working on this project.

Gordon Vorster finished *The Storyteller* with these lines about his friend, Herman Bosman:

> *I don't believe in his death ...*
>
> *We in South Africa have learned to love him. He's part of our scene and he's part of our culture. And these ephemeral things – culture and poetry – are perhaps written on the wind and blown away easily, and yet they are the most permanent things a nation has. Much more permanent than any of your great buildings – or any of your great cities – because it is a permanence of the soul – of the spirit – and that is the only permanence a nation really has.*
>
> *The best thing I can say about him, is that he is as much a part of South Africa as the thorn-trees, and the wind, and the running of the grass over the hills.*

But the story doesn't end there. The future ages that Bosman promised would never go wrong now celebrate the annual Herman Charles Bosman festival every October in the little dorp of Groot Marico, which is actually well over an hour's drive away from Zwingli near the Botswana border where Bosman taught school.

The Bosman Festival lasts a couple of days and actors Patrick Mynhardt and David Butler do their shows, and Bosmanophiles Craig MacKenzie and Stephen Gray spread the gospel and sell the books they have edited, and everybody drinks peach brandy. In 2004 I had the privilege of attending it for the first time. It was probably the most enriching experience of my entire life.

And, like all other Bosmanophiles, I think Herman Charles Bosman, who died too soon, must be somewhere in the sky smiling down at it all – and perhaps his eyes are even a bit full.

# The Estate

Herman Bosman died intestate. The estate was large enough, though, for his brother Pierre to come forward with a claim as second heir. He demanded part of his brother's literary heritage. For five years there was an unrelenting battle between him and Helena. Bosman's works had no specific monetary value, though, and in order to determine one, the Master of the Supreme Court ruled that they be put up for auction.

A short column in *The Star* of 12 October 1956 reported:

*For what is believed to be the first time in the Union, an author's copyright was put up for public auction in Johannesburg today.*

*The author was Herman Charles Bosman, author of* Mafeking Road *and* Cold Stone Jug, *who died in 1951. The rights to all his published and unpublished works, including a new book of essays to appear shortly, fetched £155. The buyer was a Johannesburg attorney, Mr Lewis Meskin, acting on the behalf of the widow, Mrs Helena Bosman.*

*The only other bidder was an attorney representing another member of the family.*

# Sources

**Personal:**

Abrahams, Lionel – pupil of Bosman and editor of his works (taped interviews, 1973)

Bates, C. V. – Editor, *Potchefstroom Herald* (taped interview, 1972)

Bekker, Thys – Marico resident (taped interview, 1973)

Blignaut, Aegidius Jean – Bosman's close friend and colleague (taped interview, London, 1973)

Boshoff, Tom (Dr) – fellow teacher of Helena Bosman (taped interview, 1972)

Callaghan, John – principal of Heimweeberg farm school (taped interview, 1973)

Delport, Captain – Department of Prisons (for information provided in 1973, archive memo 19730)

Eglington, Charles – Bosman's friend and critic (taped interview c. 1970)

Flattery children – Joey, Flo and Willie (taped interviews with the three children of Oom Jim Flattery, Marico family head, and his wife, Kitty Flattery, District Nurse, 1973)

Folland, Ada – Pietersburg friend (taped interview, 1972)

Geel, At – (Marico resident, taped interview, 1973)

Grovê, Zita – Bosman's first cousin (taped interview and SABC documentary, 1973)

Howard, George Frank – friend of Bosman (taped interview 1972); also 'Herman Charles Bosman: A Portrait from Memory' (undated).

Hudson, Elmore (Dr) – Inspector of Schools, Pietersburg (taped interview 1972)

Lake, Helena – Bosman's third wife (taped interviews, 1972/3)

Malan, Lex – Bosman's cousin (taped interview, 1972)

McKibbin, Edwin – Bosman's school friend (taped interview 1972)

Oberholster, Reinhardt (Rip) – Bosman disciple (taped interview, 1972)

Sachs, Bernard – Bosman's school friend and biographer (taped interview, 1972)

Sawyer, Vera – Bosman's first wife (taped interview, 1972)

Snyman, Willie – Principal of Pietersburg school where Helena taught (taped interview, 1972)

Stegmann, André – Helena's brother (taped interview, 1972/3)

Stegmann, Johan – Helena's brother (taped interview, 1972/3)

Vorster, Gordon – artist and writer, and friend of Bosman (series of taped interviews, 1973-5)

Waldman, William – Editor of *The Umpa* magazine (taped interview, 1973)

Weeks, John – Elisa Malan's pupil at Potchefstroom Primary School (taped interview, 1972)

**Newspapers and periodicals:**

*The African Magazine*
*The Cape Times*
*The Forum*
*The New L.S.D.*
*The New Sjambok*
*On Parade*
*The Rand Daily Mail*
*The Ringhals*

*The South African Opinion*
*The Sjambok*
*Spotlight*
*The Sunday Critic*
*The Sunday Times*
*The Touleier*
*Trek*
*The Umpa* (Wits student magazine)
*Zoutpansberg Review and Mining Journal*

**Companies / institutions consulted:**

African Publishers
Afrikaanse Kulturele Leserskring
Afrikaanse Pers-Boekhandel (correspondence 24 January 1946)
Central News Agency
Department of Home Affairs
Harry Ransom Humanities Research Center, Austin, Texas – holder of Bosman papers
Johannesburg Public Library
State Archives, Pretoria
State Library, Cape Town
State Library, Pretoria

# Index

Published by Struik Publishers (a division of New Holland Publishing
(South Africa) (Pty) Ltd)
New Holland Publishing is a member of Johnnic Communications Ltd
Cornelis Struik House, 80 McKenzie Street, Cape Town 8001
86 Edgware Road, London, W2 2EA, United Kingdom
14 Aquatic Drive, Frenchs Forest, NSW 2086, Australia
218 Lake Road, Northcote, Auckland, New Zealand

**www.struik.co.za**

Publishing manager: Linda de Villiers
Managing editor: Cecilia Barfield
Designer: Helen Henn
Proofreader: Neilah Miller

Reproduction: Hirt & Carter Cape (Pty) Ltd
Printing and binding: Kyodo Printing Co (Singapore) Pte Ltd

ISBN 1 77007 163 6

2 4 6 8 10 9 7 5 3 1

www.imagesofafrica.co.za

IMAGES OF AFRICA
P H O T O     L I B R A R Y

Log onto our photographic website www.imagesofafrica.co.za for an
African experience